AN INCIPIENT MUTINY

AN
INCIPIENT
MUTINY

The Story of the U.S. Army
Signal Corps Pilot Revolt

DWIGHT R. MESSIMER

Potomac Books
An imprint of the University of Nebraska Press

Library of Congress Cataloging-in-Publication Data
Names: Messimer, Dwight R., 1937– author.
Title: An incipient mutiny: the story of the U.S. Army
Signal Corps pilot revolt / Dwight R. Messimer.
Other titles: Story of the U.S. Army Signal Corps pilot revolt
Description: Lincoln, NE: Potomac Books, an imprint
of the University of Nebraska Press, [2020] | Includes
bibliographical references and index.
Identifiers: LCCN 2019010306
ISBN 9781640122123 (cloth: alk. paper)
ISBN 9781640122567 (epub)
ISBN 9781640122574 (mobi)
ISBN 9781640122581 (pdf)
Subjects: LCSH: United States. Army. Signal Corps. Aviation
Section—History. | Air pilots, Military—United States—
Biography. | United States. Army. Signal Corps. Aviation
Section—Corrupt practices. | United States. Army. Signal
Corps. Aeronautical Division—History. | United States.
Army. Signal Corps—Biography. | Air pilots, Military—
United States—History—20th century. | Aeronautics,
Military—United States—History—20th century.
Classification: LCC UG573 .M47 2020 | DDC 358/.24—dc23
LC record available at https://lccn.loc.gov/2019010306

Set in Minion Pro by Mikala R. Kolander.

To Luke Lutton, a good friend

CONTENTS

List of Illustrations ix

Introduction 1
1. The Army's Balloons, 1892–1908 7
2. Benjamin D. Foulois, 1909–1911 15
3. Paul Ward Beck, 1911–1912 22
4. The Benjamin Foulois–Paul Beck Feud, 1911–1913 36
5. The Flying Club, 1911–1912 43
6. The First Signs of Trouble, 1912 54
7. Upheavals, 1913 63
8. An Incipient Mutiny, March 1913 79
9. Beck Makes His Move, 1913 85
10. Cowan's Flight Pay, 1913–1915 94
11. The Seeds of Rebellion, 1911–1914 102
12. William Lay Patterson, 1914–1915 116
13. The Rift, 1914–1915 128
14. Rebellion, 1915 145
15. The Reaction, 1915 164
16. The Turnaround, 1915 176
17. Court-Martial, 1915 186
18. The Garlington Board and the Kennedy Committee, 1916 207
19. Separation Achieved, 1917–1918 220
Epilogue 239

Notes 249
Bibliography 269
Index 277

ILLUSTRATIONS

Following page 144

1. Brig. Gen. Adolphus W. Greely
2. Brig. Gen. James Allen
3. Brig. Gen. George P. Scriven
4. Brig. Gen. George O. Squier
5. Aeronautical Acceptance Board at Fort Myer
6. 1st Lt. Thomas Selfridge and Alexander Graham Bell
7. Capt. Charles DeForest Chandler
8. 1st Lt. Benjamin D. Foulois and 1st Lt. Frank P. Lahm
9. 1st Lt. Myron Crissy
10. McClaskey, Curtiss, Beck, Towers, and Ellyson
11. Capt. Charles DeForest Chandler and 1st Lt. Roy Kirtland
12. 1st Lt. Harold Geiger and 1st Lt. Thomas Milling
13. Joseph D. Park
14. Roy C. Kirtland
15. 1st Lt. Robert H. Willis
16. Ned Goodier
17. Lt. Col. Sam Reber
18. Lt. Col. Lewis E. Goodier
19. Capt. William "Billy" Mitchell
20. 2nd Lt. Walter Taliaferro
21. Wing warping
22. Two-stick control system
23. Wright Model B and C wing warping and rudder lever
24. Single-stick system for left- and right-hand pilots
25. 1st Lt. Hap Arnold
26. Wright Model C
27. Tom Milling sitting in a Curtiss D-IV

AN INCIPIENT MUTINY

Introduction

This book covers the eleven years from the creation of the Signal Corps' Aeronautical Division on 1 August 1907 to the establishment of the Air Service of the National Army, better known as the Air Service, on 29 May 1918. The focus is on the men and events that created the Goodier court-martial in 1915, brought about the Garlington Board and the Kennedy Committee in 1916, and ended with the U.S. Congress's aircraft production hearings in 1918. Those were the historical waypoints that led to army aviation's total separation from the Signal Corps, the first step toward establishing an independent U.S. Air Force on 18 September 1947.

When the Signal Corps bought the Wrights' *Military Flyer* (sc-1) on 2 August 1909, there was no legal or operational justification for the Signal Corps to have an airplane. There was only a vague idea that airplanes would somehow fit into the Signal Corps' communications mission, leaving reconnaissance as the only possible use an airplane might have beyond carrying messages. But in 1909 reconnaissance was not included in the Signal Corps' mission.[1] More important, until 2 March 1913 there was no funding for this new undertaking. Until then, "aviation was carried on by officers of the Signal Corps and officers detailed from the line without any recognition by law."[2]

The first public indication that the chief signal officer (cso) had no plan for developing military aviation appeared in his 1909 annual report, in which he wrote, "The United States does not at present possess a modern aeronautical equipment, and it is believed that a systematic plan for the development of this military auxiliary for national defense should be inaugurated without delay."[3] The word to note here is "systematic." Because military aviation had been a part of the Signal Corps since 1907, it follows that the corps should have been already developing a systematic plan for military aviation. One can infer that the CSO was waiting for the War Department to formulate one, probably on the assumption that any plan the War Department came up with would be funded.

As it was, Brig. Gen. James Allen and the two following CSOs, Brig. Gen. George P. Scriven and Brig. Gen. George O. Squier, focused on reconnaissance as army aviation's sole mission. They excluded arming airplanes with bombs and guns because weapons were not part of the reconnaissance mission. The result was discontent among the army's pilots over the "lack of progress" that grew into open rebellion and a movement to separate army aviation from the Signal Corps and make it the "fourth arm" of the line.

An obstacle to developing the airplane's full military potential stemmed from the conventional wisdom of the time: "The United States, due to its isolated position, is not likely to become involved in a war, and therefore the most economical procedure, in aerial navigation, is to wait until other nations have determined upon the types best suited to military purposes, thus shifting the expense of experimentation and development to other nations."[4]

In addition to that lackadaisical attitude were four other stumbling blocks. The first was the Congress's lack of interest in army aviation, which produced the second stumbling block, a reluctance in Congress to appropriate funds for its growth and development. The third stumbling block was the War Department's ongoing modernization of the army that gave new field artillery, improved ammunition, and modern small arms a higher priority on the budget ladder than aviation. The result was that other than a $5,000 appropriation for aviation in 1908, there were no congressional appropriations between 1908 and 1911. The fourth stumbling block was the "Manchu Law" that limited a line officer's detail to aviation to four years.[5] In his 1911 annual report, Brigadier General Allen wrote, "In order to develop aviation it requires two essential things, namely, money and officers and men; either one of these without the other brings all adequate development to a standstill."[6] In 1956 Thomas Milling wrote that the United States was "consistently first in developing a military use for the airplane while being consistently last in utilizing these capabilities. This result was directly attributable to a lack of official support and money."[7]

Milling had it half right. The United States was not "consistently first in developing a military use for the airplane." The people leading the way were the French, who by the end of 1911 had 150 qualified pilots, forty of whom were rated as military aviators, and had 170 airplanes in service. Their pilots were already flying reconnaissance missions in army maneuvers, were experimenting with fire control at Verdun, were equipping some of their airplanes with wireless radiotelegraphy and were experimenting with a machine-gun-armed airplane.[8] But Milling was definitely right about the lack of adequate funding.

In his memoirs Henry "Hap" Arnold implied that the War Department was the main stumbling block to aeronautical progress. He wrote, "In general, however, our purpose had to be the vague one of developing the airplane into a military weapon as best we could, for we certainly received few if any, suggestions from the War Department."[9] Arnold had touched on the heart of the problem, which was that army aviation was in the wrong place, like a shoe on the wrong foot.

Army aviation went to the Signal Corps, and was not placed directly under the War Department, as the French and Germans had done, and the British did later, because of a 1 August 1907 Signal Corps memorandum that created a Signal Corps Aeronautical Division and put the corps in "charge of all matters pertaining to military ballooning, air machines, and all kindred subjects." There is disagreement among several authorities as to who was actually responsible for the memorandum, but the strongest evidence is that Brigadier General Allen wrote it at Maj. George O. Squier's suggestion.[10]

The Signal Corps was the smallest corps in the army, with just forty-six officers and 1,212 enlisted men.[11] Since there were not enough Signal Corps officers to fill the need for pilots, the corps had to rely on officer volunteers from the line (Coast Artillery, Field Artillery, Cavalry, and Infantry) to provide the necessary manpower. But those officers could remain on aviation duty for just four years before they were returned to their regiments. The constant arrival of new officers and the loss of trained pilots created a severe restraint on growth and development.

There was also the reality that flying was so dangerous that by 1914 one in four of the officers who volunteered for aviation were dead, a casualty rate that created a serious recruiting problem. The death rate was an indication that the airplanes the Signal Corps was buying were poorly designed and built, a state of affairs that the officers in charge of army aviation refused to believe or admit. But the pilots believed it, and that belief fed the fires of discontent.

The Signal Corps was also the army's most technical corps, which on its face made it the right place to put a new organization that was also highly technical. But the technologies involved in the two fields were entirely different. The Signal Corps' area of expertise was primarily electrical signaling and communications devices of all sorts. Aviation was all about aerodynamics and things that flew. But that critical difference was not obvious in 1907 because the science of aerodynamics barely existed then.

The Signal Corps' rational for being in charge of military aviation was first openly questioned in 1913, when Congressman James Hay asked Brig. Gen. George O. Scriven to give the reasons why the Signal Corps should have control of army aviation. The CSO answered: "The Signal Corps is composed of a number of men of undoubted scientific ability, recognized as men of great electrical knowledge, of strength of materials, and the working of gasoline engines, of the action of natural forces—men of the kind that it is absolutely essential to have in an aviation corps, as the staff and directing heads of the corps and its scientific departments."[12] The Corps of Engineers could have made the same argument.

The fact that army aviation was under the Signal Corps' absolute control became a major source of discontent among the pilots, who viewed their leaders as incompetent, self-serving, and short-sighted. But the other side of that coin is the old adage, "Where there is smoke, there is fire."

The pilots were not alone in condemning the Signal Corps leaders for sitting on their hands. In 1914 Col. John L. Chamberlain, inspector general for the Western District, wrote in his inspection report: "What has the government to show for these years of work and for the money expended? First, the death of twelve officers and several enlisted men; second, a paper organization for one aero squadron; third, an aviation school consisting of seventeen officers; fourth, several aeroplanes of various designs and makes, all of which are out of date, obsolete, and unfit for field service, and all of which, with the exception of three or four Burgess-Wright tractors and one Curtiss tractor, are unfit and unsafe for use for any purpose whatsoever."[13]

A year later, the Senate recognized there was a problem with the Signal Corps management of army aviation. Senator Joseph T. Robinson told the Senate Military Affairs Committee on 21 February 1916, thirteen months and two weeks before the United States entered World War I:

> The inefficiency and unsatisfactory results of the present manage-
> ment of the Aviation Section is disclosed by the fact that during
> the eight years in which the Signal Corps has had control of avia-
> tion only about twenty-four qualified fliers with the military rating
> have been produced. The service has no bombs, no bomb-sighting
> device, no method of mounting a gun on an aeroplane, no armored
> aeroplanes, and the machines on hand are not efficient for military
> flying. During the eight years above referred to, which have netted
> about twenty-four qualified fliers, there have occurred seventeen
> deaths in connection with military aviation, fifteen officers having
> been killed. Six of these aviators were killed within ten months,
> and it is believed that their deaths were due to the fact that they
> were required to attempt flights in antiquated biplanes known to
> be defective and dangerous.[14]

George W. Mixter and H. H. Emmons were aware of the management problem right up to the time the United States entered the war on 6 April 1917. "No Airplane made in America up to this time had mounted a machine gun or carried other than the simplest instruments. Radiotelegraphy and telephony, cameras, bombing equipment, night flying lights, aviators' clothing, suitable compasses, and other instruments were practically unheard of."[15]

It all started in 1892 when the Signal Corps bought a balloon.

1

The Army's Balloons, 1892–1908

Army aviation started out in 1892 with a single captive balloon for use as an aerial platform from which enemy movements could be seen and reported. Observation and reporting by visual and telegraphic means was the balloon's sole purpose. The Signal Corps was not a line formation, and combat was not its primary role. It was a situation that allowed balloons to fit nicely into the Signal Corps table of organization and equipment, which was not the case with airplanes that came seventeen years later.

The Signal Corps had been created during the Civil War, with Col. Albert J. Myer as the chief signal officer (cso).[1] The army's Civil War balloon corps was actually a civilian organization that never successfully integrated into the army, and in 1863 the balloon corps was disbanded.[2] The only connection the Signal Corps had with balloons during the war was Signal Corps officers occasionally going up in a balloon to make observations and send their reports to the ground with signal flags or telegraph. Following the disbandment of the balloon corps in 1863, there were no balloons in the army until 1892.[3]

After the war, the Signal Corps lacked a clear-cut mission,[4] and in 1886 Congress passed legislation that allowed personnel for the Signal Corps to be drawn on the detail system from the Battalion of Engineers. In the meantime, Col. Benjamin F. Fisher had replaced Myer as the cso and held that position until Myer successfully lobbied his own return to office on 21 August 1867.[5]

The years immediately following the Civil War were marked by the growth of agriculture, the national economy, and westward migration. Together, those developments created a need for a national weather service. On 2 February 1870 Congressman Halbert E. Paine introduced legislation authorizing the secretary of war to provide for the taking of meteorological observations at military posts and stations throughout the United States and its territories. Seeing an opportunity to stave off dissolution of the Signal Corps, Chief Signal Officer Myer lobbied Representative Paine to assign the execution of the law to him. The legislation passed on 9 February, and Colonel Myer's lobbying was rewarded on 15 March 1870 when Secretary of War William W. Belknap assigned the weather duty to the Signal Corps.[6]

The Weather Service, officially known as the Division of Telegrams and Reports for the Benefit of Commerce, became the Signal Corps' primary responsibility, and under the recently promoted Brig. Gen. Albert J. Myer, everything went well.[7] The civilian personnel and military staff melded seamlessly and functioned efficiently until 1880, when Myer died. His contentious replacement, Brig. Gen. William Babcock Hazen, served a seven-year tenure marked by discord, scandals, and, in 1881, allegations of fraud involving the Signal Corps disbursing officer, Capt. Henry W. Howgate.[8] The captain was accused of embezzling $237,000 by using fraudulent vouchers. Notably, another scandal thirty-four years later involved a Signal Corps officer, Capt. Arthur Cowan, who allegedly filed fraudulent vouchers for flight pay.

Brigadier General Hazen was also rocking the boat by insisting that the Signal Corps should be treated as a separate branch rather than part of the War Department, a precursor of Capt. Paul Beck's attempt to separate army aviation from the Signal Corps in 1913. Hazen cited the Corps of Engineers as the example of how the Signal Corps should be treated. In the process of wrangling with the War Department over the status of the Signal Corps, coupled with the discontent among the civilian weather service employees, the War Department became increasingly unhappy with the Signal Corps in general and the weather service in particular. Brigadier General Hazen died abruptly on 16 January 1887, having been taken ill during a reception given by President Grover Cleveland.[9] His replacement was Brig. Gen. Adolphus Washington Greely.

Upon taking his post in 1887, Brigadier General Greely inherited an unruly lot of Signal Corps officers that he could not satisfy, nor could he quell the discontent among his civilian weather service employees. Increasing criticism from Congress and the press could not be stifled. By 1889 Greely was convinced that there was no hope of settling the contentiousness that had grown up under Hazen. That same year President Benjamin Harrison recommended transferring the weather service to the Department of Agriculture, and Congress agreed.[10] The act making the transfer was passed and signed on 1 October 1890. Greely now found himself in the same spot that Brigadier General Myer had been in twenty-one years earlier: the Signal Corps lost its primary responsibility, and he needed a replacement before someone decided there was no more use for the corps.

The 1 October act that transferred the weather service to the Department of Agriculture also gave the Signal Corps the responsibility for collecting and transmitting information for the army, a duty that Greely interpreted to include having a balloon section.[11] That line of thinking probably sprang from an 1889 report in which 1st Lt. Richard E. Thompson described how several European armies had observation balloon units.[12] Greely's plans for a Signal Corps balloon section might also have stemmed from the precedent set during the Civil War when telegraph-equipped captive balloons were used to communicate with field commanders. Having come up with the idea, he had also to come up with a legal justification for a Signal Corps balloon section.

The closest thing to a legal justification was found in the 1891 *Field Service Regulations*, under "The Service of Information," article 3, paragraph 61, part of which read, "The commanding officers of independent forces and of separate columns should use *all available means* [emphasis added] to secure necessary information concerning the enemy and the ground over which operations are to take place." And article 85, paragraph 1537, in the 1891 *Regu-*

lations for the Army of the Unites States assigned the Signal Corps the duty of collecting information for the army by telegraph or otherwise, and *all other duties* (emphasis added) usually pertaining to military signaling.

Greely arranged through the secretary of war, Stephen Benton Elkins, to have 1st Lt. William A. Glassford assigned as the military attaché to the U.S. embassy in Paris, with orders to gather as much information as possible "on the aeronautic equipment of the principal nations and manufacturers." He also authorized Glassford to buy a captive balloon complete with all the necessary equipment.[13]

At the time, Greely did not have a specific appropriation for the purchase, and he never got one. Having sent Glassford to buy a balloon, Greely asked Congress for $11,000 to create a balloon service. Congress turned down the request, and Greely went to the commanding general of the army, Lt. Gen. John M. Schofield, and Secretary of War Elkins, asking for authorization to use existing Signal Corps funds. It was a "Rob Peter to Pay Paul" sort of financing, but his request was approved.

Meanwhile, Glassford surveyed French army balloon activities, visited French manufactures, and bought a balloon from the Paris firm Lachambre. The balloon arrived in the United States in 1892, was christened *General Myer*, and the Signal Corps had a balloon detachment, which was the sum total of army aviation. There had been no congressional act creating an army balloon service, no *specific* authorization for a Signal Corps balloon service, and no mention of a balloon service or balloon trains in either the *Regulations for the Army of the United States* or the *Field Service Regulations* prior to 1901.[14]

In 1896 the *General Myer*, already deteriorating from long storage, was destroyed at Fort Logan, Colorado, while being inflated during a windstorm. Sgt. William Ivy and his wife made a new balloon, using rubber sandwiched between two layers of silk. The homemade balloon was used in Cuba during the Spanish-American War in 1898 and was destroyed during fighting on San Juan Hill.[15] Signal Corps balloon operations during the Spanish-American War, though limited, were sufficient to inspire Congress to allot

The Army's Balloons

$18,500 for a balloon shed and other buildings in establishing a balloon detachment at Fort Myer, Virginia, in 1900. But getting the balloon detachment off the ground was not easy.

A German kite balloon, three French silk balloons, and five small cotton signal balloons that had been bought before 1898 were in storage at Fort Frankfurt, New York. But that on-hand equipment had deteriorated during storage. In 1902 Carl Edgar Myers, a nationally recognized authority on all aspects of balloon design and construction, was hired to repair the damage. Myers used Signal Corps soldiers under Maj. Samuel Reber to construct the needed hydrogen-filled captive balloons at Fort Frankfurt, and directed their use during the army-navy maneuvers on the Atlantic coast during the summer of 1903.[16]

In the years following the maneuvers, the Signal Corps made little use of balloons, though more were bought. The problem was that the small size of the Signal Corps created a serious shortage of officers and men to work with balloons. And the Signal Corps did not have a hydrogen-generating plant, forcing them to rely on "hydrogen bottles," which were in short supply until 1906. In that same year, theoretical and practical instruction in balloon operations became a requirement in all three service schools, but the extreme shortage of equipment limited the instruction to theory only.[17]

In February 1906 Brigadier General Greely was promoted to major general, and Brig. Gen. James Allen replaced him as cso.[18] One of Brigadier General Allen's first acts was to buy a "complete military captive balloon with all the appurtenances and an ordinary spherical balloon . . . for preliminary instruction of officers and enlisted men of the Signal Corps in the elementary principals of aeronautics."[19] On 1 August 1907 Allen established an Aeronautical Division within the Signal Corps, putting it "in charge of all matters pertaining to military ballooning, air machines, and all kindred subjects." The memorandum staffed the newly created Aeronautical Division with Capt. Charles DeForest Chandler and two enlisted men, Cpl. Edward Ward and pfc Joseph E. Barrett.[20] Allen now had the organizational structure in which to develop army aviation; he just did not have the financing.

In October 1907, CSO Allen attended the St. Louis air meet, where he met and watched a dirigible flight made by Thomas S. Baldwin. Allen saw the military future of the dirigible, but Congress would not give him the money for one because the Aeronautical Division did not legally exist at the time.[21] Fortunately, in those days, the annual appropriation for the Board of Ordnance and Fortification included money the board could use to buy weapons and equipment for practical trials. Following the air meet, Allen applied to the board for a $25,000 allotment to purchase "one experimental non-rigid dirigible balloon." The Board granted the request on 7 November 1907, and the still unofficial, but now temporarily funded, Aeronautical Division of the Signal Corps was off the ground and growing.[22]

When Brigadier General Allen signed Office Memorandum no. 6, the focus was on balloons, which had found a comfortable niche in the Signal Corps. But when he included "air machines" in the list of things that were to be under Signal Corps control, he laid the cornerstone for the turmoil that soon followed. The problem was that the Signal Corps' justification for having a balloon detachment was its responsibility for reconnaissance, observation, and communications, a multiple role the Signal Corps applied to airplanes when the time came. Though it went unrecognized at the time, the airplane had a greater potential and was more suitable for offensive combat than it was as an adjunct to balloons.

It seemed logical to put both lighter-than-air aircraft and heavier-than-air aircraft under Signal Corps control, because the potential for waging an offensive campaign against the enemy with airplanes was not then recognized. Soon after the army bought its first airplane in 1909, the airplane's offensive capabilities became apparent, and not much later they were demonstrated. Nevertheless, from 1907 to 1918, army aviation remained under Signal Corps control. It happened because General Greely took the initiative, Brigadier General Allen expanded the program, and nobody with authority questioned their actions. As 1st Lt. Paul Beck later said, "They just reached out and took it."[23]

In 1907 1st Lt. Frank Lahm was in France, where he had achieved international recognition by winning the first Gordon Bennett International Balloon Race in 1906. On 8 August 1907 Lieutenant Lahm was attending the French Cavalry School at Saumur when he was detailed to the Signal Corps for two years, making him the first line officer detailed to the Signal Corps for aviation duty. His orders directed him to first go to London and Berlin to see what progress the British and Germans were making in aeronautics. Upon arrival in Washington in December, he was assigned to work with Captain Chandler.[24]

Chandler and Lahm made several free balloon flights together and prepared information bulletins on balloon construction, hydrogen manufacturing methods, and many other balloon-related topics for distribution to officers and men who were attending the Signal Corps school. In the meantime, Signal Corps Specification no. 486, detailing what the army wanted for its first airplane, had been issued on 23 December 1907.

Through its balloon activities, the Signal Corps became closely associated with the newly formed Aero Club of America (ACA), the governing body for sport ballooning and, subsequently, heavier-than-air aviation in the United states. Being the governing body meant the ACA represented the Fédération Aéronautique Internationale (FAI) in the United States, which made it possible for the ACA to issue balloon and airplane pilot's certificates and competition licenses under the auspices of the FAI.[25]

In 1907 the ACA, with ground support from the Signal Corps, made a series of demonstration ascents with captive balloons to drum up public interest in sport ballooning. The ACA also created the Lahm Trophy Race to honor Lahm's 1906 victory in France. The Lahm Trophy was a cup that went to the pilot of the first balloon to exceed 402 miles, the distance Lahm had flown in 1906.

Capt. Charles DeForest Chandler won the first Lahm Trophy Race, which started from St. Louis on 17 October 1907. A week and a half later, Chandler and his copilot, Maj. Henry B. Hersey, were in St. Louis for the 30 October start of the second Gordon Bennett International Balloon Race. Of nine balloons in the race, three were American. Chandler flew as the copilot in a balloon piloted by a civilian, James C. McCoy, and Major Hersey piloted the third balloon. The Germans won the race, and Chandler and his pilot came in fourth.[26] The balloon race marked the entry of army balloonists into competitive flying and air meets, forming the basis for what became a sort of balloon fraternity in the Signal Corps.

During Brigadier General Allen's tenure, six Signal Corps officers, Lt. Col. Samuel Reber, Maj. Edgar Russel, Maj. George O. Squier, Captain Arthur S. Cowan, Capt. Charles DeForest Chandler, and 2nd Lt. Frank Lahm, held ACA committee positions.[27] The result of this close association was twofold: it provided a conduit for the ACA's intrusive involvement in army aviation, which as early as 1911 was already showing signs of becoming more of a flying club than a military unit. The involvement was made more intrusive by the fact that the ACA's founding members were enormously wealthy, politically powerful men, whose influence went right to the White House.

Brigadier General Allen focused his full attention on balloons until 1907, when he also became interested in airplanes. But his continued focus on balloons until 1913, combined with the Signal Corps' primary mission of observation, reconnaissance, and communications, stifled any consideration of the airplane's potential for offensive combat. Allen remained wedded to the idea that the airplane was just another observation, reconnaissance, and communications vehicle. During his time as the CSO, the airplanes the army bought were unreliable, dangerous, and generally unimproved from 1909 to 1914, so Allen shared the conventional wisdom that balloons and dirigibles were more practical than airplanes. As a result, he did not provide the leadership and direction necessary to develop military aviation along the offensive lines then being pursued in Europe.

Brigadier General Allen did not ignore airplanes, but under his administration, army aviation remained a minuscule organization, and his efforts to advance military aviation were at best half-hearted and sporadic. To be fair, it must be said that he asked for substantial appropriations, but Congress gave him very little money with which to develop military aviation. Still, the real problem was the absence of direction from the top down.

2

Benjamin D. Foulois, 1909–1911

Benjamin D. Foulois was a good soldier. He was loyal to the army, made the maximum effort to accomplish every assignment, and accepted whatever came his way. Foulois was also an optimist, a man with a sense of humor who was nearly always smiling. But he was opinionated, thought highly of himself, and vigorously defended his turf in the army's minuscule aviation section. Despite his overwhelming self-confidence, Foulois could recognize his mistakes and shortcomings, a character trait that played an important role in France in World War I.

Foulois was not a profound thinker, but he recognized early in his career that military aviation was destined to become the deciding factor in warfare. Despite his vision, he never became a crusader for airpower, preferring to work within the system to effect change. Later in life, Foulois liked to describe himself as a maverick, but the truth is that he was a man who knew on which side his bread was buttered.

It was his early years as a soldier that defined his character. Foulois was a natural leader, the sort of man who got his hands dirty and expected nothing of anyone that he would not do himself. Despite attaining high rank, Foulois remained, at heart, a common soldier. He entered the army as a private in 1898 in the U.S. Volunteer Engineers, served in Puerto Rico until 1899, and mustered out as a sergeant. Following a brief interlude as a civilian, he reenlisted as a private in the regular army and was sent to the Philippines with the 19th Infantry in August 1899.[1]

In September 1905 Foulois entered the Infantry and Cavalry School at Fort Leavenworth, Kansas. The Signal Corps school was also there, and according to his memoirs, it was discussions with members of the Signal Corps School class of 1905–6 in the officers' club that fired his interest in aviation and prompted his decision to transfer to the Signal Corps. In September 1906 he applied for admission to the Signal Corps School and was accepted for the 1907–8 academic year.

In the year between his graduation from the Infantry and Cavalry School and enrollment in the Signal Corps School, Foulois was sent to Cuba as part of the Army of Cuban Pacification. During that assignment he came under the direct command of Maj. Mason M. Patrick, making what was the first of several valuable career connections. In May 1907 Foulois was promoted to first lieutenant and ordered back to Fort Leavenworth to await the September start of the Signal Corps School academic year.

When he arrived in Fort Leavenworth, his four-year detached service under article 6, paragraph 40, of the 1904 *Regulations for the Army of the United States*, known as the "Manchu Law," started. The Manchu Law said that "an officer will not be detached from his corps or arm of the service unless he has served at least two years of the preceding six years therewith." Translated into everyday language, it limited detached duty to four years. But Foulois believed that he was actually transferring from the infantry to the Signal Corps, which would have exempted him from the Manchu Law's provisions. He was wrong.

While he was a student at the Signal School, Foulois wrote a thesis titled *The Tactical and Strategical Value of Dirigible Balloons and Aerodynamical Flying Machines*, in which he predicted the rapid advance of heavier-than-air aircraft. Foulois's thesis was largely theoretical and, as he admitted, drew heavily on the Bible and Jules Verne, but not all his predictions were taken from those sources. He based several of his concepts on experiments that had already been shown to be practical. Among those predictions was that air fleets would battle for control of the sky over the battlefield, and that the army that controlled the sky would control the battlefield. He discussed technical subjects such as airborne radio and the possibility that reconnaissance photos would be transmitted "by wireless over a considerable distance." As he said many years later, he lived to see some of his predictions come true.

Though general in nature and largely theoretical, his thesis, dated 1 December 1907, came at an opportune time because he submitted it four months after the chief signal officer, Brig. Gen. James Allen, had established the Aeronautical Division, and just three weeks before the Signal Corps issued specification no. 486, dated 23 December 1907, for a "Heavier-Than-Air Flying Machine."[2]

As a result of those events, the cso assigned Foulois to the Aeronautical Board that was to conduct the acceptance trials for the army's first dirigible and first airplane. Foulois's colleagues on the Aeronautical Board were Signal Corps officers Maj. George O. Squier, Maj. Edgar Russel, Maj. Charles McKinley Saltzman, Capt. Charles S. Wallace, and Capt. Charles DeForest Chandler. Two naval officers, Assistant Naval Constructor William McEntee and Lt. George C. Sweet, plus army line officers 1st Lt. Tom Selfridge and 1st Lt. Frank P. Lahm, rounded out the list. Foulois was the lightweight member on the board.[3]

Thomas S. Baldwin built the dirigible that the army accepted on 28 August 1908. The purchase contract included the requirement that Baldwin train three officers to fly the airship, and Foulois, Selfridge, and Lahm became the army's first qualified airship pilots. While Baldwin was training them to fly, Orville Wright arrived at Fort Myer with the Wright Model A that was also called the *Wright Military Flyer*, to undergo the acceptance tests in September 1908.

On 8 September Foulois and Selfridge were pulled off the Aeronautical Board and detailed to take Dirigible no. 1 to St. Joseph, Missouri, to exhibit it at the Missouri State Fair. In the event, only Foulois and his ground crew made the trip, Selfridge remaining at Fort Myer to observe the trials as a member of the Aeronautical Board. For the next nine months, Foulois piloted Dirigible no. 1 and trained three new dirigible pilots at Fort Omaha, Nebraska.

While Foulois was away, the 1908 acceptance trials came to an abrupt end on 17 September 1908, when the Wright plane crashed, killing Lieutenant Selfridge, the first U.S. Army officer to die in an airplane crash. He was a West Point graduate, class of 1903, and twenty-six years old when he was killed.

The fatal crash did not change the army's mind about buying an airplane, but it did delay the final acceptance tests until the following year. Orville Wright, together with his brother, Wilbur, arrived at Fort Myer on 20 June 1909 with the repaired Model A. The repairs included changes to prevent the propellers from hitting the wire braces, but in all other respects it was basically the same plane that had been tested in 1908. The tests were successful, the 1909 Model A exceeded the speed requirement, and the Aeronautical Board submitted its final report on 2 August 1909.[4]

By the time the rebuilt Model A arrived at Fort Myer, Foulois had rejoined the Aeronautical Board in time for the continued trials. There was also a new member, 2nd Lt. Frederick E. Humphreys, of the Corps of Engineers, who was the board's new lightweight member.

The army accepted the *Wright Military Flyer* as Signal Corps no. 1 (SC-1) on 2 August 1909. As with the dirigible, the contract called for the Wrights to train two pilots, and the CSO designated Lahm and Foulois to receive the training. But there was a problem with that decision. Lahm's orders assigning him on detached duty to the Signal Corps were written on 8 August 1907, meaning that six days after SC-1 was accepted, he was supposed to return to the 6th Cavalry. He does not say in his memoirs how he got the time extended so that he could take flight training in October and November, but he did.

The pilot training did not start until 8 October, by which time Allen had detailed Foulois to attend the International Conference on Aeronautics at Nancy, France. Foulois left on 8 September and did not return to the United States until 17 October. In his absence, Brigadier General Allen selected Humphreys to fill Foulois's slot as the second pilot trainee.[5] Allen knew that Humphreys was under orders to return to the engineering school upon completion of his temporary duty.

Benjamin D. Foulois

The situation on 8 October when Wilbur Wright started teaching Lahm and Humphreys to fly was that on completion of their flight training both Lahm and Humphreys would be relieved from detached duty and returned to their non–Signal Corps organizations, leaving the army with an airplane and no pilot. This was the sort of short-sighted mismanagement that was to create dissension in 1913 and cause an open revolt in 1915.

In the meantime, Wilbur Wright, who was under no obligation to take on a third student, agreed to train Foulois, who started his training on 23 October. He flew on six days, acquiring a total of three hours in the air, almost the same as Lahm and Humphreys had when they soloed. Though he did not solo, he could definitely fly; he just could not land.[6] On 5 November while Lahm and Humphreys were flying, Lahm made a turn too near the ground and crashed. Neither Lahm nor Humphreys was injured, but the army's only airplane was heavily damaged and out of service. The crash brought Foulois's training to an abrupt end.

Following the crash, the army's two qualified pilots, Lahm and Humphreys, were returned to their units, leaving the army with only one partially trained pilot, Foulois. Nevertheless, in early December, General Allen ordered Foulois to take the army's only airplane, SC-1, to Fort Sam Houston, Texas, where he was to complete his flight training on his own.

Foulois's thesis had gotten him into army aviation on the ground floor, and though his place in aviation history was assured, he manufactured two enduring myths about himself. The first was that he taught himself to fly. The second myth was that he was the first pilot who learned to fly through a correspondence course. It was in Texas that the myths about Foulois teaching himself to fly and learning through correspondence were born and found their way into the popular folklore of early aviation history.

The taught-himself-to-fly myth stems from the directions that General Allen allegedly gave Foulois when he ordered the fledgling pilot to go to Fort Sam Houston in December 1909. General Allen reportedly said, "You pack it up, take plenty of spare parts, and go down to Texas and teach yourself to fly."[7] Foulois promoted the myth in the first of three articles that appeared in the *Airpower Historian* in 1955.[8] The truth was that he already knew how to take off and fly; he just could not land very well. Foulois's problem was that he was "ground shy," which caused him to come in too high and literally fall to the ground.[9]

The myth that he learned to fly by correspondence, making him the "only pilot in history who learned to fly by correspondence," comes from his 1968 memoirs.[10] He can be forgiven for overstating the nature of his correspondence with the Wright brothers while he was in Texas. Though he had already learned to fly under Wilbur's and Humphreys's tutelage, like many fledgling pilots he just needed more landing practice, and in Texas, there was not a more experienced pilot present to coach him. But he was definitely not the first person in the world to take a learn-to-fly correspondence course.

In 1910 and 1911 several flying schools offered correspondence courses in flying. Many were frauds, but a few, such as the International School of Aeronautics, which had been in business since January 1908, regularly offered correspondence courses "for resident and correspondence students in ballooning and aviation." In 1911 the American School of Aviation was offering a six-month correspondence course on flying. The founder, K. M. Kasmar, claimed that as of April 1911 his correspondence course had one hundred students enrolled, two of whom were building their own machines.[11] That was all happening at the same time Foulois was corresponding with the Wrights.

Whether or not he taught himself to fly or did it through correspondence, the fact is that while he was in Texas, Foulois was truly on his own, to the extent that he had to buy fuel and parts out of his own pocket. Being a hands-on person, he made several modifications to sc-1 that reflected changes the Wrights had made to their subsequent models. Foulois moved the elevator from its front-mounted position to the rear, where it belonged, and he equipped the Model A with wheels, which freed him from the cumbersome tower catapult that characterized the early Wright airplanes. He also designed a seat belt made from harness leather,

Benjamin D. Foulois

which in view of the number of times he crashed was probably a matter of self-preservation.

And Foulois did crash frequently. His inability to make consistently good landings meant that Signal Corps no. 1 spent more time being rebuilt and repaired than it did flying. In fact, he crashed it so often that by February 1911 Signal Corps no. 1 was beyond repair and the army had to accept an offer from the millionaire Aero Club of America member Robert F. Collier to borrow his Wright Model B. The Model B, which was the model the army started buying in 1911, was outwardly identical to the model A with the exception of the control system, which featured the small hinged lever that controlled the rudder, and an integrated rudder and wing warping device. Wright Company pilot Phillip O. Parmelee accompanied the Model B to Fort Sam Houston to teach Foulois to operate the new control system.

By February 1911, while he was mastering the Model B's control system, he was no longer the army's only pilot. He might not have known about it at the time, but he was about to find out. On 11 March 1911 Maj. Gen. Leonard Wood, chief of staff of the army, ordered the assembly of the Maneuver Division under the command of Maj. Gen. William H. Carter at Fort Sam Houston, Texas. It was the first time that the army had assembled an entire division in peacetime, and Secretary of War Henry L. Stimson directed that all the army's aircraft and aviation personnel were to join the Maneuver Division at Fort Sam Houston. The secretary of war's order to gather all four army fliers at Fort Sam Houston set the stage for a bitter feud that would play a major role in the events that followed.

So long as the army had only one pilot and one airplane the possibility of any serious dissent developing was pretty remote. Foulois was perfectly happy being the army's lone eagle and was unquestionably loyal to the Signal Corps. In fact, he was operating under the delusion that having graduated from the Signal Corps School at Fort Leavenworth, he was now a Signal Corps officer, and he thought that his future in army aviation was secure. He was wrong on both counts. Before Foulois's error became evident, he would meet 1st Lt. Paul W. Beck.

3

Paul Ward Beck, 1911–1912

First Lt. Paul W. Beck was either a far-sighted prophet or a manipulative politician out for personal gain. The truth is that he was probably both. But whatever his true character was, Lieutenant Beck was the man who made the first attempt to put army aviation on the road to becoming an independent air force, the fourth branch of the U.S. Armed Forces.

Paul Beck was born on 1 December 1876 at Fort McKavett, Texas. His father, William Henry Beck, was a first lieutenant in the 10th Cavalry, which is famous for having been one of the army's black cavalry units, the so-called Buffalo Soldiers. During the Apache Wars (1871–87) Paul's father served with many officers who later rose to high rank in the army, and during the Spanish-American War (1898) he made several important political connections. The military and political connections that the senior Beck made were passed on to his son.

On 20 April 1896 Congressman Finis E. Downing informed Paul that he was the alternate candidate for an appointment to West Point for the academic year beginning in September 1897. All that Paul had to do was pass the entrance examination, which was to be administered at Jefferson Barracks, Virginia, on 1 March 1897, and hope that the regularly appointed candidate, Charles Burnett, would fail. At the time Paul received the alternate appointment, he was living on the Winnebago Indian Reservation, Nebraska, and had lived only briefly in Franklin, Illinois. Nevertheless, on 9 July 1897 he signed an affidavit stating that he had been a legal resident of the Sixteenth Congressional District in Illinois for nineteen years and seven months. He asked the secretary of war to send all future correspondence to his Winnebago address. The change of address did not cause a problem, but something else did.[1]

In May 1896, one month after he had been notified that he was an alternate candidate, Paul got Ruth Everett pregnant. Ruth was two years older than Paul and a schoolteacher. Contrary to nineteenth-century custom, Paul did not marry Ruth, because he was only nineteen and his parents would not give their consent. But he did not abandon her.

In January 1897 Paul and Ruth moved to Fort McPherson, Georgia, where Paul had obtained a job as a civilian clerk in the Adjutant General's Office, Mail and Record Division. On 20 January he wrote to the secretary of war, asking that his place of examination be moved from Fort Jefferson, on the Dry Tortugas, to Fort McPherson.[2] But Paul Junior's birth on 27 February 1897 effectively ended the senior Paul's chances of becoming a cadet at the U.S. Military Academy. In any event, the regularly appointed candidate, Charles Burnett, passed the entrance examination, so having an illegitimate child did not become an issue for Paul.

His congressional appointment to West Point was out the door, but there was another, though less certain, way for Paul to obtain a commission. He could enlist as a private, serve two years, and take a competitive examination for a commission as a second lieutenant. Having an illegitimate child would not pose a problem for an enlisted man, since the regulation required only that the enlisted man be "a citizen of the United States, unmarried, and under 30 years of age."[3] But there was, nevertheless, a problem with that solution—Paul was underage for enlistment.

On 7 August 1897 1st Lt. William Horne, the 9th Cavalry recruiting officer at Fort Duchesne, Utah, sent a telegram to the adjutant general requesting authority to enlist Paul, who was underage. He added that Paul's parents consented. The adjutant general, at the direction of the secretary of war, refused the request. On 11

August Capt. William Beck wrote to Col. J. C. Gilmore, the assistant adjutant general, asking his help in getting the secretary of war to grant Paul an exception. On 20 August Colonel Gilmore informed Captain Beck that Secretary of War Russell A. Alger would not allow an exception to regulations forbidding enlistment of minors between eighteen and twenty-one.[4]

The failure of their second plan to have Paul commissioned did not deter the Becks. In April 1898 Paul's father, his mother, Rachel, and Paul launched a letter-writing campaign to secure a direct commission for Paul.[5] The letter-writing campaign lasted two and a half years. William Beck worked the army's old-boy circuit and called on his congressional friends for help, while Rachel used her membership in the Daughters of the American Revolution to reach President William McKinley. William Beck gained support and letters of recommendation for Paul from several high-ranking officers, including Brig. Gen. Leonard Wood and Maj. Gen. Joe Wheeler. Paul's mother actually got President McKinley to take an interest, with the result that Paul's name was placed on the preferred list of applicants.[6]

In the meantime, Paul moved to Denver, Colorado, where he took a job as a reporter for the *Denver Times*, and in April 1898 he married Ruth Everett, eliminating the obstacle of having an illegitimate son.[7] While he was in Denver, Paul developed a close relationship with Brig. Gen. Edwin V. Sumner, who commanded the Colorado Department, making the first in a lengthy list of highly placed contacts. But Paul also exhibited what at best could be called questionable ethics.[8]

On 1 July 1898 Paul wrote to Brig. Gen. Henry C. Corbin, adjutant general of the army, asking for his help in obtaining a direct commission. In his letter he wrote, "Having no political influence and possessing some experience in military affairs from having been brought up on the frontier with regular troops, participating in a number of scouts in Arizona and Utah, I take the liberty of addressing you in the hope that you may see fit to assist me."

The claim that he participated in a number of scouts in Arizona and Utah is hard to believe, since he would have been only twelve years old when the Apache Wars ended, and most of his time after the close of the Apache Wars was spent on the Winnebago Indian Reservation and attending high school in Sioux City, Iowa.

When describing his accomplishments Paul frequently used the ploy of claiming to be more that he was. In most cases, his claims had a degree of plausibility. His technique was to imply something that no one would bother to check. But in this case his letter went beyond simply overstating his experience. He used stationary bearing the letterhead of the State of Colorado, Supreme Court Chambers, Denver. Beck was not a court employee, and he listed his return address as "in care of the Times," meaning the *Denver Times*. That was not the only time he used purloined stationery to write a letter. On 9 August 1898 he wrote to Secretary of War Alger. This time he used the letterhead of the Treasury Department, State of Colorado, and restated what he had written to Brigadier General Corbin.[9]

By 1899 the Becks' letter-writing campaign was starting to take effect. Several congressmen and senators had written letters supporting Paul's direct commission, and on 9 May 1899, President McKinley directed the secretary of war to appoint Beck a second lieutenant, "subject to the usual examination." The examination was set for 29 May 1899 at Fort Monroe, Virginia.[10]

At the time Beck was again employed as a civilian clerk in the Adjutant General's Office, Mail and Record Division, this time in Washington DC. On 15 May he took a twenty-one-day leave to prepare for the written exam, but fate intervened. He came down with epididymitis, an inflammation of the testicles, which his mother described as a "severe sprain." By 27 May he was forced to ask for a postponement to 15 June. The adjutant general granted the postponement.[11]

But Paul's health problems were not over by 15 June, and when he took the physical as directed on 15 June, he failed. The doctors judged him unfit due to being "anemic and underweight resulting from epididymitis," which he still had. The medical board noted that his condition was temporary and set his reexamination date for 15 August 1899.[12]

By 21 June Paul was still sick and had exhausted his paid sick leave. He requested and received a two-month extension without pay. Three weeks later he contracted typhoid fever and was hospitalized at the General Hospital, Washington Barracks, in Washington DC. While he was there the Adjutant General's Office extended his unpaid sick leave one month and set a new date, 5 September, for his reexamination.[13]

Still not fully recovered, Paul again failed the physical examination due to being fifteen pounds underweight. He was five feet, eleven inches tall and weighed 140 pounds. But this time the medical board waived the deficiency and recommended that he be allowed to take the written examination, which Paul barely passed on 15 September. But close was good enough and on 18 September 1899 he accepted his commission as a second lieutenant in the 5th Infantry and signed his oath of office.[14]

One month later with no military training other than what he had picked up as a soldier's son, 2nd Lt. Paul W. Beck joined the 5th U.S. Infantry in Santiago, Cuba. But his field service lasted only four months before he was again on sick leave. This time it was an appendicitis attack that put him in the hospital at Morro Castle, Cuba. On 11 April 1900 he was sent back to the United States and went on extended sick leave to his wife's family home in Bancroft, Nebraska.[15]

Paul's health was poorer than the medical board had thought. On 3 May a civilian doctor in Bancroft diagnosed liver and intestinal damage due to typhoid fever. The army again extended his sick leave, and on 5 June an army doctor in Omaha reported that Paul had an abnormally rapid heartbeat caused by the fever that had accompanied Paul's appendicitis attack in Cuba. It was a lucky diagnosis for Paul, because now his medical problems were service-related. The army again extended his sick leave.[16]

On 14 July 1900 he reported to Fort Sheridan, Illinois, to await the arrival of his regiment from Cuba. He had been on active duty for ten months, five of which he was absent on sick leave. He had no formal military training when he received orders on 1 January 1901 to proceed to the Philippines, where he was to join the

5th Infantry. He served in the Philippines for two years (1901–3), and his duties were largely noncombat assignments as the regiment's acting engineering, quartermaster, and commissary officer. Despite mediocre efficiency reports, due to his lack of formal training, he was promoted to first lieutenant on 25 July 1902.[17] Three weeks later the secretary of war censured him.

The censure stemmed from a fiction short story that Paul had written in 1898 while a reporter for the *Denver Times*. He sold the story to *Ainslee's Magazine* in August 1900, while he was on active duty and just before he went to the Philippines. *Ainslee's Magazine* published the story, titled "Colonel Molkvar, Hero," in its March 1902 issue.

In the story, which was set in the Southwest in 1881, Colonel Molkvar was a recent West Point graduate who was leading a cavalry troop in pursuit of several Apache warriors. The Apaches ambushed the troop, and almost immediately Second Lieutenant Molkvar was hit in the shoulder and feigned unconsciousness, leaving the fighting to his senior noncommissioned officer, Sergeant Casey. Despite being outnumbered, with most of his men dead or wounded, Sergeant Casey rescued the troop, defeated the Apaches, and got his wounded lieutenant back to Fort Huachuca.

Lieutenant Molkvar recovered from his wound, and in his combat report he took full credit for the action, giving Sergeant Casey only faint praise. Because of his reported valiant action, Lieutenant Molkvar was immediately promoted to major and then to colonel, at which time he was assigned to the Adjutant General's Office. From that point forward his career was a succession of administrative assignments that ended in a comfortable retirement. It was fiction but not entirely.

Beck's short story was a thinly disguised version of nineteenth-century army lore regarding Col. William Jefferson Volkmar. William Volkmar graduated from West Point in 1868 as a cavalry officer. From 1868 to 1876 he served on the frontier, and it was in 1876 when the story about him was born. The exact account has been lost in time, but the evidence suggests that he was maliciously slandered in 1876 and the slander stuck through the ensuing years of his career. Volkmar did rise rapidly in rank after 1876, and he received coveted assignments, including being the aide-de-camp to Major Generals John Pope and Philip H. Sheridan. Volkmar ended his career as the adjutant general, Colorado Department, and retired in 1900. He died on 4 March 1901 at the age of fifty-four.

Despite the slanderous rumor, Colonel Volkmar had been well regarded among the army's senior officers, and when the chief of artillery read Beck's story in *Ainslee's Magazine*, he immediately recognized whom it was about despite the minor changes Beck had made. In fact, other than transposing the *M* and *V* to create the fictional Colonel Molkvar and setting the story in 1881 rather than in 1876, Beck did little to hide the fictional Molkvar's true identity. The fictional Colonel Molkvar even ended his career as a department adjutant general. The chief of artillery sent the story with a note to the assistant adjutant general, Col. Henry P. McCain, who passed it along to the acting secretary of war.

In response to the acting secretary of war's order to provide an explanation, Beck said that he wrote the story while he was a civilian, and he sold it in 1900 while he was on sick leave. His only regret was that *Ainslee's Magazine* had waited until 1902 to publish the story, though he did concede that the title was "an unfortunate choice." The letter is typical of Paul Beck, who never backed down and never acknowledged his own fault in any matter.

The assistant secretary of war also did not back down and censured Beck, writing, "Your attack on the late Colonel Volkmar is viewed with positive disapproval, and that it is unsoldierly and reprehensible." The censure might have played a part in the mediocre efficiency rating that Lt. Col. P. G. Borden gave Beck in July 1903, after the 5th Infantry had arrived at its new station, Plattsburg Barracks, New York.[18]

During the twelve months that he, Ruth, and Paul Junior were at Plattsburg, Paul's performance improved to the point that his 1904 efficiency ratings were "excellent." Part of his success stemmed from the fact that at Plattsburg he attended the garrison school, where he took and completed his first formal military training. Acting on an earlier recommendation that he would profit from attending the Infantry and Cavalry School at Fort Leavenworth, Paul applied for admission for the 1904–5 academic year, and was accepted.[19]

He graduated from the Infantry and Cavalry School on 1 July 1905 with an overall score of 94.3, which ranked him eighteenth in his class of forty-six. He immediately applied for admission to the Signal School for the next academic year, 1905–6, and was again accepted. He graduated from the Signal School on 3 July 1906 with an overall score of 95.986, which ranked him third in a class of seven. His commanding officers now recognized Paul as "a good officer of more than average ability." They also accurately characterized him as "ambitious."[20]

While he was attending the Signal School, Paul applied for immediate detail to the Signal Corps, and when his application was denied, he asked his father, who was then a retired brigadier general, to pull strings for him. The elder Beck wrote directly to Maj. Gen. Fred C. Ainsworth in the War Department, who passed the letter on to Brigadier General Allen, the chief signal officer (cso). Brigadier General Allen told the elder Beck that there were no openings available until September 1907, but Paul's name would be considered then.[21]

The fact the Signal Corps was the most technically oriented corps in the army attracted Beck, who had a strong interest in engineering. Beck left no written record of when he became interested in aviation, but he was attending the Signal Corps School at the same time that Foulois was attending the Infantry and Cavalry School. It is probable that Beck took part in the discussions in the officers' club that Foulois described in his memoirs.[22]

An opening in the Signal Corps occurred earlier than expected. Following his graduation, Beck had rejoined his regiment, which was then in Cuba, on October 1906. On 4 February 1907 he was detailed to the Signal Corps, and the Manchu Law clock started ticking. The cso placed him in charge of the telephone and telegraph lines in Cuba until 20 April, when the cso assigned him to take command of the Signal Corps General Supply Depot at Benicia, California. Beck was stationed at Benicia Barracks until November 1909 when his career made a radical change in direction.[23]

On 19 November 1909 Glenn Curtiss wrote to the CSO, inviting him to detail Major George O. Squier as the army's official observer at the upcoming First International Air Meet in Los Angeles. It was an attractive offer, because among the pilots who would perform at the meet were Glenn Curtiss, Charles F. Willard, Charles K. Hamilton, and Louis Paulhan. The presence of so many experienced American and foreign pilots, and their airplanes, would give the army's representative a first-hand look at the cutting edge of aviation as it was in 1909.[24]

At that time, the army's only airplane was a wreck at College Park and the army's only pilot, 2nd Lt. Benjamin Foulois, was cooling his heels in Washington DC. With the army's lone eagle immediately available, one wonders why the CSO detailed a nonflying officer as the army's official observer, but the answer probably had to do with money. Beck was on the West Coast, and Foulois was back east, which meant that it cost the Signal Corps less to send Beck to Los Angeles than to send Foulois. Location was the only thing in Beck's favor, because up to that point he had shown no interest in aviation. In fact, he had written three papers dealing exclusively with telephone equipment and signal unit organization, one of which, "The Proposed Organization of Regimental Signal Troops," had appeared in the September 1906 issue of the *Infantry Association Journal*.[25] On 23 December the CSO detailed Paul Beck to be the army's official representative at the air meet.

The observer title implied that Beck was to do just that—observe and report. But Beck had no intention of being just an observer; he intended to be a participant. Though he had never said or written anything about military aviation, Beck had been giving the subject some thought. Among his ideas was the concept that aerial bombardment was a battlefield role for airplanes, and he intended to test his idea in Los Angeles.

Beck was thirty-three years old when he arrived in Los Angeles intent on conducting an aerial bombing experiment. The first pilot he approached was Glenn Curtiss, who took him up twice, but for an unexplained reason, no bombs were dropped. But on 19 January 1910 Beck rode with the French pilot Louis Paulhan, who was flying a Henry Farman. Beck's bombs were three "small bags containing dirt," there was no sighting device, and there was no so-called bomb-dropping device. His original plan was to have Paulhan fly right over the target, which was a strip of white canvas stretched on the ground, while Beck judged the time of release by eye and dropped the bags from between his legs. But in order to see the target, Paulhan had to fly to the right of it while Beck tossed the "bombs" over the side. The result was a wide "lateral deviation." And none of the "bombs" came close to the target.

Very few spectators saw the demonstration, and the press gave it scant attention because there was little excitement to watching a dirt-filled bag hit the ground. But Beck was not deterred by his failure to hit the target or the lack of public attention to his test. Following the 1910 International Air Meet at Los Angeles, he wrote an article titled "Flying-Men-O'-War," which appeared in the March 1910 issue of *Sunset Magazine*.[26]

Beck's article was at the time an amazing document in which he showed an exceptional understanding of aviation development and its potential for future application. In the article Beck described the problems to be expected when employing airplanes as bombers. Though his conclusions were not entirely accurate with respect to what constituted a safe altitude and speed for bombing, his vision of the future was on the mark. His article also provided the lay reader with an easily understood explanation of the various aircraft types, their advantages, and their shortcomings. The article established Beck as an authority on military aviation, especially in the area of theoretical application.

Because he had shown no previous interest in aviation, his sudden expertise in the field came as a surprise to everyone, including himself. But Beck was always quick to recognize an opportunity, and military aviation offered a potentially large opportunity for advancement. Aviation also offered Beck a way out of the infantry, a move he had been trying to accomplish since 1905 while attending the Infantry and Cavalry School. It is evident that Beck learned a great deal while attending the Los Angeles air meet, and he was able to apply what he learned to military aviation. His exceptional writing skills and his ability to quickly assimilate information cemented his new reputation as an expert on aviation.

Following the air meet at Los Angeles, Beck returned to the Presidio of San Francisco and resumed his duties with the Signal Corps, but he was never very far away from aviation matters. There was already talk in San Francisco about holding an international air meet there, and Beck made sure that he was in on the ground floor. While he was at the Presidio Beck met and became friends with two young officers, 2nd Lt. John C. Walker, 8th Infantry, and 2nd Lt. George E. M. Kelly, 30th Infantry. Both men became only briefly involved in aviation, but Kelly's involvement created the confrontation between Beck and Foulois that grew into a bitter feud.

Beginning in the summer of 1910, the San Francisco newspapers began reporting plans for a San Francisco air meet, and in November 1910 Maj. Gen. Tasker H. Bliss, commanding officer of the Western Military Department, detailed Beck to work with the air meet committee. Beck was appointed secretary of the committee, which in effect put him in charge of the military part of the event.[27] With Beck in such an important position, the air meet was assured of a heavy army and navy presence.

Though the air meet was called the San Francisco Air Meet, it actually took place at the Tanforan Racetrack, which was in the city of San Bruno, twelve miles south of San Francisco. In his capacity, Beck arranged to have the Tanforan Racetrack renamed Selfridge Field for the duration of the air meet, in memory of 1st Lt. Thomas Selfridge, who was killed at Fort Myer in 1908.

Another, even more significant event occurred in November 1910, when Glenn Curtiss wrote to the secretary of war, Jacob M. Dickinson, offering to train one or more officers at his winter flight school on North Island in San Diego. Curtiss said that he would train the officers at no cost to the government. At the time Curtiss made the offer, the Wright Company had a one-airplane monopoly on airplanes used by the Signal Corps, and Curtiss recognized that if the army had pilots trained to fly Curtiss airplanes, it would also have to buy Curtiss airplanes. His reasoning was based on Wright and Curtiss aircraft having entirely different flight control systems, and a pilot who flew a Wright could not fly a Curtiss, and vice versa.

Secretary of War Dickinson accepted the offer, and on 7 November he detailed Beck, Kelly, and Walker to take flight training at the Curtiss Flying School in San Diego. They were to report to the Curtiss school on completion of the San Francisco air meet.

The meet, which ran from 7 to 26 January 1911, is most often remembered as being the venue in which Eugene Ely flew his Curtiss airplane from the Tanforan Racetrack and landed on the deck of the USS *Pennsylvania*, anchored in San Francisco Bay. Having landed successfully, Ely took off from the cruiser's deck and returned to the racetrack. The feat overshadowed the army demonstrations that included aerial photography, airborne radio transmission, scouting, and a live bomb drop demonstration.

In addition to acting as the meet's military manager, Beck was personally involved in an airborne radio demonstration in which he became the first army officer to send and receive an airborne radio message, "with a small radio set of his own design." In fact, Beck did not design the radio. Earle Ennis, owner of the Western Wireless Equipment Company, in San Francisco, designed and built the Type A-4 Aeroplane Wireless Telegraph Set that Beck used.[28]

Despite the significant accomplishment that his radio demonstration represented, Beck later embellished it, telling a congressional committee that at the San Francisco meet, "First Lt. Myron S. Crissy worked with me on the aggressive use of the Aeroplane and we devised a bomb-dropping device which worked from the Aeroplane." That was not true, and Crissy flatly denied he had collaborated with Beck, a denial that is supported by the fact that Crissy's live bomb demonstration did not involve a bombsight or a dropping device. Again, Beck's claim had plausibility, but it was false. Nevertheless, the alleged collaboration has found its way into aviation history.[29]

In addition to the radio demonstration and Crissy's bomb-dropping experiment, Beck had arranged for third and fourth military performances involving aerial photography and aerial reconnaissance. Second Lts. John Walker and George E. M. Kelly drew those assignments. Lieutenant Walker flew in the morning with Walter Brookins and took aerial photos of Selfridge Field. Later in the day, Brookins and Kelly flew over the San Bruno hills on a reconnaissance mission to locate a First Cavalry troop and a battery of the Fifth Artillery that were marching from the Presidio of San Francisco to attack the 30th Infantry at Selfridge Field.

Following the 1911 Second International Air Meet at San Francisco, Beck published another aviation article in *Sunset*. Titled "The Doves of War," Beck's second article was a rehash of his earlier one except for the addition of a section on the development of military aviation under the Signal Corps. He wrote, "It is hoped that the Government of the United States, through Congress assembled, will see fit to appropriate . . . a sufficient sum of money to enable the Signal Corps to purchase the necessary aeroplanes to complete these investigations."[30]

This passage is important for two reasons. The first reason is because Beck had recognized that the lack of funding for aviation development was already a serious problem, and the other because in 1911 he was supporting the Signal Corps' official position that the corps should be responsible for developing military aviation. It was a position he would abandon in the following year.

Beck, Kelly, and Walker arrived at the Curtiss Flight School on North Island on 31 January 1911 to begin flight training. A situation was developing that was very similar to the one Lahm and Humphreys faced in 1909. Under the Manchu Law, Beck was scheduled to return to the infantry on 4 February 1911, five days after he arrived in San Diego to learn to fly. On 11 January the War Department assigned him to the 30th Infantry stationed at the Presidio of San Francisco. But Beck remained at the Curtiss Flying School in San Diego, becoming the first line officer on four-year detached service to the Signal Corps to be assigned to military aviation. There is no explanation among his military records to explain how that happened, but it is safe to assume that Beck had pulled some strings somewhere.[31]

On 11 March 1911, the same day that the chief of staff established the Maneuver Division at Fort Sam Houston, Texas, Beck was promoted to captain and assigned to the 18th Infantry at Fort Sam Houston. The choice of his infantry station is interesting, because two weeks later, the War Department ordered the three Curtiss students to report to Fort Sam Houston for duty in the field with the Maneuver Division.[32]

Foulois would have followed the order without comment, but Beck protested the order on the grounds that none of them were trained well enough to operate in the field. Beck took the position that they were only seven weeks into their flight training, and though they had all soloed according to the Curtiss method, none of them had taken the FAI pilot's certificate tests. They could not be rated as pilots by any standard. Considering what happened in Texas eight weeks later, one must admit that Beck's objection was well founded.

In response, the War Department, with Signal Corps concurrence, dismissed Beck's objection on the grounds that a Curtiss instructor, Eugene Ely, would accompany the Curtiss D-IV that was being delivered to Fort Sam Houston. What training they still lacked could be made up in Texas.[33] The War Department's decision, and the Signal Corps' agreement with the decision, illustrates a situation that became a festering sore among many army aviators in the following years. Men who could not fly an airplane and had almost no understanding of what flying actually involved, were making potentially life-and-death decisions for pilots. In this case the potential became a reality.

4

The Benjamin Foulois–Paul Beck Feud, 1911–1913

Beck, Kelly, and Walker arrived at Fort Sam Houston on 1 April 1911 and the Beck-Foulois feud started on 5 April when Major George O. Squier organized the Provisional Aero Company and placed Paul Beck in command. Beck was appointed because he had been promoted to captain and was senior to Foulois, who was a first lieutenant. Feeling that he was the old hand at flying, First Lieutenant Foulois resented being placed under Beck's command.

But the Provisional Aero Company was a paper organization in which Beck did very little commanding. When formed, the company consisted of one airplane, Robert F. Collier's Wright Model B, so only Foulois did any flying. On 27 April 1911 the Curtiss Company pilot Eugene Ely arrived with a new Curtiss D-IV "Military," designated SC-2. Beck, Kelly, and Walker had flown the D-III at North Island. The D-IV had a more powerful engine than the D-III and greater load-carrying capability, which resulted in the airplane's military designation. The D-IV also featured two sets of elevators, a single elevator mounted forward of the wing and two elevators on the tail, the latter of which changed the airplane's aerodynamic characteristics. The D-IV also carried two people, the pilot in a seat forward of the wing and a passenger directly behind him in a seat mounted on the wing.[1]

The Wright Company also sent a new airplane to Fort Sam Houston, a Model B exactly like Collier's. Wright Company pilot

Frank T. Coffyn and the new Model B, designated SC-3, arrived on 18 April. The two company pilots were to instruct the four army pilots, Coffyn teaching Foulois, and Ely teaching Beck, Kelly, and Walker. By this time Foulois was experienced enough that he probably did not need Coffyn's help, but the three novice pilots sorely needed Ely's help. They did not get it.

Major Squier, the Maneuver Division's CSO, had decided to accept eighteen volunteers from the Maneuver Division for minimal flight training, which amounted only to demonstration rides. The eighteen volunteers received no meaningful instruction, but they used up training time that Beck, Walker, and Kelly needed. Nevertheless, two of the eighteen went on to become pilots.[2] By the time the eighteen volunteers had completed their "training" and the two company pilots could devote their time to the four assigned aviators, the clash between Beck and Foulois was well developed.

Foulois derided the D-IV as being "dangerously unsuitable for tactical operations with troops in the field, especially when called upon to operate out of the critically restricted flying field at Fort Sam Houston." He based his opinion on having allegedly "flown with Glen Curtiss in an identical type of airplane at San Antonio in 1910," which he did not do.[3]

Foulois's criticism of the D-IV has to be weighed in light of his not actually having piloted the Curtiss, and he was a Wright pilot. His biased criticism indicated that as early as 1911 the rivalry between Curtiss and Wright pilots was starting to develop. It was a rivalry that in this case had as much to do with Foulois's dislike of Beck as it did Foulois's preference in airplanes.

Foulois appears to have been the one carrying a grudge. There is no indication that Beck and Foulois argued or had any disputes from the date Major Squier formed the company until Kelly's death on 10 May. In fact, there was very little opportunity for the two men to run afoul of each other, since Foulois was occupied with the Wright Model B while Beck, Kelly, and Walker were concerned with the Curtiss D-IV. Nevertheless, Foulois's resentment over Beck having command was palpable. Foulois did not openly criticize the three Curtiss pilots, but he definitely believed they didn't measure up to his standard. He commented, "It frightened me to watch them operate. . . . They did many things I had learned not to do and practiced their mistakes time and time again." This was probably not sour grapes but an honest observation based on his experience.[4]

The first warning that the Curtiss pilots' minimal training in the more powerful aircraft had turned dangerous occurred on 8 May. Lieutenant Walker was making a too steeply banked turn in the D-IV at about two hundred feet when his aircraft stalled, side slipped, and very nearly hit the ground. Walker recovered at the last moment, made one turn around the field, landed, and walked away from the airplane. He never flew again and returned to the 8th Infantry at his own request.[5]

The next day, Beck went up in the D-IV and performed a series of low-level maneuvers that Foulois criticized. Everyone who watched Beck fly that day agreed that he was too low as he approached the landing strip. He throttled back his engine, probably too far, and it stopped at the critical moment. Before he could recover, the Curtiss crashed among the mesquite and rocks that covered the area. The airplane was heavily damaged, and the crash left Beck momentarily stunned.[6]

The nature of the D-IV repairs brought the feud into the open. Foulois was openly critical of the material used to make the repairs, how they were done, and Beck's performance in supervising the repairs. While no. 2 was being repaired, the Wright Company mechanic Oliver Simmons and Foulois watched and made comments to Beck about how the work was being done. According to Foulois, some of the wood being used to replace the broken front fork was cross-grained and knotty and was "obviously" inferior to the quality used in Wright airplanes. Foulois and Simmons also saw what they believed was an unnecessary bolt hole that had been drilled in the fork when the Curtiss people originally installed the cross-brace.

Foulois said he and Simmons told Beck about the poor-quality wood and the unnecessary hole, but Beck made no effort to replace the defective parts. In 1968 Foulois added that when he told Beck about the wood and shoddy construction, Beck "just shrugged them off." In his one-sided criticism, Foulois ignored the possibility that Beck might have had no other replacement parts to use. And Foulois's criticism loses credence in view of the fact that a Curtiss mechanic, James Hennig, was actually making the repairs. In any event, the allegedly shoddy parts were still in place when Kelly took the plane up on 10 May 1911.

That morning, the D-IV was again ready for flight, and Lieutenant Kelly was scheduled to fly it. Captain Beck did not make a test flight following the repairs, a point that became an issue with Foulois. One onlooker said that Kelly appeared nervous before the flight. He took off at 0600 on the clear, windless morning, climbing in a wide spiral until he reached about three hundred feet. The general assumption was that he was going to attempt to practice the dead-stick landing the FAI test required for the pilot's certificate. Witnesses' accounts about what happened next are varied, but all agree that Kelly did not kill his engine when he started his descent from three hundred feet. Some say he reduced his power about 50 percent, and others say he came down at full power. In any event, his initial angle of descent appeared to the onlookers to be about right, and the trouble started as he neared the ground.[7]

Some witnesses said that his descent became too steep and he had too much power on as he came in to land. Foulois, who witnessed the crash, said that Kelly "came in hot and high" and put the nose down sharply, causing the front wheel to hit the ground "with a sickening, wrenching sound." Other witnesses said his decent was "perfectly normal," and the accident review board said that "he made a not abnormally hard landing." All agree that the initial impact tore away the front wheel, broke both wheel forks at a point in front of the pilot and damaged the forward elevator.

The SC-2 bounced back into the air and roared across the field in a "wavering, uneven dash straight for the tents of the 11th Infantry." Kelly was in real trouble now. He had no forward elevator, it having been destroyed on impact, and he was flying only a few feet above the ground at full power, headed directly toward a row of heavy tents and equipment. Unable to climb over the obstruction directly ahead of him, he apparently tried to bank left. His left wingtip hit the ground and the airplane cart wheeled, "reducing the machine to fragments," and catapulted Kelly headlong from his seat. His head hit the ground twenty feet from the crash, and he died an hour later of a massive head injury. Foulois put the blame entirely on Beck.

Immediately following Kelly's death, an accident investigation board was formed. The board consisted of Major Squier, Beck, Walker, and Foulois, since they were the only people at Fort Sam Houston who knew anything about flying, but Foulois declined to serve. He told the division CSO that he had watched the repairs being made to SC-2 and that he had pointed out to Beck "the inferior materials and workmanship." Foulois had already decided that Beck lacked "the professional competence to realize a potentially unsafe airplane when he saw one," and had not made a test flight in no. 2 before allowing Kelly to fly it, thus making Beck culpable.[8]

Foulois may have been right about the poor-quality wood used to repair the D-IV. He certainly had enough experience putting a wooden airplane back together after a crash, having done it himself several times. But Curtiss Company mechanic James Hennig was in charge of repairing the D-IV, and if anyone was qualified to judge the quality of the materials and the repairs it was Henning. And Henning was certainly competent to recognize whether the airplane was safe to fly.

The issue was what caused the catastrophic damage to the front wheel and fork. The accident investigation board concluded that "the front wheel must have struck an abrupt depression in the ground or some obstacle, which resulted in the break." Other than Foulois, only the aviation magazine *Aero* suggested that the quality of the repairs and the material used played a part in Kelly's death. *Aero* told its readers that the front axle "was torn from the wood which held it, owing to the laminated members of the forward fork of the landing chassis having been weakened previously by a hurried job of repairing made necessary by some slight damages of the day before." On the other hand, the D-IV hit the ground so hard that even the highest-quality wood would have failed on impact, a point that Foulois, from ample personal experience, probably recognized but refused to admit.[9]

Foulois was especially critical of what he described as Beck's failure to make a test flight before he allowed Kelly to take off in the D-IV. Despite the lack of any requirement for a test flight, he strongly believed that Beck had shirked his duty by not taking the plane up. The reality was that there was no requirement that Beck make a test flight before Kelly flew the plane. Although Beck was Kelly's superior, he was at best only a marginally better pilot, and he was not Kelly's flight instructor. The Curtiss flight instructor, Eugene Ely, was present but was also under no obligation to make a test flight.

Foulois was so biased against Beck that no amount of practical experience would have made him a useful board member. The basis for Foulois's animosity is evident in the statement he made to Major Squier after the crash. He said he had "three years practical air experience as compared to Beck's five months experience," a circumstance that gave him no confidence in Beck's "qualifications to command the Provisional Aero Company." In a fit of pique, Foulois recommended that Squier either relieve Beck or Foulois from duty with the Provisional Aero Company. Major Squier recognized that Foulois resented Beck having command of the 1st Provisional Aero Company and did not call him as a witness.[10]

The accident board, now consisting of Major Squier, Beck, and Walker, did not list the repairs or the absence of a test flight among the causes of the crash. Instead, they attributed the crash to a combination of three factors: pilot error that resulted in the first impact, the initial impact that damaged the controls and set up the conditions that resulted in the second impact, and Kelly's heroism in sacrificing himself to avoid the encampment that resulted in the fatal crash. Not everyone agreed. James Hennig, the Curtiss mechanic who witnessed the whole event, sent a report to Glen Curtiss that placed the blame on Kelly for "bringing his machine to earth at full speed."[11]

Following Kelly's fatal crash, Brig. Gen. William H. Carter stopped all flying at Fort Sam Houston. On 12 June Brig. Gen.

James Allen requested that Beck be ordered for duty at College Park, and on 22 June, Beck left Fort Sam Houston. Foulois remained on the ground at Fort Sam Houston, where on 11 July 1911 the Manchu Law caught up with him and the War Department assigned him to the Militia Bureau. Foulois blamed his assignment to the Militia Bureau on his clash with Paul Beck. While untrue, the fact that he believed it illustrates the ill feeling that Foulois had toward Beck. It was an ill feeling that would again become apparent two years later.

5

The Flying Club, 1911–1912

Nineteen eleven was the year in which army aviation actually got its start. It was also the year that the separation movement got its start. The Signal Corps had leased land at College Park, Maryland, for use as a flight school. The first future pilot, and future dissident, to arrive at College Park was 1st Lt. Roy C. Kirtland, who arrived on 3 April with orders to supervise the "establishment of buildings, receive the shipments of material, and otherwise take charge of the new flying school project."[1] Kirtland was a "mustang," meaning that he had come up through the ranks. At thirty-seven, he was an elderly first lieutenant and was probably not cut out to be a pilot, as events during the next few years indicated. But he was a good straw boss, as his efficiency in getting the College Park aviation school into operation showed.

In the meantime, the next future pilots, 2nd Lts. Henry "Hap" Arnold and Thomas DeWitt Milling, were detailed for flight training at the Wright school and factory near Dayton, Ohio, arriving there in early May. When they had completed their flight training they reported to College Park on 15 June; the arrival of their commanding officer, Capt. Charles DeForest Chandler, followed on 20 June. A medical officer, 1st Lt. John P. Kelly, a civilian mechanic, Henry S. Molineau, and fifteen enlisted men arrived on 18 June. Arnold and Milling were both twenty-five when they arrived at College Park, and both were destined for stellar careers in the army.

Arnold projected a happy, outgoing personality with a large dose of good sense. Milling was described as having a winning personality and one of the first "natural-born fliers."[2]

In the spring of 1911, Congress appropriated $25,000 for military aviation, $5,000 of which was immediately available. That money allowed the Signal Corps to lease the land at College Park and buy five new airplanes, two Wright Model B's, a Burgess-Wright that was a Model B built under license, and two Curtiss D-IVs. The purchase of these five airplanes was another example that the men who were running army aviation were either not qualified for the job or were not paying attention to what they were doing.

The Wright and the Curtiss airplanes had entirely different control systems, which meant that a pilot who learned to fly one type could not fly the other. And the difference in control systems created a fierce rivalry between Wright and Curtiss pilots that at times became dangerous.[3] To further the difficulty, the Wright Model B that came out in 1911 created right-hand and left-hand pilots, which created an additional problem: a right-hand pilot could fly a Wright plane alone, but a left-hand pilot had to have a passenger, or put 150 pounds of bricks on the empty left-hand seat to maintain the plane's lateral balance. It had to do with which hand the pilot used to operate the wing-warping and rudder lever that was located between the seats. Speaking of the Wright control system in 1915, Grover Loening, the school's aeronautical engineer and a former Wright employee, said, "None of the controls had the proper movement and sensitivity, and the large warping wings were so hooked-up as to be ineffective on lateral control."[4]

Curtiss airplanes had two seats but only one set of controls and used ailerons instead of wing-warping to achieve lateral stability and to roll the plane right and left. The single set of controls made it more difficult to learn to fly, since the student pilot was alone in the machine from the day he started his flight lessons. As we shall see, it also created a situation that was ripe for abuse when flight pay was authorized in 1913.

Paul Beck and the remains of SC-2 in which Lieutenant Kelly had died arrived at College Park on 25 July. Like Arnold and Milling, Beck needed practice to pass his FAI pilot's certificate tests, but first he had to put SC-2 back together. His arrival brought the entire U.S. Army military aviation component together and marked the start of the "flying club" days. Several factors, all of which were present at College Park, made that possible.

The first factor was the absence of direction from the top down. Hap Arnold commented, "Our purpose had to be a vague one of developing the airplane into a military weapon as best we could, for we certainly received few, if any, suggestions from the War Department. It was a routine of flying a bit higher or a bit farther or mounting some communications gadget or weapon on our flying machine in an endeavor to give the airplane a military value."[5] Arnold was describing a flying program with no substance or direction, one that was simply an extension of Brigadier General Allen's order to Foulois to teach himself to fly. It was a situation that, over time, created dissatisfaction and dissent.

The presence of a permanent press corps on the airfield was a major contributor to the clublike atmosphere. Every flight made headlines, every flight was fraught with danger, and disaster was narrowly avoided.[6] Crowds of civilians came to the field every day when the weather was fair to watch the army pilots fly and perform "stunts." The army flights soon became a daily air show, the pilots became instant celebrities, and the press gushed. The Aero Club of America (ACA) created a special army and navy members section with reduced dues.[7] Membership in the ACA was not a bad thing per se, but it became intrusive and created a problem that brought dissatisfaction and dissent into the open in 1913.

The five pilots became qualified for the FAI pilot's certificate in the following order: Arnold on 29 July 1911, Milling on 30 July, Beck on 3 August, Kirtland on 17 August, and Chandler on 20 September. Following Chandler's qualification, the ACA contest committee, of which Signal Corps officer Lt. Col. Samuel Reber was the chairman, appointed Chandler as the ACA "representative to observe and report qualifications of officer candidates" for the FAI pilot's certificate. In effect, the ACA assumed the authority to judge when a man became a qualified army pilot.

Lacking an organized and structured training program, the pilots were free to do as they liked. Initially that involved flying from point to point, landing to watch a ball game, have lunch, or take part in some sort of festive occasion. On 7 July Arnold and Kirtland flew to Washington, circled the Capitol building at 2,400 feet, and flew back to College Park. On 21 August Arnold and Chandler flew forty-two miles to the District of Columbia National Guard annual encampment at Frederick, Maryland. They arrived at Camp Ordway at 0723 and were greeted by the Frederick volunteer fire department. The firemen had headed toward Camp Ordway as soon as the plane flew over the town. In the meantime, all the offices and stores in Frederick were closed for the day so that the population could go see the airplane. Before flying back to College Park, Arnold and Chandler were "pleasantly entertained." Other than gaining flying experience, there was no training involved.

Air meets in which professional exhibition pilots flew for cash prizes were held frequently throughout the United States from January 1910 to the end of 1912. In his memoirs, Hap Arnold wrote, "During 1911, we were encouraged to attend the civilian air meets, where we not only renewed aviation acquaintances, but took part in the events. Army and Navy pilots were required to pay their expenses at these meets—not easy on $124.00 a month."[8]

Though officers who took leaves of absence to attend air meets had to pay their own expenses, their expenses were offset by wages they received from the Curtiss and Wright companies for whom they flew as members of the companies' exhibition teams. Those wages were $25 a day for being on the team and $50 for every day they flew. A pilot who simply attended a seven-day air meet as a team member, and did not fly, received $175 for the week. If he flew every day, his take was $350 for the week, either amount greatly exceeding his army pay. On top of their daily draw, pilots received generous cash prizes for contests they won while flying for the company exhibition teams.

Paul Beck was the first army pilot to fly in an air meet for pay and cash prizes. He flew for the Curtiss exhibition team in the International Aviation Meet at Grant Park, Chicago, 12–20 August 1911, and won $900 for remaining the longest time aloft: one hour, three minutes, and fifty-three seconds.[9] Paul Beck and Thomas Milling attended the Harvard-Boston Aero Meet, 26 August–4 September.[10] On Labor Day, 4 September, Milling, flying for the Burgess-Wright Company, competed in the Tri-State Race and took the second-place, $5,000 prize.[11]

Arnold, Beck, and Milling flew at the Nassau Boulevard Meet on 23–30 September 1911. Beck again flew with the Curtiss team, and Arnold and Milling flew for Wright. The highlight event was the "establishment of the first airmail service in the United States." Beck's role in this event was to fly Postmaster General Frank Hitchcock from the post office tent at Nassau Boulevard to the Mineola Post Office, with Hitchcock sitting in the right seat, a mail bag on his lap. Once over the Mineola Post Office, Post Master Hitchcock, set the bag in front of him and pushed it over the leading edge of the wing with his foot, reportedly dropping the bag in "the proper spot." In all, 32,415 postcards, 3,993 letters, and 1,062 circulars were carried during the meet. The closing event was a relay on 30 September with three teams—one army team and two civilian teams—competing. The army team, with one civilian member, won and split $1,000 four ways. The crowd loved it.[12]

Second Lt. Hap Arnold and his infantry officer friend 1st Lt. Jacob Fickel teamed up for a shooting contest against two British aviators, Douglas Campbell and Thomas Sopwith. The target was a tin dinner plate in the center of the field, and the altitude was two hundred feet. Fickel, an expert rifleman, put six rounds through the dinner plate. Campbell and Sopwith, who had no known marksmanship skills, scored zero, giving Arnold and Fickel a "clear cut victory," and $700 to split.[13]

Milling won the solo duration event and, together with other successes, flew away with $2,550 in prizes, and Beck was right behind him with $1,150. Arnold, who said he was flat broke, sold rides for $50 a person, and following the air meet, he flew the aerial stunts in the low-budget, silent two-reeler *The Military Air-Scout*, starring Earl Williams, Edith Storey, and Alec B. Francis. Arnold stood in for Williams, who played Lieutenant Wentworth, an army pilot. The next day he was a stand-in for another silent movie, *The Elopement*, released in 1912 and staring Florence Baker.[14]

By 1911 many people, both civilian and military, recognized that the airplane had a big potential for waging aggressive warfare, which meant arming them with bombs and guns. Ever since Beck dropped dirt bags on a target during the International Air Meet at Los Angeles in 1910, a bomb-dropping event was a regular feature at almost every air meet. The "bombs" used for those events were anything from oranges to flour-filled bags. The live bombs that 1st Lt. Myron S. Crissy dropped during the 1911 San Francisco International Meet were more dramatic, but that was showmanship rather than a practical exercise, and was of no value insofar as producing useful information for the advancement of aerial warfare. The first bombing demonstration that should have been the start of an aerial bombing development program occurred at College Park on 10 October 1911.

Riley E. Scott was a West Pointer who graduated in the class of 1904 and was commissioned a second lieutenant in the Coast Artillery Corps. On 4 May 1910 the U.S. Patent Office granted Riley Estel Scott patent number 991,378 for "Projectiles from Aerial Craft, a Means for Dropping."[15] The following year, Scott entered the Michelin International Bomb-Dropping Contest at Villacoublay, France, that began on 11 January 1912. The prize for the bombardier who scored the most points for accuracy was $5,000. In the meantime, Scott needed to conduct practical tests of his bombsight and bomb-dropping device, and on 10 October 1911, he was at College Park with his equipment. No previous arrangements had been made, other than Scott showing up at the field and asking his friends at College Park for their help. The testing of the Scott bombsight and dropping device in 1911 was unofficial.

Scott won the $5,000 at Villacoublay, and the U.S. Army Ordnance Department set up live bombing tests in April and May 1912 at North Island, San Diego, to try Scott's bombsight with one-hundred-pound live bombs. But the Ordnance Department did not follow up on the tests, and it did not buy Scott's bombsight. The next bombing tests were done at North Island in August 1914.

Those tests showed that accurate bombing from a relatively high altitude was feasible, and Capt. Arthur Cowan, together with the pilots, recommended that bombing training be regularly taught to selected officers. But the CSO, Brig. Gen. George Scriven, disagreed, because he believed that the principal role of the airplane was reconnaissance.[16] The result was that the United States entered the war without a bombsight, and remained without a bombsight until the army adopted the British MK I and IA bombsights in December 1917. The American Expeditionary Force's Air Service used the British MK I extensively in 1918.[17]

It can be said in defense of Brigadier General Allen and his successor as CSO, George Scriven, that both men appear to have had a legal and moral objection to equipping airplanes with bombs. Allen was the CSO when the Second International Peace Conference, held at The Hague 15 June to 18 October 1907, issued its declaration prohibiting the discharge of projectiles and explosives from balloons. The United States ratified the declaration on 10 March 1908.[18]

In his 1914 annual report, Brigadier General Scriven wrote that "there can be no doubt of the value of the aeroplane in rapid and long-range reconnaissance work."[19] He acknowledged the airplane's worth in spotting and directing artillery fire, and then addressed aerial bombardment of troops in the field and economic and industrial centers, starting with a reiteration of reconnaissance as aircraft's proper role.

> But the useful, approved, and most effective work is probably to be found chiefly in reconnaissance and transmission of information in the theater of military operations; for this reason, aviation must be reckoned as a vastly important branch of the Signal Corps of the Army. The use of aircraft for these purposes cannot be open to the charge of inhumanity and cruelty. But as to the service and value of aircraft in offense, much doubt remains, except where an overhead attack on troops can be made effective—a condition that probably does not often arise, although many isolated instances of its value in attack are cited. When used in General

destructive work against noncombatants, dislike of this method of attack must always exist. A fire sown broadcast upon the earth or employed under conditions which make specific aim useless is at least distasteful.

It may be said however, that if the future shows that attack from the sky is effective and terrible, as may prove to be the case, it is evident that, like rain, it must fall upon the just and the unjust, and, it may be supposed, will therefore become taboo to all civilized people; and forbidden at least by paper agreements.[20]

Proposals to arm airplanes met with equal resistance. It was on this issue that the movement to separate army aviation from the Signal Corps got its start. The pilots had no problem accepting reconnaissance as a battlefield mission, but they also believed there would have to be a parallel effort to stop the enemies' reconnaissance planes from flying over friendly lines. The only way to accomplish that mission was with gun-armed airplanes.

In the spring of 1912, Secretary of War Henry L. Stimson issued a plan for expanding army aviation that, if implemented, would change how the Aeronautical Division was being run. Stimson wanted a structured pilot training program that included the study of meteorology, wireless telegraphy, military topography, sketching, and reconnaissance as they applied to aviation. He wanted training in "dropping projectiles, and the use of small arms and machine guns from aircraft." He also wanted training in the design of military aircraft and "all other matters to improve military aviation." The secretary of war's vision for the future went far beyond the Signal Corps' reconnaissance mission, and it was not fully implemented before the United States entered the war.[21]

A month after the secretary of war's plan for army aviation was published, Lt. Col. Isaac N. Lewis (ret.) showed up at College Park with a Lewis gun that his company, Automatic Firearms Company, had in production. He was hoping to test the firing of his gun at a ground target from an airplane during flight. But this was not an official test. When Colonel Lewis arrived at College Park, several examples of his machine guns were already undergoing test-

PRAYER FOR THE CANONIZATION OF THE VENERABLE SERVANT OF GOD MICHAEL McGIVNEY

Founder of the Knights of Columbus

God, our Father, protector of the poor and defender of the widow and orphan, you called your priest, Father Michael J. McGivney, to be an apostle of Christian family life and to lead the young to the generous service of their neighbor. Through the example of his life and virtue may we follow your Son, Jesus Christ, more closely, fulfilling his commandment of charity and building up his Body which is the Church. Let the inspiration of your servant prompt us to greater confidence in your love so that we may continue his work of caring for the needy and the outcast. We humbly ask that you glorify your venerable servant Father Michael J. McGivney on earth according to the design of your holy will. Through his intercession, grant the favor I now present *(here make your request)*. Through Christ our Lord. Amen.

Please report all favors received:
The Father McGivney Guild
1 Columbus Plaza
New Haven, CT 06510-3326 · USA
www.fathermcgivney.org

10502-A 3/17

ing and evaluation by the Ordnance Department, together with the British Vickers machine gun, and the army's standard M1909 Benét-Mercié light machine gun. The tests were not going well for the Lewis gun.[22]

Captain Chandler, who undoubtedly had read Secretary Stimson's plan in the *Register*, including the part about machine guns and bombs, agreed to the colonel's request, and though the test was unofficial, he sent a report of the test to the chief signal officer that was published in the September—October 1912 issue of the *Journal of the United States Artillery* under the title "The Lewis Airplane Gun."

When Col. George Scriven, the acting CSO, read Chandler's report on the impromptu Lewis gun test, he sent a letter to Brig. Gen. William Crozier, chief of ordnance, on 17 July, asking for five thousand rounds of service rifle ammunition for "trying the Lewis Gun with the aeroplanes during the coming maneuvers to be held . . . in August next." Colonel Scriven was talking about the army-militia maneuvers in Connecticut that were scheduled for 10–17 August 1912. Brigadier General Crozier responded ten days later.

> Replying to letter from your office dated 17th instant, in regard to the supply of five-thousand rounds of ammunition for the purpose of trying a Lewis Gun with aeroplanes during the maneuvers to be held next month in the vicinity of New York City, I have the honor to inform you that this Department would not be authorized ammunition for the trial of a gun not under test with reference to its adoption in the service, and that the representatives of the Lewis Gun have not accepted the offer of the Board of Ordnance and Fortification to test their gun with reference to that object.[23]

Commenting on the issue sometime later, Brigadier General Crozier opined, "The Signal Corps was not the agency for making tests of machine guns, had no experts or facilities for doing so, and undoubtedly wished only to test the firing of a machine gun from an aeroplane."[24] The truth was that Crozier and Lewis were in the middle of a heated feud, and the chief of ordnance was not about to let the Signal Corps test the gun during the upcoming maneuvers. In any event, it was a lost opportunity, because such a field test would have shown the Signal Corps what was needed to mount a machine gun in an airplane and what sort of design changes would be needed for a machine-gun-armed airplane.

Following the firing of the Lewis gun, the school asked, through channels, that the Ordnance Department provide three Lewis guns for further testing. The request was turned down because the Lewis gun was still being tested and was not in the army's inventory. Instead, Ordnance provided three M1909 Benét-Mercié light machine guns.

The Benét-Mercié, which was two pounds lighter than the Lewis gun, was good for what it was designed to do, but its design and the design of the Wright and Curtiss airplanes made the gun unworkable for use in an airplane. The gun was tried in both the Curtiss and Wright airplanes, and the pilots quickly saw that the Benét-Mercié, as is, would not work.

The gun could be modified for use in aircraft, but there was a catch-22; the CSO did not want a gun, period. And the ordnance people did not want to modify the gun from its intended purpose. The impasse left the choice of taking "the Benét-Mercié or nothing."[25] There was no future push by the Signal Corps to mount a machine gun in an airplane.

Given that army aviation was part of the Signal Corps, and the CSOs were opposed to considering any mission for aviation beyond reconnaissance, artillery spotting, and fire control, one would assume that training in reconnaissance would take up a lot of the aviation school's time. It did not. The only two instances in which reconnaissance was seriously practiced were at Fort Sam Houston in 1911 and at the Scranton, Connecticut, maneuvers in 1912.

In addition to reconnaissance, the Signal Corps had an obligation to provide the field artillery and coast artillery with spotting and fire control systems. When the airplane came along, it fit neatly into that obligation, but only two of the army's pilots, Arnold and Milling, received any sort of training in that role prior to the United States' entry into World War I.

With the purchase of the first airplane in 1909, the Aeronautical

Division's focus had shifted to the airplane. But the shift in focus did not include an interest in developing the airplane's offensive capability. The stumbling block was the dominant position the balloon fraternity held in the Aeronautical Division's administration, all of whom believed that reconnaissance was aviation's primary mission. The fact was that many senior army officers agreed with General Allen's opinion that the airplane was just another reconnaissance vehicle, but one with greater mobility than a captive balloon. And in 1910 the *Field Service Regulations* were amended to include "reconnaissance by balloon or flying machine" as a Signal Corps responsibility.

A role expanded to include bombing and aerial combat was not considered technically feasible, because the airplanes the army bought were still underpowered and unreliable. And other reasons were grounded in army politics and national complacency based on geography. In any event, the army's continued fixation on the airplane's reconnaissance role, to the virtual exclusion of other combat roles, generated much discontent beginning in 1913. But the Signal Corps officers who commanded the army's aviation program were the focus of the discontent.

Mismanagement, lack of funds, ACA interference, and bullheaded resistance to developing a combat role for military aviation became the fuse on the powder keg. But it was the politics of personal advancement and turf protection that lit the fuse.

6

The First Signs of Trouble, 1912

The first public indication that there might be a problem in army aviation appeared in the February-March 1912 issue of the *Aero Club of America Bulletin*. In an article titled "Army Aviation: Its Needs," Capt. Charles DeForest Chandler opened by stating, "That the United States Army is behind European armies in the development of aviation must be admitted."[1] Chandler attributed the lack of progress to the fact that "there have been no measures taken to place aviation on a sound and permanent footing," and went on to identify aviation's two basic needs: money and men.

Chandler's article was not a cry of alarm, but it was a mild statement that military aviation was not progressing as quickly as might be desired. Though he cited money as one of the two "basic needs to a successful aviation corps," he expressed satisfaction with the funding that Congress had been providing. He credited Congress with appropriating $125,000 for aviation in 1911 and felt satisfied that they would do it again in 1912. Congress did not do it again in 1912.

Chandler did not suggest that Congress should pass appropriations to increase the size of the pilot pool and to buy more airplanes. And he said nothing about appropriations for the development of a multimission role, nor did he suggest spending money to obtain better airplanes. More than anything, Chandler's article was the official Signal Corps pitch for public support in getting Congress to appropriate more money for Signal Corps aviation.

Turning to the manpower problem he wrote, "There can be no real advance in aviation matters in our Army until such time as there may be provided sufficient officers on a sufficiently permanent basis to relieve the present dearth of flying material." But he said nothing about changing the Manchu Law. His solution to the pilot shortage was for the public to support two bills in Congress that provided aviators with increased benefits in the form of flight pay, and payments to dependents of aviators who were killed on duty. He assured his readers, "It is an absolute certainty that there can be no real advance in Army aviation in the United States until some such measure is enacted."

He made a faint suggestion that Congress should increase the Signal Corps' authorized strength so that the additional officers could handle the Signal Corps aviation responsibility. But he acknowledged that such an increase was unlikely, making it necessary to rely on volunteers from the other arms, so-called detailed officers. He noted that under the existing circumstances, volunteers were few and their time in aviation was limited to four years. In January 1912, when Chandler wrote the article, there were only six officers assigned to aviation and one of them, 1st Lt. Paul Beck, was about to be "Manchued" back to the infantry. Chandler had addressed a serious problem that contributed substantially to the lack of progress in military aviation. And it was a problem that other people who were interested in military aviation recognized.

Since 1910 the aviation magazines and the ACA had been advocating that army aviation be expanded by training the National Guard and enlisting a corps of civilian pilots who could be called to duty in the event of a national emergency. The ACA was particularly active in promoting the National Guard plan. The reasoning behind those suggestions was that the states, with federal assistance, could establish part-time aviation units that were less expensive for the federal government than maintaining a full-time regular army aviation unit.

Chandler had simply followed the Signal Corps party line that increasing the authorized strength of the Signal Corps or providing increased benefits to aviators would solve the manpower problem, thus promoting progress. What he failed to address was the larger problem that the Signal Corps had no plan for a directed development program. Chandler wrote his article during the height of the flying club period when pilot training was on an individual, catch-as-catch-can basis, and practical tests of the airplane's military potential were virtually nonexistent. Though bland and lacking real substance, Chandler's article did provide a clue that not everything was right in army aviation. But the article's tone suggests that it was really a Signal Corps ploy to deflect criticism of the army's aviation program. It also illustrated why Chandler's subordinates described him as a man who "lacked push."[2]

But a more serious sign of trouble went unrecognized: the airplanes the army was buying were dangerous to fly. From the introduction of the Wright Model A in 1908, airplanes were built on the "cut and try method" and not according to sound engineering principals. In a word, they were primitive. There was no other way to build them at the time, since aeronautical science was in its infancy and the people who built airplanes were little more than gifted amateurs. The result was that many airplanes had lethal design problems built into them, and Wright airplanes had more than their share of vicious traits, among them, an elevator that often became inoperable during a steep dive.[3] In fact, Wright airplanes were inherently unsafe, but so were the Curtiss airplanes that started entering service in 1911. The most dangerous airplane was the Wright model C, which has the dubious record of killing more army pilots than any other airplane before the United States entered World War I.

The first Model C, known as the "Wright Scout," was delivered in May 1912 to College Park, where it underwent its acceptance tests. Arthur L. Welsh, a Wright Company pilot assigned to fly the new airplane during its acceptance tests, arrived with the airplane, and between 18 May and 11 June made sixteen flights in it. The Wright Model C was slightly larger and heavier than the Model B and was equipped with the Wright 6-60 engine that was rated at sixty horsepower but actually developed closer to fifty. The Wright Model C was called a "weight carrier," which meant that it should be able to pass its acceptance trials carrying two people.

Despite its more powerful engine, the Model C had difficulty meeting the rate of climb requirement specified in the contract. Welsh had found that to meet the contract requirement, he had to climb to two hundred feet and make a steep, full-power dive to build enough air speed before pulling out to make the climb. He had performed the maneuver on earlier occasions without any problem, though to onlookers, it looked terrifyingly dangerous. It was.

The second person on board for the trials was 2nd Lt. Leighton W. Hazlehurst, an infantry officer who had been detailed to aviation on 23 February 1912. He had not yet taken his FAI pilot's certificate test. Welsh and Hazlehurst took off shortly after 1800 on 11 June 1912, climbed to about 150 feet, circled the field, and returned to approximately the spot where they had taken off when Welsh went to full power, intending to put the plane in a dive to gain the speed he needed to make the climb. The plane snapped nose down, did not pull out of the dive, and slammed into the ground, killing both men.[4] It can be argued that Welsh made a full-power dive from too low an altitude. But the cause of the crash might have been due to a design flaw in all Wright airplanes.

Benjamin Foulois experienced a sudden nose drop in a Model B on 5 March 1911. He was piloting, and the Wright Company pilot, Phil Parmelee, was the observer. They were flying at about seventy-five feet above the Rio Grande when Parmelee spotted a flight of ducks. Parmelee extended his arm and sighted along it as though he was firing a shotgun, and in the process, he tripped the engine's compression lever. The engine quit. Foulois reacted quickly, reengaged the compression lever, and the engine restarted. Abruptly, the airplane nosed down and crashed into the river. Fortunately, neither man was injured, but the plane was a total loss.[5]

The crash that killed Welsh and Hazlehurst was a major warning that something was amiss, but no one recognized it. The first indication of serious dissent over how army aviation was being managed was Paul Beck's article "Military Aviation in America: Its Needs," which appeared in the May–June 1912 issue of the *Infantry Journal*. But Beck's article was more than that, much more. Beck had a clearly defined plan for his return to aviation, and assuming control.

He had been working on his first goal, returning to aviation, since his relief on 1 May. That part of his plan involved lobbying Congress to change the Manchu Law to exempt aviators from the four-year limit on detached duty. His political ally was James Hay, chairman of the House Military Affairs Committee. Congressman Hay had assured Beck that the necessary change would be attached to the upcoming army appropriations act for fiscal year 1913. The vote was to occur on 24 August 1912. Once he was freed from the restrictions of the Manchu Law, Beck planned to lobby his congressional friends to bring pressure on the War Department to have him returned to aviation.

His *Infantry Journal* article was intended to pave the way for the second part of his plan, which was to mount a legislative assault on the Signal Corps. The article had two goals. The first was to rally the existing army aviators to the cause, and to solicit public support for his planned legislative assault. To achieve the second goal, his article appeared in two civilian publications, the ACA house organ, *Flying*, and *Leslie's Weekly*.[6] Publishing his article in the ACA house organ was clearly an attempt to gather support from among the ACA's politically powerful members. Publishing in *Leslie's* was an attempt to reach a broad audience that was mostly middle- and upper-class voters. Compared with Chandler's bland discussion of what was needed to get military aviation moving, Beck's article was a revolutionary call to arms.

He offered a detailed analysis of aviation's battlefield role, describing it as "reconnaissance, aggressive action, and transport." And where Chandler had provided two basic needs for aviation, Beck produced ten "axioms for aviation" that might be more accurately called army aviation's ten commandments. The obvious difference between the two articles was that while Chandler was recommending that the Signal Corps be expanded to accommodate aviation, Beck was calling for a complete separation of aviation from the Signal Corps. Despite short-term goals that cropped up later, total separation remained the dissidents' primary goal.

One of Beck's many political activities after he had been Manchued back to his regiment on 1 May 1912 was an effective lobbying effort to exempt aviators from the four-year detached duty limit. Beck's discussion of the evils of the Manchu Law in his article was intended to cast him in the role of a mover and shaker if and when the army regulation was changed. His ego was on display when he used his own separation from aviation as an example of the Manchu Law's negative effect on army aviation, implying to his civilian readers that army aviation had suffered a great loss.

Beck argued that military aviation required "a corps of military experts," meaning aviators, who should manage all aspects of aviation. Taking a shot at the Signal Corps aviation chain of command he stated that it would be ideal if all aviation matters "were left to the aviators . . . with no one between them and the Chief of Staff who, as representative of the Secretary of War, is the supreme commander." With accurate prescience about the future Aviation School commandant, Capt. Arthur Cowan, he wrote, "Intermediaries, particularly those who do not know how to fly and who do not care to learn, should be eliminated."

His main argument was directed toward separating aviation from the Signal Corps and setting it up as an autonomous line organization. Arguing for a separate aviation arm he stated, "Aviation belongs to the line. It is part of the line," adding that "it is a separate, distinct part of the line; it is the fourth arm." He bolstered his argument by saying that the "creation of a separate corps would more clearly emphasize the importance of aviation to these branches than is possible under existing conditions."

Beck then turned to the core of the matter, which was the growing opinion among the pilots that the nonflying Signal Corps administrators were stifling progress. "From the wholly new and untried nature of the science, it is obvious that only those who are practical aviators are competent to determine just how far and how fast experimental work can be pushed." Beck held the Signal Corps administrators responsible for the lack of progress toward a clearly defined, multirole battlefield capability. He noted, "There has been but little accomplished along military lines by the flying squad during the last fifteen months. We have turned out six licensed pilots, licensed by the Aero Club of America . . . but there has been no systematic military investigation."

But Beck made a good point when he argued that the selection system had to be more professional. Under the existing selection system several of the men assigned to aviation should not have been there in the first place. A year later, Tom Milling told a congressional committee that the army was retaining poor pilots because of the manpower shortage, the implication being that they should have been weeded out sooner or not accepted in the first place.[7] Beck may have been one of them.

He was right on the money when he decried the practice of allowing nonfliers to buy airplanes for the army. He complained that the recommendations of the aviators were not followed "in the matter of types of machines and engines ordered." That was absolutely true through 1913 and generally true until 1916. But it must be said that until about 1914, even the pilots were not entirely sure about the requirements for a military airplane. Nevertheless, the pilots had a much better understanding of what constituted a safe airplane than did the two senior officers who were in charge of aviation.

In addition to arguing for a separate air arm on par with the artillery, cavalry, and infantry, Beck recommended establishing an independent aviation school. To implement his proposal, he offered a draft of a congressional bill that would establish the school and transfer all funds and equipment from the Signal Corps to the school commandant. Beck's draft bill included all ten axioms, specifying $1,500 per year in flight pay and a payment equal to six months' pay to the surviving dependents of aviators killed "in an aviation accident." Two of the provisions included in Beck's draft bill were later enacted into law. One was a stipulation that limited the number of aviators to thirty lieutenants, and the other exempted aviators from the provisions of the Manchu Law.

In a general sense, Beck was speaking for eighteen pilots who were on duty at some time from June to December 1912. But who among those eighteen did he actually represent?

All of them supported his call for flight pay and increased benefits, and they certainly agreed that the airplane's potential was not recognized or being developed. And they all agreed that the difficulties in getting officers to volunteer for aviation created a problem that had to be addressed. So, in a broad sense, Beck's article represented the general consensus among the army aviators.

As for his insistence that aviators be in charge of aviation, there might have been agreement in principal, but complaints about nonfliers being in charge were not common in 1912. In fact, as an identifiable issue, attacks on the policy of placing nonfliers in command did not become common among the pilots until after mid-1914.

But on his call for a separate air arm there was much less support. In fact, in 1912 there was almost no support for that idea. First Lt. Roy Kirtland probably shared Beck's view on that point, and 1st Lt. Harold Geiger might have, but there was certainly no solid support for the idea among the other pilots. In fact, six months later Hap Arnold and Tom Milling openly opposed the separation idea.

While Beck was pushing his separation agenda, Foulois was still in the Great Plains, serving with the 7th Infantry at Fort Leavenworth. But the Signal Corps had not forgotten him. In addition to his reassignment to the infantry, his orders directed him to establish an aviation center at Fort Leavenworth. The assignment was what the army calls a collateral duty assignment, which meant it was done on his own time. The Signal Corps shipped a Wright Model C that had been in storage at Fort Riley, Kansas, to Fort Leavenworth, and Foulois worked a deal through the post quartermaster for a hangar. He spent the remainder of 1912 overhauling the Model C, but he never got to fly it.[8]

While Foulois was involved part-time in aviation, the army appropriations act for fiscal year 1913 was passed on 24 August 1912, and Congressman Hay delivered for Paul Beck. Included in the amended act was a change that exempted aviators from the four-year limit on detached duty under the Manchu Law.[9] Beck's efforts had made many people happy, but at the same time, and unintentionally, he reignited his feud with Benjamin Foulois.

The exemption became effective after Foulois had returned to the 7th Infantry at Fort Leavenworth and while he was overhauling

Signal Corps no. 10. Chandler and Reber immediately submitted formal requests for his redetail to aviation, and Foulois submitted his own official request under the new law sometime after Chandler and Reber had made their requests. Col. George P. Scriven, the acting CSO, turned down Chandler and Reber's requests "for some personal reason," but Foulois's request made it to the desk of Maj. Gen. Leonard Wood, army chief of staff.[10]

But Foulois was not the only ex-aviator trying to go home. Beck was lobbying his congressional friends, and they were responding. But a hard-nosed chief of staff, who did not appreciate a young captain going over his head, checked Beck's flanking movement. At the same time, he rejected Foulois's request for reassignment to aviation because of Beck's congressional lobbying. Foulois described himself as "a victim of unofficial personal politics."[11]

Whether Beck had the congressional backing to overcome General Wood's refusal to reassign him remained to be seen. But in the process, Beck had blocked Foulois's straight up the front push, and Foulois was not happy about that. Frustrated, bitter, and disappointed, Foulois settled down to being an infantryman. Beck had to modify his plan and launch his legislative assault *before* he returned to aviation. The change in plans made things tougher, but Beck felt that he had a strong ally in Congressman Hay.

While Beck's article was roiling the waters, another fatal crash of a Wright airplane occurred on 28 September 1912, killing 1st Lieutenant Lewis C. Rockwell and Cpl. Frank S. Scott. Lieutenant Rockwell was the fourth pilot killed and the third in a Wright airplane. Corporal Scott was the first enlisted man to die in a crash.

This was the second fatal crash involving a Wright airplane in three months, but it did not ring any alarm bells. Planes flew, planes crashed, things happened. Most of the active pilots' attention was focused on the developing separation movement, both those for and those against. One person who was against was Benjamin Foulois.

Whether Beck's article was an underlying cause of the open rebellions that occurred in the spring of 1913 is open to doubt. But the fact remains that within six months of his article appearing in the *Infantry Journal*, there occurred two examples of open rebellion.

The First Signs of Trouble

7

Upheavals, 1913

The first open sign that the fliers were growing tired of the Signal Corps running army aviation like a flying club occurred in January 1913 at San Diego with a dispute between 1st Lt. Harold Geiger and the ACA over the FAI pilot's certificate tests. Since July 1911 the Aeronautical Division had followed the unofficial policy of having all newly trained pilots obtain the FAI pilot's certificate by completing tests administered by the Aero Club of America.

Until the War Department created the military aviator (MA) rating on 21 March 1912, the FAI test was effectively the army's only qualifying pilot's test. The army's new MA rating came with a more difficult, six-part flight test, and since that time the MA tests were the army's official standard under which a pilot was rated as a fully qualified military pilot. Nevertheless, the Signal Corps continued to follow an unofficial policy of having new pilots qualify for the basic FAI pilot's certificate before continuing their training and taking the more difficult MA test. How obtaining the FAI certificate went from an unofficial requirement to an official requirement illustrates the intrusive nature of the ACA's close relationship with the Signal Corps.

In November 1912 the CSO separated the Curtiss and Wright pilots, sending the Wright pilots to Augusta, Georgia, for the winter, and the Curtiss pilots to San Diego. The CSO placed 1st Lt. Harold Geiger, a twenty-eight-year-old West Point graduate, in command of the Curtiss detachment. Geiger's task was to establish a school on North Island in cooperation with the Curtiss Company, which was operating a commercial school there. It was to have been a temporary arrangement, with the army subleasing part of the island from the Curtiss Company.

The four officers whom Geiger was to train to fly were 2nd Lt. Lewis H. Brereton, 1st Lt. Lewis E. "Ned" Goodier Jr., 1st Lt. Samuel H. McLeary, and 1st Lt. Joseph D. Park. All of them already had some flight training, but none of them had earned the FAI pilot's certificate. Geiger's specific orders were to get them qualified as MAS as soon as possible, and the first step in that process was to get them through the basic FAI pilot's certificate tests.

Geiger had been an ACA member since May 1912 and held both the club's pilot and expert aviator certificates, which made it possible for the ACA to designate him as the official ACA umpire in San Diego, a position that authorized him to conduct the testing for the FAI pilot's certificate.[1] Geiger's first success was Ned Goodier Jr., who passed his tests on 7 January; Brereton, McLeary, and Park followed that same month.[2]

Goodier received his pilot's certificate, but the ACA refused to grant certificates to the other three men. The reasons for the refusals were classically bureaucratic examples of absurd nitpicking.

On 28 January 1913 the ACA secretary, Mortimer Delano, wrote to Geiger, pointing out that Brereton had not complied with the ACA requirement that formal application be made to the ACA secretary *prior* to taking the tests. He insisted that Brereton retake the tests after following the correct application procedure. Delano also invalidated McLeary's tests on the grounds that Geiger had set the posts too closely together, insisting that the ACA rules required them to be placed *exactly* five hundred meters apart. Delano directed that McLeary also repeat the tests with the posts "properly" spaced. Apparently, Delano had not read the rules dealing with the distance between posts carefully. And he invalidated Park's test results on the grounds that Geiger had violated procedure by not informing the club secretary, Delano, that Geiger would be the onsite judge.[3] Here was an example of either terminal stupidity or gross incompetence; Delano *knew* that Geiger was going to be the on-site judge, because it was Delano who gave Geiger the job in the first place.

At that time, there was no army regulation requiring the FAI pilot's certificate tests be administered. In fact, there was no official Signal Corps policy that made the tests mandatory. Taking the tests was a practice that had started in 1909, when Frank Lahm, an ACA member, took the FAI pilot's certificate test after he learned to fly the Wright Model A at College Park. Since that time, nearly every army pilot had taken the FAI test on a voluntary basis. Prior to the army having its own MA test, the FAI basic test served as the standard for a pilot's minimal qualification.

Beyond that, the only practical reason for the army pilots taking the FAI test was because the pilot's certificate was a prerequisite for the ACA pilot license that allowed the license holders to "act as pilots in ACA events."[4] The ACA pilot license was important because when army aviation was more of a flying club than a military undertaking, army pilots frequently took part in ACA-sponsored events for cash prizes.

Lieutenant Geiger was one of the pilots who had been only briefly exposed to the flying club atmosphere at College Park. Geiger joined the ACA in May 1912, and three days later he, along with Chandler, Arnold, Milling, and Kennedy, was an honored guest at the ACA's Army Day celebration in New York. Joining the ACA and attending an ACA dinner in New York was the extent of his flying club activities.[5] So Geiger clearly did not consider the ACA a part of the U.S. Army. But his response to Delano's letter indicates that he was not sure of his ground, and it illustrates the degree to which the ACA intruded into army aviation. Geiger wrote:

1. In the case of Lieutenant, Brereton, would state that in our course of instruction we do not consider a man qualified to handle an aeroplane when he has passed his pilot's tests, because he has completed not more than half the course.

To wait until a letter of application has been acted upon by the Aero Club and returned to this station would necessitate a delay of over two weeks. We cannot afford to waste that much time during our instruction period. It was for this reason that I requested to be allowed to observe the tests of the Army officers under instruction here.

Lieutenant Brereton's test was taken under the rules as I interpreted them. Lieutenant Brereton does not desire to repeat this test, nor do I desire to take the time to act as official observer. In case the Contest Committee decides that the test was not in due form and will have to be repeated, Lieutenant Brereton requests the return of his license fee and photographs.

2. In the case of Lieutenant McLeary, the distance between the posts was 1,500 feet (500 yards). Attention is called to the instruction form which states, under (C), that the circuits are indicated by two posts situated *not more* than 500 meters (547 yards) from each other. It is also stated that the responsible representative must see that the posts are located at a distance *not greater* than 1,640 feet (546.666 yards). From this I cannot understand how the rules require the distance to be exactly 1,640 feet. If the rules have been changed to that effect, we have not been advised of that fact by the Aero Club. A barograph record sheet of Lieutenant McLeary's flight is enclosed.

3. We desire to conform to all the rules and regulations of the Aero Club, but inasmuch as our chief objective is to train officers to become Military Aviators and not licensed pilots, I do not consider that we should attach primary importance to the latter.[6]

Lieutenant Geiger obviously did not feel that the ACA had any authority in the training of Army pilots, and his chain of command did not include Mortimer Delano. But his reply also shows that he was unsure whether the FAI pilot's certificate tests were an official army requirement. Geiger did not grasp how closely the Aero Club of America and the Signal Corps were linked through the balloon fraternity.

Mortimer Delano forwarded Geiger's reply to Lieutenant Colonel Reber, in an unadulterated example of the old-boy circuit in operation. Reber had been an ACA member since 1 July 1909, was at this time a club vice president, a governor of the club, and a mem-

ber of three committies.[7] In January 1913 he was the chief signal officer of the army's Eastern Division, headquartered in New York City,
just a few blocks from ACA's four-story headquarters at 297 Madison Avenue, near Forty-First Street. The chief of the Aeronautical
Division was not Reber but Maj. Edgar Russel, also an ACA member. The flying club nature of army aviation and its close relationship to the ACA are evident in the letter Lieutenant Colonel Reber
wrote to Major Russel on behalf of the ACA.

> Knowing the cordial relations that exist between the Signal Corps and
> the Aero Club of America, I think the best thing to do is to enclose
> the accompanying copy of a letter that the Secretary has received
> from Mr. Geiger at San Diego. The Contest Committee necessarily
> has established certain rules, one of which is that a person desiring
> a pilot's license [sic] must apply to the secretary and send the cus-
> tomary fee and photographs, and then a representative to supervise
> the test is appointed. Lieutenant Geiger was appointed a representa-
> tive of the Contest Committee at San Diego at my suggestion. Evi-
> dently the youngsters in your aviation detachment out there are
> feeling their oats a little bit. With respect to the case of Lieutenant
> McLeary, Mr. Geiger's report was evidently not in due form. The
> instructions printed on the blank are very specific and state that in
> case the distance is less than 1,640 feet the applicant must make a
> sufficient number of turns to give a full distance of five kilometers.
> The Contest Committee, both because this is an Army matter and
> because I have been Chairman of it, have asked me for advice in the
> matter, and I told them to suspend action until I could communi-
> cate with you and learn the views of the Department. You can read-
> ily see how they cannot allow youngsters to ride roughshod over
> their rules. I think it is very desirable for the Signal Corps and the
> Aero Club to work in harmony and the easiest way, I think, would
> be to give the youngsters a little fatherly advice.[8]

Reber's letter is the best example of the degree to which army aviation
had become a chapter of the ACA. Here we have a field grade officer
acting in his capacity as a senior ACA member, telling the chief of army
aviation that his officers need to comply with the Aero Club's rules.

Major Russel, who had been the chief of the Aeronautical Division for just eight months, did not know if the FAI tests were official requirements or not. To find out, all Russel had to do was pick up his telephone and ask Chandler, who would have told him they were useful but unofficial. With that information, Russel would have had the authority to tell Delano to take a walk. But Russel was not that kind of officer, and he was an ACA member who listened to Reber on all matters. Geiger was clearly causing a problem. In such a case, a careful officer takes no action and passes the problem up the line, which is exactly what Russel did. Russel asked for advice from his boss, Col. George P. Scriven, acting CSO.

The problem was that Scriven knew even less about the status of the ACA tests than Russel did. He was not yet an ACA member, so the club's rules did not carry a lot of weight with him, but as the acting CSO, he was not in a position to make a policy change. Scriven did what Russel should have done. He sent a letter to the commanding officer of the Signal Corps Aviation School, Captain Chandler, another ACA member, asking about the status of the FAI pilot's certificate test.

When Captain Chandler received Scriven's letter he was in Augusta, Georgia, with the Wright pilots. Little did he know, when he read the acting CSO's letter describing Geiger's rebellion, that in less than two weeks he would be facing his own rebellious pilots. Chandler responded:

> It is not known that the FAI license has had any official status for Army fliers. The FAI pilot test is international in character and is recognized, and referred to by aviators in foreign armies, as the "first pilot test." Heretofore references to Army aviators have counted only those who have qualified for the FAI license, and until an officer had passed this qualification he was not included in the enumeration.
>
> It is not believed that the FAI license should be made compulsory for Army fliers, nor necessary preliminary to securing the rating of Military Aviator, but an officer who obtains the rating of Military Aviator without first securing the ACA pilot license should not be expected to receive the rating of Expert Aviator from the

Aero Club of America, which special rating has been granted by the Aero Club to the FAI pilots who have passed the Army tests for Military Aviator.[9]

What Captain Chandler was referring to when he wrote about the ACA's expert aviator license was a certificate the ACA had created to match the tougher requirements the army had established for the MA rating. The ACA automatically awarded the expert pilot certificate to any army flier who qualified as an MA and who already possessed the FAI's basic certificate. The ACA did not require the MA to take the ACA expert aviator test. More important was the fact that the ACA's newly created expert aviator rating had no standing in the army.

There was also confusion on everyone's part about the term "license." Under the auspices of the FAI, the ACA issued *certificates* for certain levels of proficiency in balloon, dirigible, and airplane piloting. The pilot's certificate represented a basic level of proficiency for piloting an airplane or a balloon. But the ACA also issued *licenses* to complement each certificate, and a certificate holder had only to apply for the corresponding license to receive one. The certificates were simply documents that showed the level of a pilot's proficiency, whereas the license was needed if the pilot wanted to compete in any ACA sanctioned air meet, exhibition, or record try.[10]

On 5 March 1913 Colonel Scriven, acting CSO, became Brigadier General Scriven, CSO. After receiving Chandler's reply, General Scriven conducted a search of the Aeronautical Division's records, which revealed that the FAI tests had no official status and there was no written policy requiring the tests. The results of the records search confirmed Chandler's explanation that while the FAI certificate was not an official army requirement, obtaining it was common practice among army aviators. In addition to that information, Scriven had Chandler's recommendation that obtaining the FAI certificate not be made an official requirement.

Despite the absence of any official requirement, and against the advice from his school commander, on 10 March General

Scriven directed Major Russel to send this order to Geiger, which put the FAI pilot's certificate on an official footing in the Aeronautical Division.

1. A question arose last February concerning the status of the FAI pilot's license [*sic*] in the Signal Corps Aviation School's course of instruction.

2. This office deems it advisable for every officer to receive a pilot's license [*sic*] from the FAI.

3. As the Aero Club requires every aviator to qualify for, and to have, a FAI license [*sic*] before he can get his Expert Aviator's rating, the above policy is considered necessary.

4. Every officer is not required to receive the Expert Aviator's rating, but he must be qualified to receive such rating.

5. In compliance with the above policy, you are directed to have every officer pass the qualifications for the FAI license [*sic*] without delay, or as soon as his training warrants his making the test flights, and that the data required by the Aero Club of America, be sent to this office.[11]

In his order, Scriven confused the FAI pilot's certificate with the ACA license, which did not alter the meaning of the order. He was also confused about the importance of the ACA's expert aviator rating, since he justified the absolute requirement that all army pilots qualify for the FAI pilot's certificate on the basis that it was required before a pilot could receive the ACA's expert aviator rating. And then he said the expert aviator rating was not required. The goofy logic that made a civilian test mandatory so that an army pilot could receive a civilian rating he did not need and was not required to have, typified the Signal Corps' mismanagement of aviation. No wonder Geiger was frustrated and fed up.

One week later, Lieutenant Geiger responded and came very close to insubordination. On 17 March he wrote, "Returned, enclosing data for Lieutenant Park's pilot's license. The data for test of Lieutenants McLeary and Brereton has been sent to the Aero Club. There are not forms in this office to copy the data on. Lieutenant

Park's test was not approved by the Aero Club on account of the fact that no representative has been officially appointed. I can see no reason why he should be compelled to repeat this test."[12]

Lieutenant Geiger was clearly resentful of what he viewed as meddling on the part of the ACA, and he was digging in his heels despite Scriven's 10 March directive. Geiger may not have seen any reason to compel Park to repeat the test, but his immediate boss, Major Russel did. On 24 March Russel shot back a one-sentence reply attached to the 10 March directive. "As this office considers it necessary to work in conjunction with the Aero Club of America, paragraph 2 of this letter will be complied with in the case of all officers."[13] Lieutenant Park retook and passed the FAI test on 23 April 1913, and the policy requiring all army pilots to qualify for, and obtain, the FAI pilot's certificate before continuing their training, became official.

Whether it was important to have all army pilots qualify for the FAI pilot's certificate is arguable. But earning the certificate did establish a waypoint that was useful for evaluating a student's progress. And nearly everyone who had come to Signal Corps aviation prior to Brereton, McLeary, and Park had passed the ACA test, so they were not being asked to do something that was not already common practice. Nevertheless, it was not good policy to allow an outside, civilian organization to dictate the terms for qualifying an army pilot. Lieutenant Geiger had a good point, and his superiors should have backed him up.

While Geiger was having his run-in with the ACA and HR 28728 was being defeated, a more virulent dissent was taking place among the Wright pilots in Texas City, Texas. On 25 February 1913 the War Department ordered the Wright pilots then at Augusta to proceed to Texas City to support Maj. Gen. William H. Carter's Second Division. The five pilots, Captain Chandler, First Lieutenants Roy C. Kirtland and Harry Graham, and Second Lieutenants William C. Sherman and Tom Milling, left Augusta on 28 February and arrived in Texas City on 2 March 1913. Capt. Frederick Hennessy had preceded them there to make arrangements for their arrival. First Lt. Loren H. Call and 2nd Lt. Eric L. Ellington arrived on 10

March from the Burgess flight school at Palm Beach, Florida, and six more pilot trainees arrived later in March and April.[14]

While Geiger was having his fight with the ACA, Paul Beck's legislative assault on the Signal Corps opened when Representative James Hay introduced HR 28728, a bill that Beck helped write. The bill provided for an aviation corps as a part of the line of the army with one major, two captains, and thirty 1st lieutenants. The bill also authorized the detail of officers from other branches, specified the corps commander would be an aviator, provided flight pay for both officers and enlisted men, and created the ratings of military aviator and aviation mechanician, which was the early term for aviation mechanic. House bill 28728 also provided benefits to survivors of airmen who were killed in the line of duty. The bill was Beck's *Infantry Journal* article put in legislative language. The Signal Corps and the War Department immediately opposed the bill.

On 14 February 1913 Foulois received a telegram from the acting CSO, Colonel Scriven, requesting his views on HR 28728, and two days later, on 16 February, Foulois received a copy of the bill from a friend in Washington. The next day, 17 February, he sent the CSO a four-page letter opposing the bill. The letter's content formed the basis of the Signal Corps' and the War Department's arguments against HR 28728, and they bear closer examination.[15]

The main thrust of Foulois's argument was that military aviation was not well enough developed to warrant being treated as a separate corps, but he did not reject the separation idea. In fact, he told the CSO that because aviation units were combat units they should at some point in the future become an independent corps. The thing that argued against that happening in 1913 was that the army's aviators had been spending their time learning to fly, and little, or no, effort had been made to create a combat capability.

Beck was not alone in his efforts to create a separate air arm. Several aviation journalists, members of Congress, and the ACA shared that idea. One of the bedrock arguments for separating army aviation from the Signal Corps was that the Europeans had done it, and the Europeans were far ahead of the Americans in developing military aviation. Foulois addressed that argument in his letter when he wrote, "Our service and organizations in the United States Army are comparable only in a very slight degree to foreign standards, but we should not base our views conclusively on what is being done by French, German, and English armies."

Foulois also included a this-is-not-the-right-time argument, which was really only a delaying tactic. The Signal Corps used the argument against HR 28728, but Colonel Scriven was more impressed with Foulois's administrative argument. Here, Foulois provided the Signal Corps and the War Department with their strongest offensive weapon. He pointed out that the most senior aviator on duty was a captain, hardly enough rank to warrant commanding a separate aviation corps. Even if the War Department jumped the captain to major, as HR 28728 allowed, that would do nothing to overcome the captain's lack of administrative experience. And a major was still too junior in rank to command a corps.

Foulois's solution was to leave nonflying Signal Corps officers in command of military aviation, and to select as the commanding officer a man who had a broad general knowledge of aviation matters and extensive administrative experience. The combination of aviation knowledge and administrative experience would make him "capable of grasping and coordinating the views and ideas of the men actually engaged in flying." He lauded Major Russel's status as chief of the Aeronautical Division as "an entirely satisfactory scheme of administration for at least a year or two," the time it might take for aviation to become well enough developed for it to be made a line organization if it was not "hampered by ill-considered and thoughtless personal legislation."

Foulois's intense dislike of Beck had sharpened his senses so that he quickly saw Beck's plan to acquire personal control of aviation. This was the feature of the bill that posed the greatest threat to Foulois and offered the greatest possible reward to his enemy. It was here that Foulois struck hardest and specifically at Beck. He noted that under HR 28728 a captain who was a qualified aviator would be promoted to major and given command of the new aviation corps.

At the time, there were two captains on aviation duty and one who had been returned to his regiment under the Manchu Law. Among the other aviators were five first lieutenants on aviation duty and one who was "associated" with aviation but was back in his regiment: Foulois. Under HR 28728 one captain would be advanced to major and the other two would fill the next lower slots according to seniority. But as soon as each of the five lieutenants was promoted to captain, each one would have to return to his regiment, because under HR 28728 there were only three captains authorized for aviation. From Foulois's viewpoint, HR 28728 was a dead-end proposition. He correctly argued that such a situation would prevent the creation of an experienced pilot cadre and would stifle development.

The two captains on duty in aviation at that time were Charles DeForest Chandler and Frederick Hennessy. A third captain, who might have a shot at the prize, Paul Beck, was back in his regiment. Chandler was a Signal Corps officer, and in February 1913 he was in command of the aviation school at College Park. Given the politics and policies within the Signal Corps, Chandler would have been the most likely candidate for the corps commander slot. But that month Geiger was fighting the ACA in San Diego, and in Texas City an "incipient mutiny" was just a month away. No one, certainly not Beck and Foulois, knew that in six weeks Chandler would be caught up in the turmoil and dissent that was just unfolding, effectively putting him out of the running.

Frederick Hennessy was a field artillery officer who had been detailed to aviation since 11 April 1912, and was a dark horse for the corps commandership by any measure. In February 1913 he was not progressing well in his flight training and was about to be washed out.[16] Even if he were still on aviation duty when HR 28728 became law, it is doubtful that he would have been selected to command the new corps because Hennessy had so little time in aviation compared with the next candidate, Paul Beck.

Beck had been associated with aviation since 1910, had been assigned to aviation in January 1911, and was a military aviator. Working against him, however, was his political maneuvering to get him where he was at that point. General Wood certainly didn't appreciate Beck's behind-the-scenes maneuvering. But Beck did have powerful friends in Congress, connections that would have been useful to an aviation corps commander. In any event, Beck had written the bill to create just this situation, and he was in a good position to win the prize if HR 28728 became law.

Foulois was right on the mark when he said that under HR 28728, first lieutenants would be relieved from aviation and returned to their regiments as soon as they were promoted to captain. That was because under Beck's plan there were slots for only three captains, and in the absence of some personal or professional failing, they could not be removed. Since Foulois was a first lieutenant, that situation was a clear threat to his chances of making military aviation a career. Foulois knew that if Beck got the corps commander's slot, his chances of returning to aviation, much less a chance for promotion to captain within aviation, were zero. He acknowledged that threat when he wrote, "This bill if enacted into law will almost immediately throw out of the aviation corps several of its best and most efficient aviators, and I cannot believe that the distinguished Congressman who introduced this bill contemplate[d] any such result."[17]

But the thing that galled Foulois the most was the idea that Beck might somehow become the corps commander under HR 28728. He drew the CSO's attention to a specific section in the bill that said, "No officer shall be detailed as commandant of the Aviation Corps unless he shall have displayed especial skill and ability as a military aviator." The suggestion that Paul Beck might be considered to possess "especial skill and ability as a military aviator" was more than Foulois could take. In words that recalled his run-in with Beck at Fort Sam Houston in May 1911 he wrote, "After four years' experience in aviation and aeronautical duty, I can frankly state that there is not an individual aviator in the United States Army who has yet displayed especial skill as a military aviator, that is judging from military standards and not newspaper standards."

Foulois thought that Beck's resort to personal politics was unethical, but when Foulois tried to derail Beck's plan, he justified his own foray into personal politics by saying, "As one of the lieutenants adversely affected by the proposed HR 28728 and having been officially drawn into Army political activities on the Potomac River Cold War battle front, I deemed it appropriate to do a little personal political work of my own with a view toward starting a political backfire against HR 28728."[18]

He turned to Col. John Tilson, 2nd Regiment, Connecticut National Guard, who was an aviation enthusiast and an influential member of the Military Affairs Committee. He was also Foulois's congressional representative from Connecticut and a close friend. Understandably Foulois "believed that Tilson would be of great assistance in combating the revolutionary features contained in HR 28728."

While Foulois was organizing his counterattack from Fort Leavenworth, Colonel Scriven was organizing his counterattack in Washington. On 24 February 1913 the CSO formed a board of officers consisting of Major Russel, Captain Hennessy, and Lieutenants Arnold, Milling, and Sherman, and directed them to prepare a legislative recommendation for furthering aeronautical work in the army. Their recommendation called for an increase in the authorized strength of the Signal Corps, provided for the detailing of officers from other branches, allowed for promotions within aviation, and created a promotions board, the members of which would be selected by the CSO and approved by the secretary of war. The pilot's board recommendation also included 50 percent flight pay, which would be equal to half of a pilot's base bay, and payments to beneficiaries of airmen who were killed in the line of duty.[19]

While Colonel Scriven's group was working on its recommendation, Foulois took a fifteen-day leave and went to Washington, where he asked Scriven for authority to contact Representative Tilson. Besides granting permission, Scriven told Foulois that Beck had been Representative Hay's adviser in connection with the drafting of HR 28728, which did not surprise Foulois. Scriven also said that the Signal Corps and the War Department opposed the bill.

There was a significant difference between the way Foulois went about playing politics and the way Beck did it. Before Foulois made any move in his personal politicking, he always went to Scriven, told him what he planned to do, and got authorization to do it before he did it. Beck, on the other hand, simply worked through his congressional contacts without telling anyone in authority what he was up to. The difference in style may be a fine point, since in each case Foulois and Beck were working for personal gain under the guise of doing it for the good of the service. But fine point or not, Foulois's way of politicking gave him command of the moral high ground. Be that as it may, the fact is that Beck was playing a dangerous game, whereas Foulois was doing it pretty much by the book.

During his meeting with Tilson, Foulois learned that the army appropriation bill for fiscal year 1914, which contained the third appropriation for aviation, was stalled in the Military Affairs Committee. According to Tilson, the snag was the provision for flight pay contained in the bill. Tilson told Foulois that the flight pay provision was going to be cut unless someone could persuade the committee chairman, James Hay, to support it. Foulois told Colonel Scriven what Tilson had told him and suggested that he be allowed to do something about it. Colonel Scriven agreed and told Foulois to do what he could.[20]

Foulois arranged a four-chair game of stud poker, with Congressman Hay in the fourth chair. His agent in the matter was a female acquaintance identified only as Julie. Her strength was that she knew Congressman Hay well and had direct and immediate contact with him. Julie agreed to set up the poker game in her apartment on the next Saturday night. Foulois's role was to deliver Julie's friend, Mary, to the apartment before eight that evening and then remain to play poker. Julie told Foulois that the poker party would break up at ten thirty, "at which time Mary and [Foulois] were expected to leave the apartment."

During the two-hour-long poker game Foulois lost fifty dollars and bent Hay's ear about flight pay. As directed, the party broke up at ten thirty, and Mary and Foulois departed. The following Monday, Foulois telephoned Tilson and told him about the poker game. Tilson said that the Military Affairs Committee had discussed the flight pay issue, and Congressman Hays, after "diligent research during the weekend," supported the provision.

On 2 March 1913 Congress passed the third appropriation for aviation, $125,000 that also included 35 percent flight pay. At about the same time the secretary of war's organized opposition to HR 28728 caused the House Military Affairs Committee to abandon the bill. It appeared that at this point Foulois had been successful in his behind-the-scenes political maneuvering: HR 28728 had been defeated and flight pay had been authorized.

8

An Incipient Mutiny, March 1913

The trouble started as early as October 1912 in Augusta and had probably been simmering long before that. It came to light when a round-robin letter landed on the newly appointed cso's desk during the first week in March 1913. The letter's contents surprised, shocked, and angered the new cso, Brigadier General Scriven, who was already dealing with a two-pronged attack from his pilots. Geiger was fighting with the ACA in San Diego, and Beck was leading the charge to have Congress separate aviation from the Signal Corps. Scriven was in no mood to be confronted by a third attack from a different quarter, which might explain why he came down so hard on Geiger in favor of the ACA on 10 March.

The letter that Scriven received has long since disappeared. So what do we know about it? Hap Arnold was working a desk in the cso's office when the letter arrived, and Scriven showed it to him. Arnold later wrote, "The letter was not a request, a recommendation, or a communication to the Inspector General of the Army. It was a round-robin letter direct to the cso from the Wright pilots stating their demands, which included changes in the aviation commanders in Washington, Texas City, and San Diego. The letter even stated who was to be put where."[1]

From testimony that Scriven and Maj. Samuel Reber gave at a later date, we know that Captain Chandler was unpopular, and the Wright pilots were refusing to serve under him. The letter apparently gave the CSO an ultimatum—relieve Chandler or relieve them. The reasons for their strong dislike are at best vague. Chandler said that the problem stemmed from his having tried to enforce discipline at Augusta, and there was a reference to a problem of heavy drinking among the pilots. According to Reber, one of the pilots' complaints was that Chandler would not allow them to make cross-country flights and another was that they "did not like his way of doing business." Even Tom Milling, who made sitting on a fence an art, said that he "did not like Chandler and his methods."[2]

There is no doubt that the Wright pilots targeted Chandler for replacement. He was a weak leader. In 1913 Foulois said of Chandler, "I know of no poorer officer to be in charge of it," referring to army aviation and the school at College Park. Frank Kennedy, a former Curtiss pilot, accused Chandler of having an open bias against Curtiss pilots, and Roy C. Kirtland said that Chandler "had no push" when it came to advancing military aviation. Hap Arnold said of the Signal Corps officers who commanded aviation in 1912, "When I first joined, I do not think that they had the best men in charge of the flying station." Arnold was referring to General Allen and Captain Chandler.[3]

On 6 March General Scriven ordered Reber to go Texas City and find out what was going on. Arriving there on 10 March, Reber immediately became deeply involved in the controversy. The first man he spoke to was Capt. Arthur S. Cowan, whose obvious connection to the controversy stemmed from his assignment as the Maneuver Division's signal officer. In that capacity he was in the chain of command between Captain Chandler and General Carter for matters dealing with the 1st Aero Squadron (Provisional).[4]

Brigadier General Scriven also went to Texas City, where he found the pilots in a "very mutinous state."[5] Describing the cause of the unrest, he said:

> It seems that all these young flying officers wanted to get control themselves: get it out of the hands of the Signal Corps. They were a difficult lot of men to deal with. They have a very high opinion of themselves; of course, men of great courage, fine character

An Incipient Mutiny

as a rule, but I should say they were distinctly insubordinate; living in town at College Park, near here, without much discipline; almost no discipline, and I doubt if Chandler could have had a well-disciplined force. Each man did more or less as he thought best; undisciplined condition.[6]

Scriven singled out Hennessy and Kirtland as the ringleaders. He said of Kirtland, "He was always, I believe, very much against the Signal Corps."[7] The CSO's opinion of Kirtland's dissatisfaction with the Signal Corps was no guess. Kirtland had told the CSO that the pilots were demoralized over the lack of progress in army aviation, and that they believed that if aviation remained under the Signal Corps, no progress would be made. Kirtland said that any success they had achieved had been made "in spite of the Signal Corps."[8] It would seem that at this point Paul Beck's *Infantry Journal* article had some influence in creating the situation in Texas City.

Throughout General Scriven's time in Texas, Captain Cowan acted as the pilots' spokesman, taking their side and supporting their grievances. According to Kirtland, Cowan kept them informed about his conversations with General Scriven, and what Cowan reported to them added fuel to the fire.[9]

There were issues that the CSO and Reber did not recognize or chose not to mention. The growing number of fatalities was a large concern among the pilots. But the aviators' belief that the top aviation commanders should be men "who understood aviation" stemmed less from the death rate than it did from mismanagement. An important point is that the term "men who understood aviation" did not necessarily mean they had to be pilots. At the heart of the issue was the lack of progress in developing military aviation into an effective combat arm. Kirtland summed up how they all felt. "It was that everybody worked and worked and had put their whole heart was in the work, and we were getting nowhere. We were becoming discouraged. It got to where the attitude was I'll go back to the cavalry or infantry or wherever it was rather than stay here, eating my heart out."[10]

Related to Kirtland's statement was one Milling made many years later: "At College Park we were doing nothing but diddling around, no thought being given to tactics or strategy or anything else."[11] The frequent references to College Park are significant because they indicate that the problem had started there and came to a head in Texas City.

While Cowan was acting as the go-between for the dissidents and the cso, Reber was talking to Benjamin Foulois, who was then stationed with the 7th Infantry at nearby Fort Crockett. Foulois still had not returned to flying duty, but he had managed to work out an arrangement in which he could go to Texas City and fly on his own time. While he was stationed at Fort Crockett, the controversy erupted and Foulois had an inside view of what was happening. Reber naturally turned to Foulois for advice and information because of Foulois's long involvement in army aviation but also because he and Foulois were close friends. The latter situation assured Reber that Foulois was in the Signal Corps camp on the issue.

Despite his anger at the letter writers, General Scriven recognized the seriousness of the situation and issued orders that initially seemed to solve the problem, or at least dampen the fire of dissent. On 25 March 1913 he replaced Captain Chandler with Capt. Arthur S. Cowan. At the same time, he let it be known that on 10 September 1913 Major Reber would replace Major Russel as chief of the Aeronautical Division. The pilots had gotten what they demanded.[12] George Scriven was the cso, Arthur Cowan was in command of the 1st Aero Squadron (Provisional), and Samuel Reber was scheduled to replace Russell. Changes in San Diego were not mentioned, but circumstances would soon resolve that problem, if there was one.

In Washington Hap Arnold thought that the changes were a good sign that things would improve.[13] Arnold was wrong. In Texas City, Foulois was thrilled with the news that Russel was out and Reber was in. The changes meant that Foulois had a good shot at returning to aviation. He later said, "Major Reber and Captain Cowan are as good men as we ever had in charge and we will go a long way to find better." Nothing could have been farther from the truth. Kirtland said that the pilots greeted with enthusiasm the news that Reber would take over from Russel. "Now, everyone said, we have got new blood now. Colonel Reber knows something about it. He is going to take charge, and we won't have any more trouble." Kirtland was also wrong.[14]

While the situation at Texas City was being resolved, two more army aviators were killed in April and May in San Diego. First Lt. Lewis H. Brereton and 2nd Lt. Rex Chandler crashed a Curtiss flying boat in San Diego on 8 April 1913, killing Chandler and injuring Brereton. Brereton was making a steeply banked turn close to the surface when a gust of wind struck the plane, increasing its bank so that the wing touched the water and the plane slammed into the bay. Lt. Joseph D. Park was killed on 9 May 1913 in a Curtiss D-IV, SC-2, while trying to take off from a field of shoulder-high barley. The airplane managed to rise about ten feet and hit a tree, destroying the plane and killing Park.

The deaths of Chandler and Park raised the army's aviation fatalities, including Corporal Scott, to seven men in five years, but six of them had been killed during the previous twenty-four months. The airplanes involved were evenly divided at three Curtiss and three Wright, but that ratio was about to change.

On 6 June 1913 the War Department relieved Cowan of command at Texas City and sent him to San Diego "for duty at the Signal Corps aviation school."[15] The language used in the orders sending him west would come under close scrutiny two years later. Nine days later, on 14 June, most of the squadron personnel and equipment followed Cowan to San Diego, leaving First Lieutenants Kirtland, Graham, and Loren H. Call with two Wright Model Cs, SC-11 and SC-20, in Texas City as the Maneuver Division's aviation section. On 30 June Graham was seriously injured in a motorcycle accident and was relieved from aviation on 13 October. A week later, a Wright Model C killed Lieutenant Call.[16]

Call's death raised the count to eight dead and placed Wright airplanes in the lead as the biggest killers of army pilots. Call's crash marked the start of a series of fatal crashes that would kill an additional six aviators during the next fifteen months. And all those crashes would involve the Wright Model C.

The loss of his two subordinates and an airplane left Kirtland alone in Texas with one airplane, which he did not use. In fact, after Call died, Kirtland stopped flying, and did not fly again until after World War I. He waited in Texas until 28 November, when the War Department ordered him to San Diego.

9

Beck Makes His Move, 1913

On 12 August 1913 the hearings on HR 5304, which was essentially a watered-down HR 28728, opened in Washington. It was Beck's second attempt at separating army aviation from the Signal Corps, and this time he went public to press the attack. Hearings were held from 12 to 16 August, and the Signal Corps fielded an impressive three-element team to testify against the bill.

The lead element was made up of Brig. Gen. George P. Scriven, the cso; Lt. Col. Samuel Reber, who was to take over as the chief of the Aeronautical Division in September; and Maj. Edgar Russel, who at the time was still the chief. The second element included former aviators Benjamin Foulois and Frederick Hennessy and active aviators Hap Arnold and Tom Milling. The third element consisted of two outside experts, former 1st Lt. Riley Scott, inventor of the Scott bombsight, and Capt. William "Billy" Mitchell, a Signal Corps officer who was assigned to the general staff. The opposing team consisted of one man—Paul Beck.[1]

The Signal Corps team clearly profited from the arguments that Foulois had provided in February. Every point he made in his 17 February letter to Colonel Scriven was amplified during the August hearings, and the delivery was almost flawless. The bedrock argument in favor of retaining aviation in the Signal Corps was based on the proposition that the Signal Corps had the administrators and technical personnel necessary to manage and develop military aviation.[2]

General Scriven argued that administrative capability was the justification for retaining military aviation in the Signal Corps. He told the committee, "The Signal Corps is composed of a number of men of undoubted scientific ability, recognized as men of great electrical knowledge, of strength of materials, and the working of gasoline engines, and of the action of natural forces. Men who are absolutely essential to an aviation corps, as the staff, and the directing heads of the corps and its scientific departments. It also has all the important machinery for purchasing and for disbursing, including making contracts."[3] Scriven warned the committee that "to create a separate corps would be to lose years in the progress of the work of aviation," and he restated his administrative argument.

Lt. Col. Samuel Reber supported General Scriven's administration argument. Reber told the committee that the Signal Corps had the "organization for handling the question from three points of view: administration, the purchase and inspection of the necessary supplies, and the supervision and control the aviators' training as well as their actual organization and handling in the field."[4]

Captain Foulois told the committee, "It is not an absolute question that they (administrators) know how to fly. It is a question of having a man at the head of aviation who is an organizer, a man who is an administrator." Foulois told the committee, "I think it should not be separated from the Signal Corps just now, because we want older men at the head of it."[5]

But Representative William S. Howard was skeptical that the technical knowledge the Signal Corps possessed was the kind needed in aviation. Directing his questions to Scriven, he asked, "How many men," meaning officers, "have you in the Signal Corps who are practical fliers today?" Scriven told him "one, Capt. Charles Deforest Chandler." "How many men are there in the Signal Corps?" Howard asked, still meaning officers, and Scriven told him there were seventeen, plus twenty-nine detailed officers, "making forty-six in all." There was a short pause before Howard asked, "And only one of them can fly?"

Beck Makes His Move

Scriven confirmed that only one Signal Corps officer could fly and was about to launch into a long-winded explanation when Howard broke in: "I am trying to get at the practical knowledge that your Signal Corps has of aviation." The question rattled Scriven, who lamely responded, "We have theoretical knowledge, not practical knowledge."

Howard said, "Men who simply have a theoretical knowledge of flying . . ." just before Scriven interrupted: "I am talking about the general subject of aviation and aeronautics." The CSO's answer did not satisfy Howard, who was clearly not pleased with what he was hearing. Raising his voice, he said, "A man might have a general knowledge of aviation, but if he could not fly he would be worth a 'cuss' to the Army in time of trouble."

Scriven recovered and scored: "I am trying to make the distinction clear between the theoretical and the practical sides of the matter, and that is just the difference between the ability of the man who manufactures the gun and the man who uses it." Howard nodded and sat back in his chair. Scriven saw that he was back on track and talked about reconnaissance being the airplane's battlefield role.[6]

Assistant Secretary of War Henry Breckinridge told the committee that the War Department's official view was that the airplane was "nothing but another branch of the service of information, which includes all communication, observation, and recognizance [*sic*]" that ought to be "coordinated with, and subordinated to, the general service of information, and not erected into an independent and uncoordinated service."[7]

The assertion that the airplane's role was limited to reconnaissance caused Mr. Hay to ask the CSO, "Will you state briefly what are the functions of an aviation corps in time of war?"

The general restated the scouting and reconnaissance missions and guardedly admitted to a "fighting function," which he presumed was "bomb dropping." He dismissed bombing, saying, "Of this nobody knows much of anything, but we have theories." Having opened the door briefly to the possibility that the airplane's role might actually be broader than just reconnaissance, the CSO quickly closed it by reemphasizing the airplane's reconnaissance role. "One of the main services of the aeroplane is that of reconnaissance and the collection of information."[8]

It was important to the Signal Corps' strategy to keep the airplane's battlefield role focused on reconnaissance. This hearing was really all about whether to separate aviation from the Signal Corps or leave it where it was. Reconnaissance filled the bill as a reason for leaving aviation with the Signal Corps, whereas having a combat capability did not.

When Congressman Warren Gard asked Lieutenant Colonel Reber if he thought that "the aviation service should be simply an auxiliary of the Signal Corps," Reber replied, "That it is a part of the work of the Signal Corps; yes, sir." Major Russel stepped in to hold the line that reconnaissance was a Signal Corps function. He told the committee, "Reconnaissance and reporting are too closely related. To say that the Signal Corps is charged with the second and not the first would be to set severely hampering limitations."[9]

The importance of the reconnaissance argument to the Signal Corps strategy was evident when Captain Mitchell was called on. Mitchell was without question the biggest gun in the Signal Corps arsenal of experts, and Scriven had selected him to represent the Signal Corps for several good reasons. At that time, Mitchell was serving on the general staff, and though he had no practical flying experience, he had studied the subject and had been a lecturer at the Signal Corps school on the uses of the balloon and dirigible in reconnaissance and bombardment.[10] He was exceptionally bright and had the ability to make truly impressive factual presentations. He sounded like an expert, and his general staff assignment lent authority to what he said. Mitchell was also a Signal Corps officer, which meant that he was solidly in the Signal Corps camp. Mitchell's testimony fully justified Scriven's choice.

Mitchell's entire presentation was done without notes, and his delivery was flawless as he reeled off fact after fact with such authority that it appeared he had spent his life in aviation. He told the committee, "We know absolutely that aeroplanes are valuable for reconnaissance service." He set aside the argument that recon-

Beck Makes His Move

naissance rested solely with the cavalry, telling the committee that "every man in the Army performs reconnaissance."

He reinforced the claim that the airplane's primary role was reconnaissance and moved on to establish that reconnaissance was legally a Signal Corps function. That was somewhat more difficult to do. General Scriven lent a hand by citing a memorandum by the new secretary of war, Lindley M. Garrison, who wrote, "Under the law the Signal Corps supervises the services of communication, observation, and reconnaissance as effected through wire and wireless telegraph and telephone."

But the legitimacy claim was stronger in the 1913 *Field Service Regulations*, paragraph 56, titled "Aeronautical Reconnaissance," which said, "Military aircraft of all kinds will be employed under the direction of the commander of the forces to which they are assigned and the immediate control of the officer commanding the aero organization," and went on to say, "Dirigible balloons and aeroplane reconnaissance supplements and extends that made by cavalry." The wording made it appear to the committee members that for at least five years the army had assigned a reconnaissance role to aircraft, and during that time aircraft came under Signal Corps control.

Nevertheless, the committee members questioned the premise that the Signal Corps had a reconnaissance mission, and a heated argument went on for some time until Daniel E. Garrett asked, out of the blue, "Could any army contend with its opponents if they should have an aviation service?" Scriven, who had seen service in the Philippines, provided a hypothetical situation as his answer.

If an enemy should land at Subic Bay, and the defense was provided with aeroplanes, I doubt very much if the attack could get ashore. They must approach with their transports loaded with troops, horses, and guns exposed, and the beach open to anything that might come over it, attack from overhead—an ideal condition for dirigibles and aeroplanes, which by dropping nitrogelatin might stop the landing or at least disorganize the enemy's troops. There can be no doubt of the tremendous influence of overhead attack upon transports crowded with troops, and upon small boats and shore landings.[11]

Unintentionally, the CSO's hypothetical answer had again opened the door to the idea that there was an offensive role for airplanes. And an offensive capability, meaning guns and bombs, was definitely not a Signal Corps function. Major Russel moved in to close the door again. There was no denying that an offensive role was a possibility, but the Signal Corps' position was that any discussion on the airplane's offensive role was purely speculative, whereas reconnaissance was a solid reality.

But the discussion about arming airplanes with guns and bombs would not go away, and finally Lieutenant Colonel Reber stepped in to divert the discussion away from bombs and guns. He told the committee, "The Signal Corps is one military establishment which by law, and possibly by custom, has certain functions prescribed for it. Among those functions and duties has been military aviation." Reber added, "The thing has grown up with the Signal Corps." But he said rather ruefully, "I am sorry to say it has grown faster than the Signal Corps."[12]

Reber's statement ended the talk about guns, bombs, and offensive operations but opened the prospect that someday military aviation would grow so large that the army would have to separate it from the Signal Corps. General Scriven had also dropped that hint in his opening statement to the committee. On the future prospect that military aviation might someday become a separate line unit Scriven acknowledged that in Europe aviation was on a separate footing and a part of the line. He excused that, saying, "It is true that the countries of Europe all have an aviation corps. I refer to those that have a sufficiently large aeronautical force to maintain what may be called a fourth arm of the service."

Following a discussion on military aviation in Europe, Representative Garrett asked Foulois, "Your idea is that when our aviation department reaches that stage of efficiency now attained by foreign countries, it should be separate?"[13]

Foulois answered, "Yes, sir," and added, "There is no question in my mind that it is going to be one of the biggest things there is in the field of military reconnaissance."

Beck Makes His Move

Garrett asked, "But your idea is that if the aviation squadron grows and assumes large proportions, it is bound to separate?"

Foulois: "Yes, sir."

Garrett: "And it is only a question of time until separation takes place?"

Foulois: "Yes, sir."

Mitchell attempted to curb the talk about future separation, insisting that the Signal Corps would always be aviation's home. Warren Gard asked directly, "Ultimately this aeronautic service will develop so it will be a separate arm?" Mitchell avoided a direct answer, saying instead, "I think it will dominate the Signal Corps."[14] Gard bore in: "Would you not favor making it a separate arm?" Mitchell could not dodge that question, but he adroitly deflected it by equating aviation with the Signal Corps: "That may be proven advisable in the future. I doubt it, as the Signal Corps will itself be aviation." Mitchell's blocking maneuver did not hold, and the drift of the discussion continued along the lines that while aviation might someday become a separate arm, now was not the time to take that step.

To say that Capt. Paul Beck was outgunned is an understatement, and on top of that he did not make a very strong argument for his cause.[15] Beck was unclear on whether he advocated removing aviation from the Signal Corps for the purpose of creating a separate arm, or if he simply wanted aviation put somewhere else. He told the committee, "As to the present wisdom of using the word 'corps,' I am somewhat in doubt."

But there was absolutely no doubt that he wanted aviation taken away from the Signal Corps. His principal argument was that aviation "does not logically belong to the Signal Corps." He read paragraph 1578, saying that it "states explicitly what the duties and the functions of the Signal Corps are and Aviation is not included." He told the committee, "There never has been any specific provision giving aviation to the Signal Corps. They just reached out and took it," referring to Brigadier General Allen's 1 August 1907 memorandum.

Beck did not spend time arguing against the Signal Corps position that it had the administrative staff necessary for managing aviation. The only direct reference Beck made to the Signal Corps administration record followed a question from Representative Hay, who asked Beck how long it would take a separate aviation organization to create "a concrete plan." Beck ducked the question and took another shot at the Signal Corps. "That is something the Signal Corps has not done in five years—a plan for ultimate organization."

Beck also took a shot at the Signal Corps, calling their claim that its officers possessed the technical knowledge to handle aviation matters a "gigantic bluff." He spent too much time criticizing the Signal Corps chain of command, saying that it was too cumbersome and slow. He said, "As it stands today, we have a nonflier at the head and all recommendations come from him. They go to the Signal Office where, if I mistake not, they are always referred to Lieutenant Arnold, who is a flyer in charge of that branch of work in the office. Next, they go to General Scriven, who is the chief of the corps, and his final recommendation goes to the Chief of Staff." Beck suggested that the chain of command should go from the commandant of the school directly to an aviation officer who was assigned to the War Department. "Then the matter comes from a flyer to a flyer, to the man who acts on it, and you cut out three intermediaries, going right to the meat of the subject."

Beck tried to kill the Signal Corps argument that reconnaissance was a Signal Corps function, but at that point in the hearings the committee members had heard all they wanted to hear on that subject. What little questioning there was ended when Beck was forced to concede that paragraph 1578 contained "a more or less obscure phrase that might be construed as permitting them to do reconnaissance duty."

Beck tried to sell the idea that airplanes had an offensive role in modern warfare. He repeated the four "fundamental uses for the airplane in war" that he had described in his 1912 *Infantry Journal* article—reconnaissance, artillery fire control, "aggressive use," and "the occasional transportation use." He told the committee about his experience dropping simulated bombs at the Los Angeles air meet in 1910 and said that he had worked with Lieutenant Crissy on a "bomb dropping device" at the 1911 San Francisco air meet. He concluded with the assertion that his experience "leads me to believe that there is an aggressive use for the aeroplane." There was no discussion, and Representative Hay led Beck into a discussion of the idea that it would be better to wait until military aviation had reached a size and efficiency comparable to European aviation units.

The best Beck could do was tell the committee, "There is no certainty that it will ever attain any size or importance under the Signal Corps. They have been handling it now for five years with no appreciable results. . . . The longer they keep it, the stronger their hold will become and the less chance we will have of getting aviation into the hands of the men who actually do the work."

Beck's lame performance was steamrollered by the Signal Corps opposition to HR 5304. It was clearly obvious that when Beck walked away, the committee consensus was that the time for separation had not come and, for the time being, army aviation would remain in the Signal Corps. HR 5304 in its original form did not go beyond the committee hearings. Instead it went back to James Hay for a complete rewrite, an effort in which Beck was not included. When the new HR 5304 emerged, it had little in common with Beck's original version. As we shall see, the revised version caused more problems than it solved.

10

Cowan's Flight Pay, 1913–1915

In the wake of the March 1913 round-robin letter incident at Texas City, the CSO consolidated all flying at North Island in June 1913. Except for three pilots and two airplanes in Texas, and Lahm's part-time school in Manila, all the Wright and Curtiss pilots were on North Island by 22 June 1913, where Captain Cowan relieved Lieutenant Geiger as the commanding officer.

Cowan was optimistic about the future when he took command of the Signal Corps Flying School at San Diego on 22 June. The upheavals during the first half of 1913 were past, and shortly after being relieved, Geiger was ordered to take twelve men, a civilian mechanic, and two Curtiss hydroplanes to Hawaii, where he was to establish a flying school at Fort Kamehameha and support the First Hawaiian Brigade. That one of the airplanes he took with him to Hawaii was the school's newly acquired dual-control Curtiss hydroplane totally escaped Cowan's notice. With Geiger gone, things seemed to settle down. Most of the Texas City pilots' demands had been met, Sam Reber was scheduled to become the chief of the Aeronautical Division in September, and the weather in San Diego was fine, clear, and warm.

Cowan's new position was made more attractive by the law passed on 2 March 1913, in which Congress gave the Aeronautical Division legal standing by creating the Aviation Section of the Signal Corps, and authorizing 35 percent flight pay "for such officers as

are or may be hereafter detailed by the Secretary of War on aviation duty: *Provided* that this increase of pay and allowances shall
be given to such officers only as are actual flyers of heavier-than-
air craft, and while so detailed."[1]

Cowan believed that the secretary of war's order, SO131, assigning him to command the flying school, had detailed him "on aviation duty" as the new law required. But when he took command
of the aviation school in San Diego, he had no intention of learning to fly and there was nothing in his orders directing him to
do so.[2] The decision to learn to fly was Cowan's alone, and on 10
July 1913, he made two "grass-cutting" runs in a flightless Curtiss
trainer.[3] He did not immediately follow up on the initial lessons,
and he said nothing to his instructor, Tom Milling, about wanting
to learn to fly. Most of the pilots thought he had done it for a lark.

But beginning on 31 July, Captain Cowan signed a pay department voucher on which he typed, "I certify that I am an actual flier
of heavier-than-air craft," and said he made his first flight on 10
July 1913. From that date forward, he drew flight pay at 35 percent
of his pay, earning an extra $113.63 per month until 31 March 1915.[4]

Cowan always insisted that his flight pay claim was legal according to the army regulation in force at that time. That regulation read:

An officer shall be considered an actual flier of heavier-than-air
craft from the date of his first flight after reporting by order of the
Secretary of War for duty at an aviation station or to the commanding officer of an aeronautical organization in the field until relieved
of such duty. An officer entitled to the increased pay on account of
duty as an actual flier of heavier-than-air craft will certify on each
pay account, during the time the increased pay is claimed, that
he is an actual flier of heavier-than-air craft, under detail for aviation duty by the Secretary of War. The first voucher upon which
the increased pay is claimed will be the date of the first flight. A
copy of the order detailing the officer for aviation duty will be filed
with this voucher and the order cited on all subsequent vouchers
so long as the increased pay is claimed.[5]

Cowan had certified that he had made his first flight on 10 July

1913, which was correct, but how did a single-seat "grass-cutter" run constitute a flight, since he never left the ground? Because running across the field in a flightless trainer that did not leave the ground was the first flight lesson in the Curtiss flight-training syllabus, and the policy at the Signal Corps flying school was that a Curtiss student's first lesson in the grass cutter was his first flight.[6]

All Curtiss students started their flight training on the flightless grass-cutter, and all of them started drawing flight pay immediately following their first lesson. The situation was different for Wright students because the Wright planes were two-seaters that had either semi-dual controls or dual controls depending on whether they were a Model B or a Model C. Wright students *flew* on their first lesson.

Given the policy, one might infer that Cowan could legitimately draw flight pay from the day of his first lesson in the Curtiss grass-cutter except for the additional requirement in Paragraph 1291½ that he had to be "under detail for aviation duty." His orders sending him to San Diego said that he was there "for duty in the Signal Corps Aviation School," whereas the orders assigning line officers to aviation duty said that they were to report "for aviation duty." And after the passage of the 18 July 1914 act that created the Aviation Section of the Signal Corps and the rating of junior military aviator the orders included the phrase "on duty requiring him to participate regularly and frequently in aerial flights." The sticky question was, did being assigned "for duty in the Signal Corps Aviation School" mean the same as being detailed "for aviation duty?" It was a matter of semantics. Did being assigned to command the aviation school mean that Cowan was being assigned "aviation duty" with an attendant duty to fly?

Besides the question of semantics, the critical difference between Cowan and regularly assigned student pilots was that the regularly assigned students followed a structured flight-training program that started immediately following their first flight lesson, whether it was in a flightless Curtiss grass-cutter or a dual-control Wright Model B or Model C. But Cowan did not follow the standard training syllabus and flew only when it suited him or circumstances made it imperative that he take another lesson or two.[7] Cowan might have acted in good faith when he decided to draw flight pay after 10 July, but he started questioning the legality of his decision during the HR 5304 hearings in August 1913.

During the HR 5304 hearings Brigadier General Scriven told the House committee twice that the post of school commandant was an administrative assignment that did not involve flying.[8] But at the same time, when Representative Maurice Connolly asked if it would be better to have a flier "at the head of the thing," Scriven told the congressman, "Other things equal, it would be."[9] That was the closest Scriven came to saying that Cowan's position could be a flying position. But it was all that Cowan had to work with, and he made the best of it a month later.

Connolly was actually asking about the chief of the Aeronautical Division, who at the time was Maj. Edgar Russel, but the question could be applied to the school commandant too. Given the ambiguity of the language in his orders and Scriven's rather open-ended reply to Congressman Connolly, Cowan's position became more precarious when 2nd Lt. Moss L. Love was killed in a Wright Model C at North Island on 4 September.[10]

Love's death, the first at North Island since Cowan had taken command of the school, did nothing to encourage Cowan to learn to fly. But the cso's testimony before Congress in August had put him in a tight spot with respect to drawing flight pay. Up to this time, the legality of Cowan's drawing of flight pay was questionable but defensible, and he set out to strengthen his position.

On 21 September Lt. Col. Samuel Reber, now the chief of the Aeronautical Division, spent three days inspecting the school at North Island. During the visit, Cowan asked Reber if he, Cowan, should learn to fly as a part of his duties at the school. Hooking his wagon to the cso's answer to Congressman Connolly, Cowan added that it would be a good idea for him to "know enough about flying to be able to supervise the work of his instructors." Reber agreed but said that the amount of flying was entirely up to Cowan.[11]

Reber had attended the HR 5304 hearings the previous month and had heard the cso describe Cowan as an "administrator" on two occasions. Knowing the CSO's position on the matter, Reber stressed that Cowan's "principal duty was to build up the school and supervise the work of the others."[12] Cowan now felt that despite the ambiguity of his orders detailing him to the school, Scriven's reply to Connolly, and Reber's qualified authorization provided him with the justification he needed to continue drawing flight pay. It also became the basis for the trouble that followed. Cowan had entered a gray zone, which left him open to the charge that he was fraudulently drawing flight pay. So far no one knew he was drawing flight pay, and he continued to keep that to himself, a strong indication that he knew he was on thin ice.

Reber, unaware that Cowan was already drawing flight pay, remained focused on seeing that the army flight school was run the way he wanted it run. Knowing exactly what had happened at Texas City and having been involved in the Geiger-ACA confrontation in early 1913, he was intent on preventing a recurrence of the Texas City incident, and on stifling the move to separate aviation from the Signal Corps. He told Cowan to keep a lid on things, which meant tighter control and closer supervision. Thus the week of 21 September 1913 marked the start of Cowan's troubles with the pilots. He said, "When we started to tighten up and require officers to do more work . . . some of them did not accept it." That was true.[13]

When Cowan returned to San Diego in September 1913 following the HR 5304 hearings, he ran into his first of several problems. He discovered that Geiger had taken two of the Curtiss airplanes, one of which was the school's only dual-control Curtiss, with him to Hawaii. Geiger was gone several months, during which the absence of two Curtiss planes seriously hindered the training of Curtiss pilots at North Island and irked Cowan because Geiger hardly flew while he was in Hawaii and accomplished nothing during the fourteen months he was there.[14] And then there was Ned Goodier.

Cowan's dislike for Goodier developed soon after Cowan returned from the HR 5304 hearings. At that time Goodier was the chief instructor for the army's Curtiss students and he worked closely with the civilian employees at the Curtiss Company Flying School at the south end of the Island. Lieutenant Goodier was in charge of virtually all aspects of Curtiss airplane operations and maintenance at the army's flying school, which meant that he also spent a lot of time in and around the nearby Curtiss Company Flying School.[15]

The issue was the close, even cozy, relationship that the army's Curtiss pilots had with the Curtiss employees. The relationship was so close because the army's Curtiss camp was right next to the Curtiss Company School, hangars, and engine shop. Not only did the Curtiss Company School provide free occasional instruction to the army officers; the army officers also provided occasional instruction to the Curtiss School's civilian students. And the relationship was not limited to sharing instructional roles. Curtiss allowed the army fliers free access to its machine shops, spare parts, and airplanes. Cowan believed that Ned Goodier's close relationship with the Curtiss school employees was corrupt and bad for discipline.

The school commandant was also concerned about the rivalry between the Curtiss and Wright pilots that the arrival of Wright pilots from Texas had reactivated. Cowan soon developed the opinion that Ned Goodier was the instigator of the "banter going on between the Curtiss and Wright pilots." Initially, banter was about the limit of the rivalry, but it quickly went from banter to more serious and dangerous behavior that created a them-against-us atmosphere between the two camps.[16]

When Cowan arrived at the school, Goodier had just returned from Letterman Army Hospital, where he had been treated for injuries sustained in a near fatal crash on 18 February 1913. Because of his injuries, which included a compound skull fracture and a serious concussion, Goodier was still weak. He regularly visited the hospital at Fort Rosecrans for outpatient treatment of chronic fatigue, and he had back problems. Cowan unfairly commented on Goodier's frequent trips to the hospital, saying, "Goodier has to either do the work, go to the hospital, or get off the job."[17]

Despite his instant dislike for Goodier, there was no serious friction between Cowan and the other pilots during that time, and there is ample evidence that he enjoyed a congenial relationship with his subordinates. One of the most active dissidents, 1st Lt. Townsend F. Dodd, said, "Captain Cowan has been extremely nice to me personally and socially, and our official relations have always been of the very best. Although many of his ideas about technical subjects were different from those held by me, I have always felt that such differences were simply those due to a different viewpoint."[18]

The records suggest that Cowan was a conscientious officer who tried his best to administer the aviation school. He went to bat for the pilots on many occasions, did his best to obtain airplanes and replacement parts, and promoted technological experiments.

But Arthur Cowan was not a fighter. Above everything else, he wanted to avoid appearing to be an obstacle to General Scriven's policies and decisions, whatever they were. He made those feelings clear in a letter he wrote to Samuel Reber. "I hate like everything to appear in the light of opposing any project that the Signal Office wishes to carry out. I hate to appear as an obstructionist. I want to be loyal to the Signal Corps and to the officers of the Signal Corps who are conducting this work."[19]

Outwardly, Cowan was an honest man, and being honest, he disapproved of the relationship the army's Curtiss pilots had with the Curtiss Company School, which he believed was unethical and possibly criminal, especially that the army pilots were given free access to the Curtiss tools, machine shop, and, occasionally, aircraft. But Cowan's indignation at what the Curtiss pilots were doing, or appeared to be doing, did not prevent him from taking flight pay under questionable circumstances.

On 1 November 1913 Lt. Col. Lewis E. Goodier arrived in San Diego to visit his oldest son, Ned. Lieutenant Colonel Goodier was the judge advocate for the Western Military Department, headquartered in San Francisco. Though the flying school came under the CSO's direct command, the Western Military Department had jurisdiction over the school for discipline and courts martial.

The parental visit attracted no special attention, but several of the aviators were glad to see Colonel Goodier and renew old

Cowan's Flight Pay

acquaintances. The senior Goodier's visit was more than a social call. For one thing, he wanted to see how his son was getting along following his return to duty at North Island in June. The senior Goodier's concern was prompted by the fact that Ned Goodier had returned to duty before he was completely recovered from the head injury he sustained in his 18 February crash.

But the more important purpose for the visit was to have a first-hand look at how the school was being run. Colonel Goodier's visit was entirely unofficial, but Ned had been writing to him, telling him about some of the things that were going on, which included increasingly frequent confrontations with Cowan. The senior Goodier's motive for the November visit was evident when he said, "We were deeply concerned in everything touching Ned's progress."[20]

Cowan had filed vouchers for flight pay in September and October 1913 but didn't take up flight lessons again until November. On 14 November he actually got off the ground by making four "straightaway" hops, during which he rose from fifty to eighty feet and remained in the air for about a hundred and fifty feet. That same day, shortly after Cowan had made his last hop, 2nd Lt. C. Perry Rich was killed in in the Philippines, the ninth fatality in the 1913 series of fatal crashes. Rich's death had less immediate impact on the men in San Diego because the crash occurred in Manila Bay and Rich was not a member of the San Diego Wright fraternity, having done all his flying in the Philippines. But his death did disturb the San Diego pilots because it was the fourth fatality in a Model C.[21]

On 16 September 1914, ten months after Lieutenant Rich was killed, Cowan resumed his flight training. During that ten months he never left the ground, but he had continued to draw flight pay.[22] None of the pilots knew for sure that Cowan was drawing flight pay on the basis of his irregular lessons, but there were rumors.

11

The Seeds of Rebellion, 1911–1914

A strong rivalry between the army's Curtiss and Wright pilots stemmed from the pilots' close personal relationship with the two manufacturers. The army's earliest pilots all received their initial flight training from either the Wright or the Curtiss Company on a one-on-one basis. In the process, some of the rancor between Wright and Curtiss was adopted by the pilots. The pilots' rivalry was about specifics such as which company was the better at design, better for flying, and safer, which had the better training methods, and which was the better for military flying. With regard to design, flying qualities, construction, safety, and flight training methods, there was room for discussion. As for which one was more suitable for military aviation, the answer was neither one.[1]

The rivalry started at Fort Sam Houston in 1911, lasted until mid-1914, and took the form of demonstrating the superiority of the Curtiss or the Wright airplanes. In its initial form, it was harmless.[2] When new students arrived, each camp tried to persuade them to fly either the Curtiss or the Wright airplane, describing the superior teaching methods of the respective builders and flight characteristics of the respective aircraft. The recruiting was on the same level as a fraternity rush. Although harmless enough in the beginning, there were many instances in which each side took unnecessary risks to prove the superiority of their respective design.[3] The differences between the Wright and Curtiss flight controls was the heart of the argument.

The discussion turned on the question of which airplane was easier to learn to fly. The Wright airplanes' side-by-side seat configuration made the plane a better trainer because a Wright student always had an instructor in the seat beside him. In that respect, the Wright would seem to be the easier plane in which to learn to fly, but having an instructor aboard was not all there was to it. The Wright and Curtiss airplanes had entirely different flight control systems and the only features they shared were that the pilots were able to control the airplane's pitch, roll and yaw, and the pilots sat in front of, or on, the lower wing.

The most important feature that the two control systems had in common was that both achieved lateral control, which allowed the pilot to keep the wings level in flight and to roll the airplane right and left. The Wrights used wing-warping to achieve lateral control, which involved bending the outboard, trailing wingtip edge on one wing up and bending the trailing wingtip edge on the other wing down to the same degree at the same time.[4]

But the Wright controls were not instinctive. The Wright Model B had three levers. one on the left of the left-hand seat and one on the right of the right-hand seat. Those two levers were interconnected and controlled the elevators: pull back to climb and push forward to dive. Those movements were instinctive. The third lever that controlled the wing warping and the rudder was between the seats, so the instructor and the student shared it: push forward to turn left and pull back to turn right. Those movements were not instinctive. The wing-warping and rudder movement were linked to the single stick by an ingenious wheel-and-chain device so that wing-warping and rudder direction functioned together to accomplish a coordinated banking turn.[5] A short wooden lever was attached by a hinge to the top of the wing-warping and rudder lever. This short lever allowed the pilot to operate the rudder independently of the wheel-and-chain device, and was used when making tight, spiral descents.

The three-stick arrangement of the controls in the model B created the problem of right-hand and left-hand pilots. If the instructor sat in the left seat, he controlled the wing-warping and rudder stick with his right hand and the student controlled it with his left hand. This resulted in having left-hand pilots who could only fly in the right seat, which upset the airplane's balance in flight because the pilot and the engine were both to the right of the wings' center.[6]

The Model C "Speed Scout" that went into service in 1912 was a truly dual-control aircraft. The layout was the same as on the Model B, but each seat was provided with a complete set of controls. The elevator stick was on the left side of each seat, and the warping and rudder stick was on the right side of each seat. This change eliminated the problem of having either right- or left-hand pilots. Men who learned to fly in the Wright C were all right-hand pilots, and it did not make any difference which seat they occupied. Though it provided dual controls that made flight training easier, the Model C was a vicious airplane that killed more army pilots before August 1914 than any other type.

The Curtiss D-IVs the army bought in 1911 had a second seat that was squeezed in behind the pilot and in front of the engine. That seat had no controls, making it unsuitable for an instructor's or student's seat, and visibility was awful, making it largely useless as an observer's seat.[7] A Curtiss student pilot was alone in the plane from the moment he started his flight training and remained solo throughout his primary and basic training.[8]

His flight training started by running at takeoff speed across the field in a plane called a "grass-cutter" that had the throttle blocked so that it could not develop enough speed to lift off. Once the student had mastered going straight ahead without ground-looping, the instructor replaced the throttle block with one that allowed the plane to lift off but could not sustain prolonged flight. The student could make only short hops of about one hundred to two hundred yards at an altitude of about fifty feet. Those hops taught him to take off, keep the wings level, and land. For the final stage, the instructor removed the throttle block, allowing the student to fly oval circuits around the field and figure eights around two posts set in the ground. Throughout the training period, the instructor was planted in a chair, firmly on the ground, taking notes.

The Seeds of Rebellion

Curtiss used ailerons to roll left or right. A padded aluminum frame called the "shoulder brace aileron control" encased the pilot's upper arms, just below his shoulders. Leaning left against the frame caused the plane to roll left. Leaning against the right frame had the opposite effect.

A wheel and column between the pilot's knees controlled the rudder and the elevators. Turning the wheel left or right turned the rudder left or right. Pulling the column back caused the plane to climb, and pushing forward caused it to dive. A controlled left, banking turn was made by leaning left and turning the wheel left. Leaning right and turning the wheel right had the opposite effect. When you recall that Curtiss got his start building and racing motorcycles, you see where the idea came from. Despite being solo throughout their training, students had an easier time mastering the Curtiss control system because it was more instinctive.

Since the days of the big air meets in 1911 and 1912, the army's pilots knew that there were better, safer airplanes on the market, having seen them firsthand at the air meets they attended. The Signal Corps' policy of buying only Wright and Curtiss airplanes became a sore point with them as the death toll among army pilots climbed, reaching one in four in 1914. The obvious defects in the designs and construction of the Wright and Curtiss planes actually heightened the rivalry between the two camps and fueled the growing dissent, especially among Curtiss pilots.

The arrival of the Wright pilots and their planes in San Diego in June 1913 exacerbated the rivalry between the two camps, and the competition between the Curtiss and Wright pilots became dangerous. Grover Loening, whom Colonel Reber hired in July 1914 to be the army's aeronautical engineer and to address the aircraft problems at North Island, wrote, "The vicious Curtiss versus Wright rivalry that existed in the commercial game had, like an insidious disease, fastened itself upon the Army fliers. The rivalry started out as good-natured kidding. Once, the Wright pilots asked the Curtiss pilots to not fly over the Wright hangar because parts fell off Curtiss airplanes and endangered the people on the ground.

Cowan felt Goodier was responsible for that sort of banter. But the rivalry grew into deadly serious jealousy and spite, affecting everyone, even down to the mechanics."[9]

By the fall of 1913 the rivalry had become so intense that it interfered with the school's efficiency. After Cowan relieved Chandler and took the Wright pilots to San Diego, the Curtiss pilots began viewing themselves as underdogs in the manufacturer-based rivalry. They believed that Cowan was a Wright supporter because of his open dislike for Geiger and Glenn Curtiss. That might not have been the case, but if Cowan leaned either way it was probably toward the Wright people because of his closer association with them, and because of the Signal Corps love affair with the Wright Company airplanes.

The sense of inferiority among Curtiss pilots also stemmed from the inescapable fact that the Signal Corps consistently bought more Wright airplanes than Curtiss airplanes. In 1911 and 1912 the ratio was two to one, and in 1913 the ratio increased to three to one. By December 1913 the number of Curtiss aircraft at North Island had dropped to three compared with seven Wright and Burgess airplanes. The drop in Curtiss numbers was due to natural attrition, and the Signal Corps' attempt to establish a school in Hawaii, without buying replacements. As the number of Curtiss airplanes on hand dwindled, a rumor started among the Curtiss pilots that they would have to become Wright pilots.[10]

The rumor was unfounded. In fact, circumstances over the following four months would have exactly the opposite effect, forcing all Wright pilots to convert to the Curtiss control system. The truth in December 1913 was that the awkward Wright control system would be completely eliminated in about seven months. The move away from Wright airplanes started on 9 February 1914, following the last fatal crash in the bloody series that had started ten months earlier.

The final victim in the series of fatal crashes was 2nd Lt. Henry B. Post, or "Postie" to his friends, who was killed flying a Wright Model C, SC-10. He was enormously popular with all the pilots, and his death in a Model C that nearly everyone agreed was inherently dangerous angered the pilots at North Island. Two days after Post's death, 2nd Lt. William Nicholson visited Ned Goodier in San Francisco.

On 11 February Nicholson told Colonel Goodier that the enlisted mechanics who were preparing SC-10 for Post's 9 February flight told him the airplane was unsafe because "the engine section was weak." The mechanics thought that the airplane should not be flown. Nicholson said that he went to Foulois with that information, and Foulois responded, "No matter. The machine will have to be flown." If the story is true, Foulois was guilty of the same neglect of duty that he charged Beck with in 1911 at Fort San Houston.[11]

True or not, the story fit the Curtiss pilots' belief that they were increasingly at the mercy of the Signal Corps' bias in favor of Wright airplanes. Colonel Goodier asked Nicholson if he would tell that story to Col. John L. Chamberlain, the department's inspector general (IG). Nicholson readily agreed, and Colonel Goodier sent Nicholson upstairs to talk to the IG.

Later that day, Goodier told Chamberlain that Lieutenant Nicholson's report should be investigated, emphasizing that the Wright airplanes were the source of the problem. Chamberlain agreed. But he told Goodier that he had already conducted the first annual inspection and any order to return to San Diego had to come from the IG's office in Washington, because the Western Department had no authority over the aviation school to make an unscheduled inspection.

While Colonel Chamberlain applied for authorization from Washington to reinspect the school at San Diego, General Scriven grounded the remaining Wright Model B and C airplanes on 16 February 1914. He appointed Foulois to head a board made up of four other pilots, Carberry, Chapman, Dodd, and Taliaferro, with instructions to report on the suitability and safety of the Wright airplanes. The order was soon extended to include the Curtiss pushers.

The board did not report on the suspected design flaws associated with the Wright Models B and C but, on 24 February 1914, condemned all pusher airplanes, those that had the engine and propeller facing rearward, and recommended that the school use only tractor airplanes, those that had the engine and propeller facing forward. The decision was based on the fact that in a crash the pusher engine was thrown forward and hit the pilot. That conclusion applied only to Curtiss airplanes that had the engine mounted on its stand directly behind the pilot. The Wright engine rested on the wing *beside* the passenger, and if and when it tore loose, it went forward, past the passenger. Nevertheless, the decision effectively ended the army's love affair with the Wright Company and established the Curtiss Company as the army's prime contractor for training airplanes. The decision also opened the door for the Glenn L. Martin Company.

Colonel Chamberlain arrived at the school on 25 February to conduct the second inspection, which resulted in a critical report. Chamberlain noted the rivalry. "The school is divided into two general camps separated from one another by about one and a half miles. The rivalry between the two camps has been very keen. In fact, so keen that it has resulted in more or less friction." Chamberlain handled the second inspection as an expansion of the inspection he had made on 5 February. The second inspection was conducted from 25 to 27 February, and both inspections were covered in the 19 March report as one inspection. But his report on the school's airplanes was the most damning of the Signal Corps administration of aviation. At the time of his inspection, only four tractor airplanes were in service, all with Wright controls. In his report he posited, "What has the government to show for these years of work and the money expended? First, the death of twelve officers and several enlisted men; Second, a paper organization for one aero squadron; Third, an aviation school consisting of seventeen officers; Forth, several aeroplanes of various designs and makes, all of which are out of date, obsolete, and unfit for field service."[12] He allowed that the three or four tractor airplanes in the school's inventory were at least suitable for training.

During Chamberlain's interviews, pilots and civilian instructors complained about the poorly designed and shoddily constructed airplanes the Signal Corps was buying. They heaped their heaviest criticism on the Wright airplanes, and much of the criticism

The Seeds of Rebellion

came from the Wright civilian instructors. But Curtiss airplanes were also criticized for being out of date. Second Lt. Joseph E. Carberry, a Curtiss pilot, told Chamberlain, "The machines we have in our camp are almost exactly the same as the one that Mr. Curtiss flew down the Hudson in 1910."

Colonel Chamberlain also noted, "During the period mentioned there have been forty-eight officers detailed on aviation duty," and he listed all forty-eight, showing dates of assignment, dates of relief, and ratings accomplished. He concluded with, "Of these, sixteen are still on duty, twenty have been relieved for various reasons, and twelve have been killed. Of those living, there are perhaps a dozen, more or less, who are competent pilots, and a few others who have secured more or less skill. But, so far as I am able to learn, the Army has produced no one who may be regarded as having mastered the art of aviation."

Colonel Chamberlain finished his inspection on 27 February, and his report, submitted on 19 March 1914, was a fourteen-page exposé of the Signal Corps' mismanagement of military aviation since 1909. The responsibility for every problem cited in his report went straight back to the chief of the Aeronautical Division and the cso. But Chamberlain did not place the blame on anyone. He concluded, "It would be very easy to criticize individuals and policies, but such criticism would in all probability be unjust, since to arrive at any satisfactory conclusions would be extremely difficult, if not impossible."

The IG avoided naming anyone in the Signal Corps as being responsible for the sad situation in military aviation, but General Scriven did not miss the implications in the report. He rebutted Colonel Chamberlain's findings by saying, "In spite of the shortcomings and accidents, the results obtained are believed to be fully commensurate with the means provided for the establishment of this new art in the Army." That attitude, combined with a change in management style at North Island, fueled the third and most serious open rebellion.

Following Colonel Chamberlain's investigation, Cowan made a sound decision when he consolidated the Wright and Curtiss camps in one location and terminated all contact with the Curtiss Flying School. The move was done to reduce the rivalry, and to eliminate what he believed was an unhealthy relationship with the Curtiss employees. Shortly afterward, the Curtiss School closed and left the island.[13]

Post was the twelfth army officer to die in a crash since 17 September 1908, bringing the casualty rate among army aviators to exactly 25 percent. His death opened the floodgates of dissent and unrest and caused the pilots to take a hard look at their commanding officer, Capt. Arthur S. Cowan. Cowan drew flight pay, but he could not fly.

At the same time Cowan's demeanor changed. No longer the congenial, concerned advocate for pilots, he started castigating officers for petty derelictions and mistakes. But Cowan's change in management style, in combination with the existing low morale, distrust, and paranoia, brought him into direct conflict with the pilots and further exacerbated the situation. He probably equated mistakes, omissions, and inattention to details on the ground to similar errors, omissions, and mistakes in the air that were killing pilots. He also probably believed that if he tightened discipline on the ground he would reduce flying accidents.

Captain Cowan began a crackdown on pilot discipline even as the deadly crashes subsided. His attitude toward the officers under his command can be seen in what he told Colonel Chamberlain during the latter's inspection of the school in early 1914. Following the long string of deaths, Cowan considered suggesting that the army "discontinue all Wright machines" but instead felt that the problem might be with the pilots who "were really nothing but amateurs."[14]

This nearly contemptuous belief could not have been easily hidden, and by this time the pilots were aware that Cowan was drawing flight pay without making a serious attempt to learn to fly. But the thing that hardened their dislike for him was that he began criticizing and disciplining the pilots for what they considered to be petty issues. One of the first pilots Cowan went after was Ned Goodier over some missing tools.

The Seeds of Rebellion

The tools disappeared sometime between June 1912 and June 1913 when an enlisted mechanic, Sgt. James F. Hartman, lost or sold some of his army-issued tools.[15] Shortly after Lieutenant Brereton became the school maintenance officer in March 1913, an inventory showed the tools were missing, and it fell to Brereton to write the report of survey. He wrote the report and filed it away until the army granted his request for relief from aviation on 24 June 1913. As Brereton went out the door to return to the Coast Artillery, he handed the long overdue report of survey to Goodier, who was the new maintenance officer.

Goodier sat on the report for eight months, until 24 February 1914, when he learned that Colonel Chamberlain would be arriving the next day to conduct an IG inspection. Goodier did not want to be written up for the unfinished business of the lost tools, and on 24 February he endorsed Brereton's recommendation, which was to "relieve the responsible officer from all responsibility" and make Sergeant Hartman pay for the tools. Goodier submitted the report through channels and forgot about it.

When the long-delayed report arrived in Washington, Reber denied the recommendation that Sergeant Hartman pay for the tools and rejected Goodier's endorsement. He returned the report of survey with his own endorsement, stating that since Hartman had already been discharged on 28 February 1914, Lieutenant Goodier should be held accountable "in view of the long delay in submitting the report of survey."

Reber went after Goodier because he sat on the report for eight months. Although Reber could reach either Geiger, now in Hawaii, or Brereton, back in the Coast Artillery, Goodier was immediately accessible. There was also the fact that Captain Cowan disliked Goodier, and Colonel Reber adopted the policy that Cowan's dislikes were his dislikes—if for no other reason that discipline and stability needed to be maintained in the construction of their "empire."

In Cowan's view, Goodier's heel dragging in the missing-tool incident typified the general disregard for military procedure that Cowan was trying to eliminate. Goodier and Cowan clashed so often that he became "a pain in Cowan's ass." Also working against

Goodier was his openly stated view that to advance, army aviation had to be removed from Signal Corps control. He had been expressing that opinion since the Wright pilots arrived from Texas City in June 1913, which brought him into direct conflict with everyone in the chain of command from Cowan to the CSO. Both Reber and Cowan were looking for reason to send Goodier back to the Coast Artillery.

Lieutenant Colonel Reber's reply to Brereton's recommendation and Goodier's endorsement represented the new reality at North Island. The tools had disappeared during the flying club days, when Russel and Chandler ran the aviation program with a lackadaisical attitude and the pilots were not held accountable for such mundane things as lost tools. But after Post's death, Reber and Cowan began demanding greater accountability for the day-to-day running of the aviation school. During the spring of 1914 the pilots became aware that the rules had changed, and Goodier was one of the first to feel the pressure.

The second pilot to feel the pressure was an infantry officer, 1st Lt. Robert H. Willis Jr., who had been assigned to aviation on 6 August 1913.[16]

Willis lived in Coronado with the other pilots, and every day he rode his horse from there to the landing, where he caught the ferry for the trip across Spanish Bight to North Island. His attire for those daily rides was "a civilian cap, civilian coat, Army riding breeches, leggings, and tan shoes." In fact, army regulations authorized that attire "for riding purposes," and Cowan had no complaint about that. The trouble arose on Friday, 13 March, after Willis arrived at North Island "wearing his mixed uniform around the school during duty hours."

Cowan called him on it and gave him a standing order to change into the proper uniform "the very first thing upon arriving at the school." A few days later, on Tuesday, 17 March, Cowan caught Willis in front of a hangar at 1000 wearing his spiffy riding clothes. The captain asked the lieutenant why he had not changed into the proper uniform, pointing out that the duty day started at 0730. Willis offered Cowan a lame excuse that Cowan did not buy.

The next day Cowan again spotted Willis wearing his riding attire, this time aboard the contract ferry bringing officers across Spanish Bight to North Island from Coronado. Cowan, who clearly felt that the regulations did not include wearing riding clothes in a boat, sent word to the dock for Willis to report to him immediately.

When Willis entered the office, Cowan was standing behind his desk and Benjamin Foulois sat at his desk in the same room. Willis reported correctly, and Cowan demanded, "What do you mean by wearing that uniform through town and on the boat? Especially in view of the fact that I have spoken twice to you about this uniform!" When Willis came up with yet another lame excuse, Cowan told him that the explanation was "entirely unsatisfactory," and there followed a nasty exchange.

Cowan said, "From this time forward, you will not wear that uniform on this post. You can wear it in town while you're riding, but there is no authority for wearing it on duty and I don't propose to have you do it!"

Willis flared and snapped back, "Well, I'll get authority." He clarified his intention when he added that he would take his complaint to the IG.

"Good. You get authority," Cowan replied. "But until you do, don't let me see you on this post wearing that uniform. You're dismissed."

After Willis left, Foulois told Cowan, "You should charge him with insubordination. That was the worst case of insubordination I have ever seen." Cowan agreed that Willis had gotten out of hand but declined to have him charged. Instead he wired Reber, requesting immediate relief for Willis from aviation and return to his regiment. The next day, 19 March 1914, Cowan received orders relieving Willis, effective that day. Cowan kept track of Willis during the next nine months to see if his attitude showed improvement. When Willis applied for reassignment to aviation, his application included a letter of apology. Cowan forwarded the application and the apology to Reber with a recommendation that Willis be reinstated. Reber agreed, and Willis returned to North Island on 3 December 1914.

In April 1914 Cowan dealt with another attitude problem, this time with a twenty-six-year-old cavalry officer, 2nd Lt. Byron Q. Jones, a 1912 West Point graduate. Jones and another officer were in a hangar, working on an airplane with some enlisted mechanics, when Cowan heard Jones "burst out with the most filthy, obscene, profane lot of language that I have ever heard an officer or an enlisted man in the Army use." Cowan, a West Pointer himself, was shocked that an officer would use such language. "It had been reported to me previously that Lieutenant Jones was in the habit of doing this," Cowan recalled, and he called Jones outside and "reprimanded him severely."[17]

During the reprimand, Cowan said that Jones exhibited the disregard for military courtesy common among the pilots. "When I began to talk to him he assumed a very nonchalant air and started to roll a cigarette. I ordered him to throw away the cigarette and stand at attention while I was talking to him. He became very angry and showed it plainly. When I got through, he announced in a very insubordinate voice that he was going to apply to be relieved. I told him to submit his application and assured him that it would be approved."

Jones did not submit an application for relief, and the next day he apologized to Cowan for "making a fool of himself." Cowan accepted the apology, telling Jones, "We will consider the incident closed, but remember that that sort of thing will not be done as long as you serve under me." Jones got the message. Cowan kept his word and a year later sent Jones to the Massachusetts Institute of Technology to study aeronautical engineering.

In Cowan's view the pilots were "temperamental," and many believed that "because they were flying, risking their lives every day, they should not be subject to the ordinary rules of military discipline." He believed that the pilots' poor attitude stemmed from their early association with civilian pilots, which was especially true of the army's Curtiss pilots. It seemed to him that the civilian attitude had rubbed off on the army pilots so that a pilot "wanted to come to work in the morning, ask the sergeant if the machine was all right, and if it was he got in, made his flight, landed, got out and walked away, his day's work done." Grover Loening, who as the army's civilian aeronautical engineer was a neutral observer, agreed with Cowan's opinion. Loening said, "The aviators in many ways thought that they were above routine discipline. Flying officers never realize that they are members of the U.S. Army."[18]

Although inexcusable, the pilots' attitude came a from the belief that having learned to fly they were unique, they had an uncommon skill. And until the spring of 1914, their chances of dying in a flying accident were one in four. In fact, it was so dangerous that insurance companies refused to issue life insurance policies to army pilots.[19]

Their skill and the danger they faced, led the pilots to assume an air of self-confidence and swagger that public adoration fueled. In his memoirs, Hap Arnold commented on pilot arrogance, saying, "The glamour part of the early flying days was enough to spoil a man if he let it," and many of these early pilots were clearly spoiled.[20]

Cowan, a nonpilot and virtually a nonflier, was caught between recognizing the source of the pilots' attitude and maintaining military discipline. He managed the tightrope act fairly well, but being a nonpilot did not help. Being a nonflier prevented Cowan from understanding the pilots, because he was not one of them. He did not experience what they did, because he did not want to fly. All he wanted was the flight pay. In his ignorance, Cowan was about to commit another act that further angered the pilots and raised the specter of criminal fraud. The reworked version of HR 5304 had made Cowan's act possible, and the man for whom Cowan did it was 1st Lt. William Lay Patterson.

12

William Lay Patterson, 1914–1915

First Lt. William Lay Patterson arrived at the school on 1 April 1914 to assume the school's administrative duties and be in charge of the enlisted men. Patterson was actually Cowan's second choice, the first having been 1st Lt. B. F. "Butch" Miller, who had served with Cowan in the Philippines.[1] Cowan told Reber that Butch Miller was "one if the best Quartermasters among the younger officers of the Army and has a relatively large amount of experience in that class of work." Miller was also a close friend of Congressman Hay.[2]

Cowan planned to use Miller as the school adjutant who would be responsible for the enlisted company and keep the school's records, a nonflying administrative position. He also planned to "get him here, have him make a pay-flight, and then go about these other tasks, and it won't be necessary for him to do any more flying."[3] As things worked out, Miller could not accept Cowan's invitation, forcing Cowan to look for someone else, who turned out to be Patterson.

Cowan had also served with Patterson in the Philippines, and when he tapped Patterson to take Miller's slot, he was filling a nonflying administrative position.[4] Cowan's offer to Patterson was the same he made to Butch Miller: take the initial flight lesson, start drawing 35 percent flight pay, "and not thereafter do any flying."[5]

From the day Patterson arrived, he enjoyed an extremely close relationship with Cowan, who fussed over him and showed favoritism apparent to everyone. Patterson was the first student pilot to start flight training after Post's death, and he had to compete for time in the school's five airplanes. He started flight training on Monday, 6 April, when Oscar Brindley, the Wright civilian instructor, took him up for a twenty-two-minute orientation flight in a dual-control Burgess tractor that was still equipped with the Wright control system. Patterson's second training flight took place eleven days later, on Friday, 17 April, in a Burgess hydro, also equipped with Wright controls. Brindley was the instructor on that twelve-minute flight. Following those initial flights, Patterson started drawing flight pay.[6]

On 26 April U.S. relations with Mexico hit rock bottom, and part of the 1st Aero Squadron was detailed to Galveston, Texas. Foulois took the 1st Company, 1st Aero Squadron, with three Burgess airplanes and four pilots, to Texas, leaving the school with two tractor-engine airplanes—a Burgess with Wright controls, SC-9, and a Curtiss, SC-22—to serve ten pilots, including Patterson. Cowan decided to have the five Wright pilots transition to the Curtiss control, probably because no. 9 was old and due for overhaul. The decision was not popular with the Wright pilots, but it was a smart move.

Because Patterson's real purpose at San Diego was to assist Cowan with the school's administration, his flying lessons did not have a high priority, and Cowan made no effort to move Patterson's training along. It was also more important to Cowan that the nine experienced pilots learn to handle a tractor-engine airplane than it was for Patterson to learn to fly. The situation suited Patterson, who did not want to fly any more than he had to, but he did go up on 27 May with Oscar Brindley for a thirteen-minute flight. The truth was that Patterson did not like to fly, and during his flights with Brindley he refused to touch the controls.[7]

The airplane shortage became critical at the end of May. The only airplane with Wright controls, Signal Corps no. 9, was at the Burgess factory for overhaul, and on 30 May Ned Goodier made a bad landing in the Curtiss that collapsed the landing gear and broke the engine crankcase. With Signal Corps no. 9 in Marblehead, the school was without an airplane.[8]

The extreme shortage of airplanes at the school gave Cowan and Patterson a good excuse not to fly, and both men used it. But Patterson was developing a pattern similar to Cowan's flight training. Both men flew only occasionally, and neither man enjoyed it. Their irregular and infrequent training flights might not have become a problem had the law not changed in July. But that was in the future, and at the moment there were more immediate problems related to change, and Cowan was the person who created them.

In June 1914 changes, both good and bad, were being planned and implemented for army aviation. The good changes were still in the planning stage, but they were already starting to take shape. The most promising change on the horizon was General Scriven's plan to create at least three new squadrons. By June 1914 it was being rumored among the pilots that at least one of the new squadrons would be formed very soon, and it would be sent to the Philippines or the Panama Canal Zone.

Cowan asked Kirtland if he wanted to be in line either to take command of the school or to command one of the proposed squadrons. Kirtland told the captain he preferred commanding the school, since he had been involved in all aspects of the training program since its inception at College Park in 1911. A week later Kirtland changed his mind. It looked as though the school opening was not going to become available in the near future, and he now preferred to be in line for command of one of the new squadrons when they were established. Cowan agreed with him that the school opening would probably not come up and said that he had made the right decision. Kirtland said, "I never heard anything else on the subject."[9]

Cowan's conversation with Kirtland took place when Congress was debating a completely rewritten version of James Hay's HR 5304. The revised bill no longer called for aviation to be removed from the Signal Corps, but it involved changes that threatened Cowan's flight-pay status and threatened Patterson's assignment to aviation. By the end of June, it was apparent to Cowan that the new HR 5304 was going to pass and become law. The reworked version was a Signal Corps–friendly bill that most of the pilots did not want. Among its provisions was a limit of no more than sixty officers assigned to aviation duty. And it required all aviation students to be unmarried first or second lieutenants who were younger than thirty years. The age, rank, and marital restrictions greatly reduced the pool of applicants and made the manpower shortage worse.

The way the law was written, the age, rank, and marital requirements affected only newly selected aviation students and not qualified aviators. Under the law, a qualified aviator was an officer who had been rated a junior military aviator (JMA), a new rating. The requirements for the military aviator rating were increased, including that an officer could be rated a military aviator only after he had served three years as a JMA. The effect was that the eleven pilots who were already rated as military aviators and still on aviation duty would be disrated to JMA.

The new law also said that the four student pilots then on duty at San Diego had to be rated as JMAs within sixty days of the law's enactment. In addition to Patterson, the students were Thomas S. Bowen, Byron Q. Jones, and Douglas B. Netherwood, all second lieutenants. The second lieutenants were farther along in their training than was Patterson, because they had been at San Diego since January. But the airplane shortage had brought their training to a standstill. To obtain the rating during the sixty-day window, the four students had to show "by practical tests, including aerial flights, that they are especially well qualified for military aviation service." When the law became effective on 18 July 1914, there was no test for the new JMA rating. The situation looked like a catch-22, but it did not work out that way.

The good news contained in the law was that JMAs automatically advanced one grade in rank and received flight pay at 50 percent of their pay and allowances. Pilots who were second lieutenants would be advanced to first lieutenant and draw a first lieutenant's pay. First lieutenants would become captains and draw a captain's pay. But flight pay was not based on the increased rank, which was temporary. Flight pay was figured for each pilot "on the grade held under his line commission . . . as increased by longevity pay." In other words, a newly advanced first lieutenant drew flight pay as a second lieutenant, and newly advanced captains drew flight pay as first lieutenants.

To receive flight pay, the JMA had to be "on duty that requires him to participate regularly and frequently in aerial flights."[10] There is no evidence that Cowan drawing flight pay under paragraph 1269 had anything to do with the more specific language in HR 5304, but there it was. Unless Cowan became a pilot overnight and started flying regularly and frequently, under the new law he was going to be ineligible for flight pay.

The new law also reinstated the four-year limit on assignment but included a provision that allowed for redetail to aviation of officers "who, during prior service as an aviation officer in the aviation section, shall have become especially proficient in military aviation."[11] The provision was intended to retain such officers who were clearly a notch above the average and would be hard to replace. One cannot help feeling that the clause was inserted for Paul Beck's benefit, since he wanted to return to aviation.

There was not much in the new law that Cowan liked, but the largest and most immediate threat was to his protégé, Patterson, who was forty years old. If he failed to qualify as a JMA during the sixty-day window and could not show "by practical tests, including aerial flights" that he was "especially well qualified for military aviation service," he would have to return to the infantry. For a person who had received only forty-seven minutes of instruction, becoming "especially well qualified for military aviation" in a short time was a tall order, especially when the school had no airplanes. Cowan wrote to Reber and expressed his concern.

> The man who is afraid he will be relieved under the bill is Patterson. He is considerably over thirty years of age, and he has received practically no training, so, he cannot be rated as anything but a student aviator. The Bill, however, provides that student officers must be under thirty years of age, at least that is the way the Bill is interpreted here.

William Lay Patterson

I do hope that you will find some way of keeping this officer on the job if the Bill goes through. He is the only man I have ever had with me since I have been connected with this work who has the faculty, ability, and disposition to get down and master details. Moreover, he is an older man of excellent judgment and is a splendid soldier. A few men of this type are absolutely essential to maintain the balance with the younger and less experienced men. I should regard Patterson's relief as little short of a personal calamity to me personally.[12]

Reber reassured Cowan in a letter dated 13 June 1914: "You can tell Patterson that he need not worry about his relief, as I think I can find a way to retain him, and I would suggest that as soon as you get a chance, you push his training as much as possible, so that you can state that he is qualified to fly, as you know the Bill gives sixty days after its passage for the classification of those now on duty."[13] That was good advice, but on 13 June there were no airplanes in San Diego for Patterson to train in.

On 20 June 1914, just a few days after he had received Reber's reassurance, Cowan placed Patterson, a man who had just forty-seven minutes of flying instruction, in command of the 2nd Company, 1st Aero Squadron. Cowan's decision was probably based on the fact that Patterson was the senior lieutenant at the school, and as such the assignment was procedurally correct. But the decision angered many of the pilots, who thought that the slot should have gone to either Kirtland or Ned Goodier.

While he commanded the 2nd Company, 1st Aero Squadron, Patterson made two flights, one on 8 July and the other on 9 July. It had been forty-two days since his last flight, and the July flights were not training flights. On 8 July he rode as a passenger in a Curtiss J with Curtiss Company pilot Raymond V. Morris. The new airplane had been delivered on 24 June, and Morris was checking out the nine experienced pilots in the airplane. In Patterson's case, there was no checkout since Patterson could not fly. Instead he just went along for a twenty-minute ride. The same was true on 9 July when Glenn Martin took him up for a five-minute ride in a Martin hydroplane. Patterson's flying time as a passenger in July totaled twenty-five minutes, and none of it counted as training time.[14]

On 13 July Foulois and the Texas detachment returned to North Island, and their three Burgess tractors arrived a few days later. At about the same time a new Martin T2, dual-control trainer became available so that the airplane problem was somewhat relieved. The school now had three Wright control airplanes and one Curtiss control airplane in service. Bowen, Jones, and Netherwood immediately started flying, but Patterson did not.

Patterson suffered a stomach ulcer that his uncertain future probably aggravated, and on 13 July 1914 he entered Letterman Army Hospital in San Francisco for observation and treatment.[15] On 18 July 1914, while Patterson was on sick leave, HR 5304 became law, and for Cowan the situation went from being a future concern to an immediate and serious problem. He had sixty days in which to get Patterson qualified, but Patterson was in a hospital six hundred miles away, and Cowan did not know when he would return.

On 22 July 1914 he wrote to Reber, explaining the situation. The tone of the letter clearly indicates that Cowan and Patterson had a special relationship, and at times Cowan's letter reads like a distraught mother pleading on behalf of her son.

I anticipate no trouble in qualifying the student aviators within the two months that we have allowed for that purpose. The only doubtful case is that of Patterson's. Poor Patterson is now in the Letterman Hospital in San Francisco undergoing treatment for some stomach trouble. He hated to leave here and in fact would have hung on if I had not insisted on his going to the hospital. I expect he will be away for at least a month, and that will leave a very short time to complete his training in order to secure a rating. I wish to recommend, however, that everything possible be done to retain him on this work. He is the only officer that has been detailed on aviation duty since I have been connected with it, who has had the preliminary training necessary to qualify him as an efficient secretary. Patterson has had an unusual amount of work for an officer of his rank. The departure of Patterson and the loss of Mr. Rinker has again upset this office.[16]

Reber, who was a very thorough administrator, remembered that a flight-pay issue was involved. Under the new law JMAS immediately advanced one rank and began drawing a 50 percent increase in pay, but the still unqualified student pilots remained in their rank and drew a 25 percent increase. Reber knew that Cowan, and the four student pilots, had been drawing 35 percent flight pay under the provisions of the 2 March 1913 act. When the new law took effect on 18 July 1914, the four students' flight pay was supposed to drop to 25 percent. And Cowan, who could not be a student under the new law, would lose his flight pay entirely. On 21 July Reber went out on a limb. "I am going to let the status of yourself, Bowen, Jones, Netherwood, and Patterson remain as it is so that you can all draw your thirty-five percent. As soon as you are prepared to certify that the above four are experienced enough to be rated a Junior Military Aviators, I will have the transfer in rating made. We have until the 18th of September to qualify these men and get them in without having them detailed as students. All you have to do is sit tight and draw your pay."[17]

Two days later Reber heard someone sawing on his limb. The quartermaster general's office had issued a directive nullifying the 2 March 1913 flight-pay regulation. The quartermaster general's order meant that the student pilots would have to be satisfied with a 25 percent flight pay until they became JMAS. But Cowan was going to be left without any flight pay, because he was not a student pilot. He was simply the school commandant who happened to be taking some unofficial, and only occasional, flight lessons in connection with his assignment. The new law did not address his situation. On 24 July 1914 Reber wrote to Representative Hay, who had authored HR 5304.

There is just one little point that has arisen, and I have been advised by the disbursing branch of the Quartermaster General's office that Captain Cowan, who is now on aviation duty, cannot receive any extra pay while flying as they hold that HR 5304 directly repeals the provisions of the Act approved 2 March 1913 that refers to the thirty-five percent increase in pay for an officer on aviation duty while flying. I claim that the Committee has clearly established the principal of extra pay for extra hazard, and inasmuch as Captain Cowan cannot be rated a Junior Military Aviator because he is a captain, he is entitled to the thirty-five percent increase allowed by the Act approved on 2 March 1913. I am sure that your Committee, having established the principal of extra compensation for the extra hazard of flying, did not intend by the provisions of HR 5304 to cut off Captain Cowan's thirty-five percent increase.

By 18 September no person can be detailed to aviation duty except in accordance with the provisions of your Bill. Between 18 July and the date of the signing of the Bill by the President, and 18 September all the officers now on aviation duty will have received the status of Junior Military Aviator or Aviation Student, which will leave only Captain Cowan the only man in the Army to whom the provisions of the Act of 2 March 1913 can apply.

If it is not asking too much, will you be good enough to give me a note stating that in drawing up the Bill it was not the Committee's intention to cut Captain Cowan out of the increase in pay allowed by the Act of 2 March 1913 so that I may show this to the Comptroller, before whom I am going to argue my case, and show Cowan's right to extra pay while flying?[18]

The next day Representative Hay sent Reber a letter saying, "The Committee did not intend to cut off the extra pay that has been allowed Captain Cowan under the Act approved on 2 March 1913, and if Captain Cowan is engaged in flying it seems to me that there can be no question that he would be entitled to the extra compensation allowed by the Act of 2 March 1913."[19]

Armed with Representative Hay's letter, Reber went to the comptroller, where he got the opinion he wanted. In a letter to Cowan following the visit, Reber said, "I had an interview with the Comptroller of the Treasury yesterday and he looks at the law the same way I do. That is, the Act approved on 18 July 1914 does not repeal the present law that gives the thirty-five percent increase but refers only to those who are Student Aviators or Junior Military Aviators."[20]

　　　　　　　　　　　　　　　　　　William Lay Patterson

While Reber was scrambling to protect Cowan's flight pay, Patterson's situation was becoming more pressing as time ran out. Apparently Reber did not know that Patterson was in Letterman Hospital and there was no indication that he was going to return soon. On 24 July Reber had written to Cowan. "I want you to push the instruction of Patterson, Bowen, Netherwood, and Jones as much as you can consistent with safety so that we can certify before 18 September that they are qualified for detail as Junior Military Aviators. In case they do not qualify as Junior Military Aviators, I can have Jones, Netherwood, and Bowen classed as aviation students, but Patterson would lose out because he is too old."[21] When Reber wrote that letter, Cowan had less time to get Patterson qualified than Reber thought. The window closed on 16 September, not on the 18th. And there was another, unrecognized problem. No practical test for the JMA rating had been drawn up. The crisis was avoided by using the old MA tests to qualify the new JMAs.[22]

In the meantime, Reber was getting ready to sail for France, and had written specific instructions for his temporary replacement, Captain Wallace. Reber instructed Wallace, "As soon as the commanding officer at San Diego reports that Lieutenants Bowen, Patterson, Jones, and Netherwood are qualified, request should be made by the Chief Signal Officer for their detail in the Aviation Section as Junior Military Aviators."[23]

On 5 August Cowan wrote to Reber. "Bowen and Netherwood are now flying alone and will be ready to take their pilot's license tests most any time now. This will clean up all the student officers now here and will leave only Patterson to be trained. He is still in Letterman General Hospital and is not expected back here before 25 August. We are planning to give him all the training he can possibly take between the time of his return and 18 September in the hope that he will be able to pass his pilot's license test by that time."[24]

Shortly after sending that letter, and before any of the student pilots had taken any sort of practical test, Cowan sent a telegram to the CSO recommending that Bowen, Jones, and Netherwood be rated as JMAs.[25] Reber, whose trip to Europe was delayed, rubber-stamped Cowan's recommendation and passed it on to General

Scriven, who made the official recommendation that went to the adjutant general for action, and the secretary of war's signature. The point is that once a recommendation got beyond Cowan and Reber, it was put into effect with no questions asked.

Based on Cowan's certification that they were qualified pilots, the secretary of war rated 2nd Lt. Thomas S. Bowen, 2nd Lt. Byron Q. Jones, and 2nd Lt. Douglas B. Netherwood JMAS on 20 August 1914. Why did Cowan and Reber jump the gun with regard to Bowen, Jones, and Netherwood? At the time Cowan recommended them be rated JMAS they were in no danger of being relieved from aviation after the sixty-day window closed. They were all second lieutenants, unmarried, and under thirty. Since they were already taking flight training, they could remain on aviation duty until a standard JMA test was created, at which time they could qualify. The answer might be that Cowan was building a precedent that he could use to support a similar recommendation for Patterson when the time came. And it was coming very soon.

Cowan later said that he had consulted Foulois, Milling, and Taliaferro about rating Patterson before he had taken the tests in order to "prevent the loss of a valuable officer for aviation duty." According to Cowan, all three assured him that there was no "question but what Captain Patterson would learn to fly and become a valuable officer for aviation duty."[26] We have only Cowan's word that he spoke with those three officers about Patterson's potential worth as a pilot, but if he did speak to them, it is unlikely that he received their support. Eight months after Cowan had allegedly gotten Taliaferro's favorable opinion about Patterson's potential as a military pilot, Taliaferro noted on 12 May 1915 that Patterson would "never make a flyer of sufficient ability to do military flying."[27]

On 2 September, just two weeks before the window closed, Cowan wrote to Patterson, who was still in Letterman Hospital.

> Briefly the situation is this. There is no authority of law for continuing you as a student aviator after 18 September. The only way you can be retained on this job will be to rate you as a Junior Military Aviator prior to that date. In order to give us some legitimate

William Lay Patterson

ground for recommending you for this rating, it will be necessary for you to receive a certain amount of training, and while this amount of training is a matter that we alone can decide, you of course will realize the propriety of your getting as much training as possible prior to the date we make our recommendation.[28]

Obviously, Cowan's math was as bad as Reber's because the sixtieth day after 14 July was 16 September.

Cowan's goading worked, and Patterson returned to San Diego on 8 September. On 10 September he made one seven-minute flight with the civilian instructor, Oscar Brindley, and that seven minutes was all the additional training Patterson received.[29] Nevertheless, on 11 September Cowan sent the telegram to the CSO recommending that Patterson be rated a JMA. At that time Patterson's total time under instruction was forty-four minutes and he could not fly an airpalne.[30]

Significantly, in the telegram Cowan did not say that Patterson was "especially well qualified for military aviation."[31] Whether Cowan accidentally or deliberately omitted the phrase when he wrote the telegram, there is no way to know. In any event, Wallace sent the recommendation along to General Scriven, who passed it along to the adjutant general's office. But a clerk there returned the recommendation to the CSO because it did not have the words, "especially well qualified for military aviation." Someone in Scriven's office amended the recommendation to conform to the clerk's wishes, and on 15 September General Scriven sent the amended recommendation to the adjutant general. Cowan's original recommendation without the words "especially well qualified for military aviation" disappeared and was never seen again.[32] The adjutant general issued the order making Patterson a JMA on 17 September 1914.[33] Patterson was advanced to captain and started drawing 50 percent flight pay.

Cowan was sitting on a powder keg, and he was about to light the fuse. The match he used was not his flight pay, nor was it Patterson's, Bowen's, Jones's, Netherwood's, and Clark's fraudulent JMA ratings. Cowan was the match. By then he had become insistent on old-style army discipline, and his subordinates were out to get him.[34]

13

The Rift, 1914–1915

Shortly after Patterson became a junior military aviator, a rift developed between Cowan and Roy C. Kirtland. It developed for several reasons, one being that Kirtland had much more aviation experience than Patterson, which would be troublesome when it came time to put Patterson in a command slot. Cowan suspected that Kirtland had been the ringleader of the 1913 flare-up in Texas.[1] He also knew there was growing support among the pilots for removing aviation from the Signal Corps, and Kirtland was a leading proponent of separation. So Cowan believed he had good reason to find a way to ease him out of aviation. And the way was at hand.

Kirtland did not always pay attention to detail, and his work showed it. It was a carryover from the flying club days when a lot of small details were allowed to slide. But most of Kirtland's sloppiness was petty stuff that collectively would not warrant kicking him out of aviation. Nevertheless, Cowan started jumping on Kirtland for just about everything.

Kirtland quickly was aware of the change as Cowan became increasingly picky and nagging. In fact, nagging was one of Cowan's characteristics about which many of the pilots complained. Cowan found ample opportunity to jump on Kirtland for not doing things right or on time, as well as holding him responsible for things that were essentially beyond his control. Kirtland believed that Cowan's criticisms were unfair and complained that he was overworked and underappreciated, to which there might have been some truth. He said he was responsible for transportation to, from, and on the island, maintenance and repair of the school's crash boat and the flying field, and the running of the storehouse. To accomplish those tasks, he had "general fatigue men who nobody else wanted and a storekeeper who did not know the names of half the articles he had in the storehouse."[2]

Kirtland was not the only officer who felt that Cowan was unfairly holding him responsible for something that was not his fault. During the tests of the Scott bombsight from 4 to 24 August 1914, Cowan called Ned Goodier on the carpet for causing a near accident. It was the first of a series of incidents in which Cowan questioned a pilot's flying, and implied that the pilot was, in some way, doing it wrong. Coming from a man who could not fly and made very little attempt to learn how to fly, the criticisms galled the pilots.

In the first instance Ned Goodier was on the ground, tuning the engine on his airplane in preparation for one of the bomb-dropping tests. As Goodier was climbing into the cockpit, Milling approached the field at a low altitude, circled the Curtiss hangers at less than one hundred feet, and landed. Milling touched down just as Goodier started his takeoff, and Milling's airplane very nearly landed atop Ned Goodier's. It was a near miss, but Ned Goodier was unaware of the close call until he returned from the bombing test and landed.

Cowan had witnessed the entire thing, including Milling's low approach across the Curtiss hangars. The pilots who also witnessed the near disaster held Milling entirely responsible for the close call, because he was supposed to have waited until the field was clear before he landed. Jones said that Milling made a regular practice of coming in low over the hangars and flying up the field at an extremely low altitude before pulling up, going around again, and landing. In this instance, the sudden landing caught everyone by surprise. When Cowan issued a letter to Goodier blaming him for the near accident and demanding a written explanation for why Goodier had let it happen, the other pilots were outraged and so was Goodier, who wrote to his father about the incident.[3]

Cowan's dislike for Goodier was obvious to the other pilots and was undoubtedly the reason for the landing and letter incident. Shortly after the letter incident Cowan told Dodd, "I don't know what I can do with Goodier unless I have him relieved."[4]

On 16 September 1914 an insignificant event occurred that was later falsely portrayed as fraudulent self-promotion. The fact that the event later became blown out of proportion reveals that when the time came, Lieutenant Colonel Goodier's emotional involvement with his son's situation blocked his ability to think logically where Cowan was concerned. The colonel's reaction to this event was at the heart of Cowan's ultimate downfall.

Captain Cowan flew out to the USS *San Diego* to pay a visit to the cruiser's captain on 16 September. The cruiser, which was anchored in San Diego Bay, had just had her name changed from USS *California* to USS *San Diego* in honor of the city. The flight out to her and the visit were part of the celebration. Cowan was the passenger, and a civilian contract flight instructor, Francis Wildman, was the pilot. The round-trip flight and visit took less than thirty minutes to complete, but the press, typically unconcerned about accuracy, made the short hop look like a transpacific crossing. Worse yet, the newspaper accounts found their way into two service publications, the *Army and Navy Journal* and the *Army and Navy Register*. The wording in both articles, though more subdued than what had appeared in the popular press, made it appear that Cowan had piloted the flying boat. There was no mention of the civilian pilot, Wildman.[5]

On 17 September Cowan made a written report to the CSO in which he described the flight and used the pronoun "we" when he referred to himself and Wildman. Though Cowan did not name Wildman in his report, Cowan not once said or implied that he had piloted the flying boat, and in the flight log he was listed as the passenger. None of the pilots thought anything about the flight, which was a routine matter under the circumstances. But a year later the flight and allegations that Cowan had misrepresented himself as the pilot were among the charges filed against him.

Cowan had a run-in with Tom Bowen on 21 September 1914 over

the way Bowen mismanaged a takeoff that caused the airplane to crash. According to Kirtland, Bowen was taking off in a 1st Aero Squadron plane that "struck a little puff of wind or something and the machine turned over, breaking it up to a certain extent." Kirtland's account was not entirely accurate and is an example of how the facts in many cases were altered to give a favorable slant to the officer on the receiving end of Cowan's anger.

What actually happened casts the incident in a different light. The airplane involved was not one of the 1st Aero Squadron's more powerful airplanes. It was a Martin T2 side-by-side, dual-control trainer that had been accepted on 7 September 1914. Bowen had tried to make a crosswind takeoff, which was a violation of school regulations, his training, and common sense.

Bowen's negligence had caused a crash that severely damaged the new trainer, putting it out of service when it was sorely needed. The loss of the dual-control trainer hindered the school's operations to a greater degree than would have been the case had Bowen damaged a 1st Aero Squadron plane, none of which were used for flight instruction.

Captain Cowan called Bowen in his office and told him that the crash was due to his carelessness, and Cowan was going to make Bowen pay for the parts. Bowen objected and told Cowan that the day he was called on to pay for those repairs "would mark the stoppage of all flying on the field."[6]

Cowan wrote to Reber, telling him what had happened and asking for his opinion on his decision to make Bowen pay for the damages. Cowan explained that his decision was based on the fact that Bowen had violated a basic safety procedure by taking off in a crosswind. Reber fully supported Cowan's decision and wrote that "the excuse offered by Bowen that he had seen other people start in a crosswind shows that he is either over-confident or lacks good judgment."[7]

In the end, Cowan relented, and Bowen did not have to pay for the damages. But much to the annoyance of the pilots, Cowan became increasingly involved in critiquing their flying. Some of his criticisms, such as that they were making turns too close to the ground and were flying too close to the hangars and other buildings, were justifiable safety issues. But his criticisms that questioned how a man landed or took off were offensive to the pilots because Cowan could not fly. He spent a lot of time on the field watching students and qualified pilots take off and land, and in nearly every instance he had something negative to say about how the pilot had handled his plane. In late September, he angered Dodd.

Dodd was a qualified pilot who had earned his military aviator rating in December 1913. Since then he had gone on to become one of the army's most competent pilots and was widely recognized for his ability. On 29 September 1914 Dodd was making an approach to land when he realized that his descent was too steep and too fast. He pulled up sharply, went around the field, and made a perfect three-point landing. Cowan caught him just as Dodd stepped out of the cockpit and tore into him for "being careless and pulling a dangerous stunt." He accused Dodd of very nearly crashing. Dodd could not believe what he was hearing and dismissed the captain's comments on the grounds that Cowan "lacked knowledge of the situation."[8]

Cowan also jumped on Ned Goodier for running up his engine in front of an open hanger and blowing dust and debris into the hangar where men were working. Ned wrote to his father about the incident and said that he was "deeply aggrieved." The senior Goodier took his son's complaint so seriously that he "was strongly tempted to take the matter up."[9] When you recall that Lieutenant Colonel Goodier was the judge advocate for the Western Military District and had court-martial authority over the school at San Diego, his urge to take up the matter assumes a serious quality. The senior Goodier was clearly becoming too deeply involved in events on North Island.

Whether he was right or wrong, Cowan's supervisory style was becoming tiresome to the pilots. Dr. Harry L. Schurmeier, the medical officer, said, "Captain Cowan got on the nerves of the Army aviators who were a tense lot, and who had to face daily problems of which Cowan had no understanding." Grover Loening also saw the change in Cowan's management style. "For weeks and months, as activities increased and the tension caused by the fatal accidents eased, Captain Cowan started to irk the aviators by what they thought were minor nuisance regulations. He became insistent on old-style Army discipline." But Loening saw the other side of the coin when he added, "The aviators in many ways thought they were above routine discipline. Flying officers never realize that they are members of the U.S. Army."[10]

By October 1914 it was apparent to most of the pilots that Cowan had it in for Ned Goodier and Kirtland, and Kirtland's run-ins with Cowan were becoming more frequent and more serious. On 7 October the school's rescue boat was put out of commission with a broken-down engine. Cowan told Kirtland to get it fixed, and Kirtland turned the job over to Netherwood, who was in charge of the engine repair shop, with instructions to get the engine repaired as quickly as possible. A few days later Cowan asked Kirtland for the status of the engine, and Kirtland told him it was being repaired. A heated exchange between the two officers ended with Cowan ordering Kirtland to "get it fixed" and walking off.[11]

A few days later there was another confrontation. Just after noon Cowan told Kirtland that he needed the truck. Kirtland told him, "I don't know if the driver is on the island or not. But I will see." The request and the reply seemed to be normal for the circumstances. The school had one REO truck assigned to it, but at that moment, the enlisted driver, along with most of the other enlisted men, was probably in San Diego having lunch. Their absence was routine and fully accepted as common practice, because there was no enlisted mess hall on North Island. Cowan knew that.

The request turned ugly. Cowan became angry and demanded to know why the driver was not immediately available and shouted, "Didn't I give you orders that a driver was to be available all day?" Kirtland did not argue but said that he would see what could be done. He sent an enlisted man to find the driver, who returned with a man who could drive the truck. Cowan was informed the truck was manned and ready, and that is when Kirtland learned the reason for the urgent need for the truck. George Dupuy, a civilian friend of Cowan's, had gotten his car stuck in the sand near

Coronado, and Cowan needed the truck to pull him out. The captain and the enlisted driver drove off to accomplish the rescue.

That afternoon the regular truck driver returned to North Island from San Diego, where he had in fact gone to eat lunch. Kirtland wrote a note stating that the driver was available for duty and placed the note on Cowan's desk. When Cowan returned to his office from rescuing his civilian friend, he read Kirtland's note and sent an enlisted man to find him. When Kirtland arrived at Cowan's office, he found the commanding officer in a foul mood.

Cowan ordered Kirtland to prefer charges against the enlisted driver for being away without leave. Kirtland protested that it was standard procedure for the enlisted men to return to San Diego daily for lunch. That excuse did not satisfy Cowan, who wanted an explanation for why no driver was available during the lunch hour. Kirtland told him, "I had a driver as soon as I knew that you wanted the truck. Had I known there would have been a need for a driver during the lunch hour, I would have had him ready." Cowan was not having any of that. He wanted the assigned driver brought up on charges for being away without leave, and Kirtland's protestations were to no avail.[12]

The truth is that Kirtland often put himself in a position to be called out for failure to do what he was told. It happened now when Cowan suddenly changed direction and demanded to know why Kirtland had not seen to the construction of a barn for the officers' horses. Again, Kirtland was caught flat-footed. Cowan had in fact ordered him to see that a barn was built, and that had not been done.

On another occasion, Cowan called Kirtland in and asked him what had happened to the school's engineer's transit and a mimeograph machine normally kept in the storehouse under Kirtland's control. Kirtland told him that the transit had been issued to Lieutenant Bowen so that he could survey the school's speed course, and Grover Loening was using the mimeograph machine to make handouts for his aerodynamics classes. Kirtland probably saw it coming when Cowan asked if he had checked on them. He said that he had not checked on them, and Cowan replied,

"Well, you go down to the storehouse and look at them! They are all covered with dirt."

Kirtland was again caught flat-footed, but not so much that he could not find a quick alibi. "Captain, I have my hands so full of things for which I'm responsible that I can't be responsible for articles that are issued to someone else. I have too much to do." Cowan played his ace. "Didn't I see you out there on the field a while ago talking to Foulois, or someone else, *smoking*?" Kirtland knew he was in a corner, and all he could say was, "Yes sir, you did."

Cowan looked directly at Kirtland. "Don't you think that instead of gabbing and smoking you might have been down at the storehouse checking on school property?" Kirtland had no answer. A few days later Dodd stopped Kirtland outside the hangars and warned him, "You want to look out. Keep your eyes open. The captain is gunning for you."

There is no question that Cowan was nitpicking and abrasive in his dealings with Kirtland. It is also true that Kirtland was letting some things slide, and in some of those cases he unfairly blamed the results on his subordinates. Kirtland's style was a holdover from the flying club days. But Cowan also let things slide, and the issue of fiscal mismanagement was a case in which Cowan threw Kirtland to the wolves.

In October 1914 the school needed a gasoline-powered generator to provide power for the machines and tools used in the training of aviation mechanics and in the repair shop. In addition to the generator, the mechanics training center and the repair shop needed additional machines and tools, such as wheels, lathes, and "numerous other articles." That month, Sam Reber visited the school and Cowan took the opportunity to present him with a list of what the school needed. Cowan wanted Reber to assign additional funds with which to make the purchases. Kirtland was present when Reber agreed to provide some extra money, but specifically turned down the request for the generator and shop machines. Kirtland heard Reber say, "We will have to let those instruction shops go for the time, as I don't want to spend the funds on them now."[13]

But a month later Cowan decided to go ahead with the shop

purchases, knowing that there was no money available. He directed Kirtland to "ascertain the costs and get the prices from the different manufacturers." Cowan told Dodd after Reber denied the additional funds, "Well, Dodd, we are going to get you your things, but how we are going to pay for them I don't know."

By 31 December 1914 Kirtland had placed orders for machines, tools, and equipment totaling $5,000. According to Kirtland, he and Cowan "understood" that there were no funds on hand for those purchases. At about that same time, Cowan told Kirtland to give him a memo "as to what funds we would need for the remainder of the fiscal year" that would end on 30 June 1915. Kirtland gave him an estimate that totaled $25,000.[14] At that point both officers were unaware that the money thing was going to mushroom into a very serious matter, in part because for the next few weeks Cowan turned his attention to personnel matters, starting with Harold Geiger.

Geiger was a source of irritation for Cowan, and he was already on Reber's list. Geiger had gone to Hawaii in July 1913 to establish a flight-training program there. For a lot of reasons, one being the combination of wind and sea conditions, the program failed completely and Geiger returned to North Island on 17 August 1914. Reber was not pleased with Geiger, but he had him placed on flying status when he reported to North Island. Geiger, however, refused to fly.[15]

His refusal reflected what Cowan believed was the pilots' prima donna attitude. Geiger was a twenty-nine-year-old West Point graduate and a Coast Artillery officer. When he returned to the school from Hawaii, the school had six airplanes available for use, four of which were equipped with Curtiss controls. But Geiger's reason for not flying was that there were no *Curtiss* airplanes for him to fly. That was not entirely true.

One of the four airplanes equipped with Curtiss controls was a new Curtiss J, Signal Corps no. 29. That meant that only three of the four Curtiss-control-equipped airplanes at North Island were not Curtiss-built. During the next three months, the school received three more Martin T-2, Curtiss-control-equipped airplanes, and Loening converted another Burgess to Curtiss controls, making six airplanes that had Curtiss controls. Still Geiger did not fly. On 28 November 1914 Cowan wrote Reber a long letter about what was going on in San Diego, and the preparations being made for the 1914 MacKay Trophy competition. "I am not sure yet as to whether Geiger will want to fly. But as he is a Military Aviator, I see no reason why he should not enter."[16]

Another Martin T2 side-by-side trainer had been received on 20 August but was not put into service until 7 December. The new Martin, Signal Corps no. 32, was also equipped with the Curtiss control system, so Geiger had no excuse for not flying the plane except that it was a Martin and not a Curtiss. On 8 December Cowan again wrote to Reber about Geiger.

Yesterday was the first time that No. 32 has been in commission. As soon as this machine was in commission I sent for Geiger and told him that it was now up to him to declare himself about flying; that he must either get out and fly, or state that he didn't want to. He assured me that he was anxious to fly, but that he had been waiting for a chance to fly a Curtiss machine. I don't quite understand this man, but I am determined to see that he does a reasonable amount of flying from now on. He made his first trip alone in No. 32 this morning. I must say that he handled the machine very well and didn't seem to have lost his flying ability through his long layoff.[17]

Cowan was exasperated with Geiger's attitude, but Reber was fed up with it. On 15 December he told Cowan, "It is up to Geiger to make good or quit. The minute you make the recommendation for his relief, I will start the machinery in motion to bring it about. I will have this matter settled in a few days."[18]

In the meantime, Cowan tried to arrange a compromise under which Geiger would be taken off flying status and given an administrative job at the school. The plan called for Geiger to relieve Kirtland of most of his duties and make Kirtland the school's executive officer. But Reber turned down the plan, and Geiger's relief became effective on 16 January 1915. Despite Geiger's refusal to fly, and Reber's explanation, the feeling among the pilots was that Geiger's relief was unwarranted. But the action made it crystal clear to everyone at the school that Sam Reber was calling the shots.

With the Geiger issue settled, Cowan's attention returned to the school's fiscal situation. On 4 January 1915, while Geiger's relief was in the works, Cowan asked Reber for funds to cover the rest of the fiscal year, asking for a total of just $20,000—$5,000 less than Kirtland's estimate. Before the request for funds was acted on, Cowan and Kirtland placed "several fairly large orders" in January 1915, expecting Cowan's request for additional funds to be granted. But on 25 January 1915 Reber told Cowan that he would authorize only $5,000 for school expenditures for the remainder of the fiscal year. When Kirtland learned about the decision, he was stunned. He told Cowan, "Why, $5,000 was already spent at the end of the last quarter." With several "fairly large orders outstanding," and no additional money available, Cowan and Kirtland were in big trouble.[19]

On 31 January 1915 Cowan submitted a written request to Washington asking that the CSO pay a $2,000 bill due to the Curtiss Company. The next day Kirtland left North Island to enter the Letterman Army Hospital in San Francisco, where he was to undergo an examination for a problem with his eyes. When he returned on 15 February the gasoline-powered generator had arrived along with a bill for $1,300. Cowan submitted that bill to the CSO, and asked Kirtland if they would have enough money left to cover the other purchases if the CSO picked up the tab for the generator. Kirtland told him that he thought so. But he was worried.

Kirtland asked his clerk, Sgt. William Collins, how they stood, and Collins told him that they had "about $2,500 to the good."[20] Kirtland then engaged in some fuzzy math that reflected his wishful thinking and came up with an end-of-year balance of approximately $2,500. A day later he asked Sergeant Collins again about their bank balance, and the sergeant revised the figure downward to $2,000. Kirtland saw that he was in deeper trouble than he had imagined or wanted to believe. The bottom line was closer to $1,700.

While the over-obligation issue was coming to a head, Cowan

received a disturbing letter from Sam Reber. On 16 February 1915 Reber wrote:

> For the past eight months, the Chief has been very anxious to put other Signal Corps officers, especially [Capt. William "Billy"] Mitchell, in the Aviation Section, and for some reason also [Maj. Carl F.] Hartman. This I have fought tooth and nail and have compromised on his telling me to write [Capt. George S.] Gibbs, asking if he would come. You need not let this worry you in the slightest as I will take care of your interests, see that you remain in command at the school, and, if necessary, put Gibbs in command of the 2nd Aero Squadron. I have made up my mind that Foulois shall command the 1st Aero Squadron and you shall not be interfered with in the slightest.[21]

This was the first mention that Billy Mitchell was being considered for an assignment in aviation, and the first indication that General Scriven was considering relieving Cowan at San Diego. Mitchell's performance during the 1913 hearings had impressed the CSO, who viewed Mitchell as a very valuable asset and an ideal choice for an aviation assignment.

There is no indication that Mitchell was lobbying for an aviation assignment, but he was interested in aviation in connection with his general staff duties. That interest and those duties had brought him into contact with the pilots, most of whom thought very highly of him—especially Hap Arnold. But Mitchell's assignment to aviation would pose an immediate threat to Cowan and a future threat to Reber, and for that reason both men opposed his assignment. Benjamin Foulois, whose position Mitchell also threatened, but to a lesser degree, strongly supported their opposition.

Mitchell had the status, style, and demonstrated ability to move up quickly. It was obvious to Reber that if Mitchell took command of the school, it would be only a matter of time before Mitchell moved up and displaced Reber as the chief of the Aeronautical Division. Mitchell certainly had the CSO's backing. Reber set himself to the task of blocking Mitchell's assignment, which he might have accomplished had the situation building in San Diego not happened.

Cowan called the pilots together for lunch on 26 February 1915 and told them that General Scriven was considering giving a new aviation command slot to a Signal Corps officer. Specifically, he told them, the cso planned to place a nonflying Signal Corps officer in command of the 2nd Aero Squadron when it was created and additional nonflying Signal Corps officers in command of all subsequent squadrons as they were created. The pilots were stunned and then outraged.[22]

Their expectations, and logic, called for any newly created command slots to go to qualified pilots. Cowan seemed to be on their side, since as the junior Signal Corps officer he could easily lose his slot at the school to a senior officer who had the general's ear. "I think the general is coming out here to sound you out as to your feelings about Signal Corps officers taking command of the squadrons," he told them. And he underscored his solidarity with the pilots by saying, "I think we will have to fight that just the same way we fought it in Texas City."[23]

Cowan described the friction that had existed between the aviators and the cso in Texas in the spring and summer of 1913, and told the officers that in his opinion, General Scriven had "not learned his lesson" at Texas City. Cowan told them that following the Texas City incident he had written to General Scriven, warning him that another blowup would result in a congressional investigation. "If that happens," Cowan warned the cso, "the Signal Corps will lose aviation." He then said he would testify before Congress that aviation would make better progress in the control of the fliers than it would under the Signal Corps.

Following his strong talk and implied support, Cowan sidestepped, telling them, "I can't say anything to the General now; being a Signal Corps officer, it is my duty to take anything that comes my way. But you men can, and I think that Foulois is the person to speak to the general." He explained that "Foulois has been promised command of the 1st Aero Squadron, so he won't be looking for personal gain by making any statement or asking questions. But I can't say anything and neither can any of you." Then Cowan withdrew his support. "I am in aviation and I'm doing my best, but I'm bound by the Signal Corps and I'm not going to hang myself for anybody."[24] At that moment, the pilots knew that they were on their own.

On 1 March Sergeant Collins had handed Kirtland a financial report that showed the school was $1,800 in the red.[25] Kirtland took the report to Cowan, who read it and asked, "How did this happen?" Clearly the school commander was not going to be saddled with this disaster that was largely his own making.

Kirtland must have seen that his own culpability stemmed from his unfounded faith in Cowan's ability to work with Reber to make things right. Instead of fulfilling his responsibilities as the officer in charge of the school's finances, Kirtland had let things slide, and he now tried to dump the blame on Sergeant Collins and the vendors. Kirtland complained to Cowan that Collins was behind in his work and had "assigned incorrect values to some of the bills." He also accused Collins of mislaying a Curtiss bill. He also accused the vendors, especially Curtiss and Martin, of failing to provide price lists until several months after the orders had been placed.

Cowan told Kirtland, "You go into this thing, and checkup personally. And make a full report to me." Cowan added, "I have troubles of my own, and you have got to get out of this thing the best way you know how."[26] Cowan had cut Kirtland adrift.

On 4 March 1915 Kirtland returned to Cowan's office with a complete report of the disaster they faced. To Kirtland's credit, he was now prepared to shoulder his share of the responsibility. Cowan looked at the report and was stunned to see that Kirtland had pegged the deficit at $4,000. "Is that correct?" Cowan asked. Kirtland told him the figure was correct and added, "I don't know exactly how it came about, but I suppose it had something to do with *your* previous over-obligation." Kirtland was unable to tell if his offensive thrust had worked or not, but he "did not hear anything more."[27]

On 6 March General Scriven arrived at North Island to inspect the school. He spent much time alone with Cowan, but the pilots never learned what was said between the school commandant and the CSO. What the pilots noted was that after the general returned to Washington, Cowan never again talked about "fighting the Signal Corps."[28] At the same time Foulois went to Texas to survey the area around Fort Sam Houston for a permanent air station there, another of Scriven's ideas that the pilots objected to. Foulois told the pilots when he left that he would find out what was going to happen, but they never heard anything more on the subject from him.

The following afternoon the pilots met to discuss the situation. Kirtland told them that two days earlier Cowan had said that aviation would be much better off if it were removed from the Signal Corps. Kirtland told his listeners that before Scriven had arrived at North Island, Cowan declared, "I would be willing to testify to that before anyone." The pilots adopted a cynical attitude toward Cowan's professed support for their interests. In their view, he had "given the aviators scant thought or anything else." But now that he saw his own position endangered, Cowan wanted "to feather his nest on both sides of the fence."[29] Seven days later Kirtland had solid evidence that the group opinion was correct.

On 14 March 1915 Cowan called Kirtland into his office and handed him a letter from Colonel Reber. Kirtland unfolded the letter and read that Cowan had requested his relief and that Reber had sent the request up the line to the CSO for action. It was Kirtland's turn to be stunned. "I asked him why he had not told me that he was going to ask for my relief." Cowan declined to answer the question until the orders for Kirtland's relief had been received. But Kirtland saw no reason for Cowan to wait until his request was granted and he had the orders in hand. "Why, Captain, you know that you have been told by Colonel Reber that any of your recommendations concerning any officer would be carried through without question."

Kirtland knew why Cowan had requested his relief, but he wanted to hear the captain say it. Cowan refused. Angry, Kirtland went to his office and typed up a formal request for an explanation of the grounds for his relief. He returned to Cowan's office and handed him the request.

Cowan read the request and asked, "What do you want?"

"My seventeen years in the service has been perfectly clear, and if I am going to have a mark against my record I want to know what it is."

"There is no reason assigned by the Secretary of War for your relief," Cowan told Kirtland and added, "Except that I don't want you on my staff."

"I want to know the basis for your feelings," Kirtland pressed.

Cowan dodged the question. "I hold that my position here is substantially the same as any commanding officer of any organization who has the privilege of choosing the officers for his personal staff." He looked at Kirtland's request again and added an open threat. "However, if you want it to go up," he said, referring to Kirtland's request, "it will go up, and it will have a reason assigned to it by the time it gets to the Secretary of War."

Kirtland immediately recognized the threat and knew that he was in a corner. "I don't see why it has to go to the Secretary of War or to the Chief Signal Officer. All I want to know is the reason the Chief Signal Officer gave to the Secretary of War for my relief."

Cowan waved the request in Kirtland's face and told him, "It will go to the Secretary all right, and it will have a reason on it by the time it gets to him." Cowan knew how to play hardball. "He tossed the request on his desk and said, "I had given you some credit for having more common sense than to try to stir up trouble. You know the results Willis got when he tried to get either an inspector or a board or a court of inquiry."

Kirtland tried to play his ace by reminding Cowan of his own precarious position with regard to Patterson. "Why Captain, it is going to look strange you having me relieved from the aviation service and you keeping Captain Patterson." Kirtland continued driving home his point. "I have flown since 1911 and Patterson can't fly. And I don't believe that he can handle the job that I have here.

Cowan waved his hand, saying, "Don't take it out on poor old Patterson."

"I didn't mean that," Kirtland replied. "I am just explaining to you that relieving me and keeping a man who can't do my job, and who can't fly, won't look square to the outside."

Cowan shrugged. "Well, there isn't any other way," he said, ending the discussion.

Kirtland recognized a brick wall when he saw one and capitulated, telling Cowan that he could tear up the request. But Kirtland was not completely finished, and he returned to his office to gather evidence against Cowan and to build his own defense. The documents that Kirtland found were not complimentary to his efficiency as the disbursing officer who should have been supervising Sergeant Collins's work. Kirtland found numerous cases in which purchase orders were undated and the item descriptions vague. Among the documents in Collins's files were several in which Cowan asked the cso to pick up the tab for some of the big-ticket items, but in every case the captain had not informed the cso why he was making the request. Among the documents that Cowan had never forwarded to the cso was Kirtland's memorandum telling Cowan that the school had expended its last $5,000.[30]

The documents left no doubt about Cowan's role on the school's over-obligation, but the fact was that Kirtland had signed every order.

1. Brig. Gen. Adolphus W. Greely, CSO, 1887–1906, led the way to establishing Signal Corps control over army aviation by creating a Signal Corps balloon section in 1892. He did it without a congressional act and without a specific appropriation. Library of Congress, B Historical Biog. file—Greely, A. W. (Adolphus Washington), 1844–1935.

2. Brig. Gen. James Allen, CSO, 1906–13, established the Signal Corps Aeronautical Division on 1 August 1907, putting it in "charge of all matters pertaining to military ballooning, air machines, and kindred subjects." Author's collection.

3. Brig. Gen. George P. Scriven, CSO, 1913–17, took command of the Signal Corps just as the rebellion was starting. Under his command, army aviation made no progress toward becoming a combat organization, and many of his decisions angered the pilots. Thomas Dewitt Milling told an interviewer in 1954 that "we were just diddling around." Library of Congress, LC-B2-3323-8.

4. Brig. Gen. George O. Squier, CSO, 1917–23, was a brilliant officer and scientist who commanded the Signal Corps through U.S. participation in World War I. Despite his honesty, he became caught up in the postwar congressional witch hunt for war profiteers. Library of Congress, LC-B2-4271-8.

5. Aeronautical Acceptance Board at Fort Myer, 1909. *Left to right*: Capt. C. McK. Saltzman, Signal Corps; 1st Lt. Frank P. Lahm, Cavalry; Capt. Charles W. Wallace, Signal Corps; Capt. Charles DeForest Chandler, Signal Corps; Lt. Col. George O. Squier, Signal Corps; Lt. George C. Sweet, U.S. Navy; 1st Lt. Benjamin D. Foulois, Infantry; 2nd Lt. Frederick E. Humphreys, Corps of Engineers. Library of Congress, LC-H261-1321.

6. First Lt. Thomas Selfridge (*left*) and Alexander Graham Bell at Fort Myer, 1908. Air Force Historical Agency, Maxwell Air Force Base, Alabama, 090710-F-1405A-020.JPG.

7. Capt. Charles DeForest Chandler, commanding officer of the Aeronautical Division, who was not popular with the pilots. In March 1913 they demanded his relief and got it. Library of Congress, LC-H261-1604.

8. First Lt. Benjamin D. Foulois (*left*) and 1st Lt. Frank P. Lahm at Fort Myer in 1908 for the Wright Model A *Military Flyer*'s acceptance trials. Library of Congress, LC-H261-1341.

9. First Lt. Myron Crissy at the Los Angeles International Air Meet in 1911, where he dropped a live bomb that he designed and built for the demonstration. The pilot is Philip Owen Parmalee, and the airplane is a Wright Model B. Parmalee was killed on 1 June 1912 at Yakima, Washington, when turbulence flipped his plane. Air Force Historical Agency, Maxwell Air Force Base, Alabama, 090713-F-1405A-092.JPG.

10. John W. McClaskey (*standing*), chief Curtiss instructor; Glenn Curtiss (*in D-IV*); *sitting*: 1st Lt. Paul Beck, U.S. Army; Lt. John Towers, U.S. Navy; and Lt. Theodore Ellyson, U.S. Navy. The picture was taken in April 1912 and illustrates the Signal Corps' mismanagement of army aviation. Beck was due to be sent back to his regiment under the "Manchu Law" on 1 May 1912. Sending him back to Hammondsport for advanced training in April was a waste of resources, the sort of mismanagement that fueled the 1915 rebellion. Air Force Historical Research Agency, Maxwell Air Force Base, Alabama, 090713-F-1405A-094.JPG.

11. Capt. Charles DeForest Chandler and 1st Lt. Roy Kirtland, 7 June 1912. The photo was posed so that the Lewis gun could be shown "mounted" in an airplane. The test firing was done on 7 and 8 June 1912, with Thomas Milling piloting and Chandler doing the shooting. Air Force Historical Agency, Maxwell Air Force Base, Alabama, 090713-F-1405A-074.JPG.

12. First Lt. Harold Geiger (*left*) and 1st Lt. Thomas Milling seated in a dual-control Curtiss D-IV training plane at College Park in 1912. On 16 January 1915 Reber sent Geiger back to the Coast Artillery. His abrupt dismissal from aviation angered many of the pilots. Library of Congress, LC-H261-1606.

13. Joseph D. Park, who was killed in a Curtiss D-IV, SC-2, on 9 May 1913, shown here seated in the same plane. Author's collection.

14. Roy C. Kirtland standing in front of a Burgess Model H tractor, sc-24, in San Diego in July 1914. Author's collection.

15. First Lt. Robert H. Willis, who had difficulty understanding what the uniform of the day was. He served with the 1st Aero Squadron with General Pershing in Texas. Author's collection.

16. Ned Goodier leaning on a Curtiss F Boat, SC-34, equipped with a Goodier strut, an addition that resulted from Goodier's near-fatal crash on 18 February 1913. This flying boat is the second Curtiss Model F the army received. On Goodier's right is the civilian Wright instructor Oscar Brindley, and to his right is 2nd Lt. Joseph C. Morrow. The two officers at the left end of the row are unidentified. Air Force Historical Agency, Maxwell Air Force Base, Alabama, 09073-F-1405A-133.JPG.

17. Lt. Col. Sam Reber. The pilots welcomed Reber when he relieved Maj. Edgar Russel as chief of the Aeronautical Division in September 1913. They soon regretted it, however, and Reber's policies were a major cause of the 1915 rebellion. Library of Congress, LC-B2-3812-10.

18. Lt. Col. Lewis E. Goodier, 1st Lt. Ned Goodier's father and the Western Department judge advocate. In the latter capacity, he helped the dissident pilots bring charges against Captain Cowan. His efforts backfired, and he was court-martialed in October 1915. Library of Congress, LC-B2-3639-5.

19. Capt. William "Billy" Mitchell was the officer who most profited from the scandal that resulted in the Goodier court-martial in October and November 1915. The ensuing fallout shook up the Signal Corps Aviation Section and put Mitchell in the catbird seat for his skyrocket rise to rank and fame. Library of Congress, LC-H261-30114.

20. Second Lt. Walter Taliaferro was supposed to have been the second signer on the charges the dissenters made against Cowan. But Taliaferro was killed on 11 October 1915 when his Curtiss Model J suddenly went into a steep dive and crashed into San Diego Bay. Author's collection.

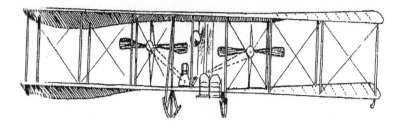

21. Wing warping. In this drawing of a Wright Model A or C that is coming directly at the viewer, its right wing is darkened and its left wing is white. The trailing wingtip edge on the dark wing is warped down, causing that wing to gain lift, and rise. The trailing wingtip edge on the white wing is warped up, causing that wing to lose lift, and drop. That combination causes the plane to roll left, and with the right amount of right rudder, the plane will make a gentle, lightly banked left turn. From Berriman, *Aviation*.

22. Orville Wright also developed a two-stick control system that was used on all Wright airplanes, starting with the Model B. The right-hand control still warped the wing and turned the rudder, but this system featured a short, flexible lever atop the warping stick. The pilot grasped the lever in his right hand and pushed or pulled the stick to warp the wings, which simultaneously turned the rudder left or right to make a controlled banking turn. Wing warping and rudder control were linked through a wheel and chain device that automatically determined the amount of rudder to add during the turn. The system was much simpler than the three-stick system, and it was easier to learn and use. Author's collection.

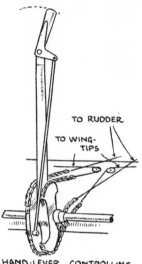

TO RUDDER

TO WING-
TIPS

HAND-LEVER CONTROLLING
RUDDER & WING-WARPING·

23. Wright Model B and C wing warping and rudder lever. From Berriman, *Aviation*.

24. Orville's new single-stick system created left-hand and right-hand pilots. This photo shows that Captain Chandler was a left-hand pilot because he took his flight training sitting in the right seat. The photo was taken at College Park, Maryland, in June 1911. Air Force Historical Research Agency, Maxwell Air Force Base, Alabama, 090713-F-1405A-088.JPG.

25. First Lt. Hap Arnold was a right-hand pilot because he took his flight training sitting in the left seat of a Wright Model B. Air Force Historical Research Agency, Maxwell Air Force Base, Alabama, 090713-F-1405A-116.JPG.

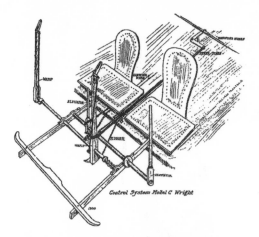

26. The Wright Model C was a true dual-control airplane, which eliminated the problem of creating left- and right-hand pilots. From *Aeronautics*, May–June 1912, 154.

27. Tom Milling sitting in a Curtiss D-IV, showing the Curtiss shoulder bars that controlled the ailerons. The pilot banked left by leaning left and banked right by leaning right. The wheel turned the rudder, and the bamboo rod connected the column to the forward elevator. Pushing the column forward caused the plane to dive, and pulling back cause it to climb. Author's collection.

14

Rebellion, 1915

On Tuesday, 16 March 1915, there were twenty-three officers, including Cowan, at North Island, and eight of them were at a meeting in Dodd's two-bedroom beach cottage that he and Kirtland shared. Those who attended the meeting were dissidents: Thomas Bowen, Carleton Chapman, Townsend Dodd, Byron Jones, Thomas Milling, Douglas Netherwood, Walter Taliaferro, and Robert Willis. Kirtland was there in spirit but did not attend the meeting, because he believed that his presence would give Cowan the ammunition he needed to discredit the group.[1]

The discussion focused on their grievances. At the top of the list was General Scriven's plan to assign nonflying Signal Corps officers to the new command positions. The four-year limit on assignments to aviation was attacked, as was the absence of any measurable progress in military aviation. On the day they met, Europe had been at war seven months, and airplanes were beginning to play an important role. Significantly, aviation in the European armies was a separate arm, and there was universal agreement among the eight dissidents that something had to be done to lever aviation away from the Signal Corps.

Post's death was still on everyone's mind, and they complained about the poor designs and construction of the airplanes they flew. Taliaferro was particularly vocal on that subject. Among the men present, Milling was the least critical of the airplanes. The talk about dangerous airplanes and fatal crashes inevitably led to the subject that was the real reasons for the meeting: the rumor that Captain Cowan was drawing flight pay and the preferential treatment he afforded Patterson. The discussion quickly went from a general gripe session to an outright declaration to get Cowan. The captain was not popular in March 1915, and every man in that room had felt his bite at one time or another. Being a nonflier and a Signal Corps officer, Cowan represented everything they detested about the Signal Corps' control of military aviation.

The conversation became particularly heated when they discussed Patterson's junior military aviator (JMA) rating. The dissenters expressed outrage and disgust over the fact that Patterson had been rated a JMA when he could not fly. The facts that Cowan was drawing flight pay when he rarely flew and Patterson enjoyed the benefits of advanced rank and extra pay when he could not fly were seen as criminal fraud.[2] The question was, What should they do about it?

It now became evident that Cowan's remarks to the pilots prior to General Scriven's visit had registered with them. Jones later said, "The question of removing aviation from the Signal Corps has been discussed by the fliers. The opinion of all the fliers has been that aviation would prosper much more out of the Signal Corps than it has in it, or would in the future."[3]

It was now that Cowan's warning to the CSO in 1913 became significant, because the fliers began forming the connection between their grievances and a congressional investigation. All they needed was a catalyst to bring the two together. If they could capitalize on Cowan's fraudulent drawing of flight pay, they could expose the Signal Corps' mismanagement of aviation and bring on the congressional investigation they wanted. The question was how to go about attracting congressional attention to the problem?

One suggestion was that all of them should put in for the 35 percent flight pay authorized under the 2 March 1913 law. They were already drawing the 50 percent increase authorized under the new law, but the old law was still in effect. They felt that if they drew flight pay under both laws, it would attract attention in Washington, and would result in an investigation that would expose Cowan's fraud. From there it was just a short step to exposing the Signal Corps' mismanagement of aviation.[4] They believed that once the public was aware of the mismanagement, Congress would move quickly to separate aviation from the Signal Corps.

The idea was rejected, because double dipping for flight pay, regardless of the reason, would constitute a serious abuse, which would probably cause the army to eliminate the benefit entirely. And the dissidents would be the only double dippers, because they would be taking their 50 percent for being JMAS plus the 35 percent authorized under the 1913 law. The ploy would certainly attract attention but toward the wrong people. Cowan, who was drawing only the 35 percent flight pay authorized under the 1913 law, would come off looking like the only honest officer at North Island.

Dodd suggested that they confer with Benjamin Foulois about the situation. Foulois was the senior pilot and was already in command of the 1st Aero Squadron. The others rejected the idea because they perceived him as "wishy-washy, afraid of responsibility, and afraid of the Signal Corps." In their view, Foulois was "anxious to feather his own nest. As long as he got that, nothing else would matter much." They also believed that Foulois was in the position he was because he "catered to the Signal Corps," and if he found out what was brewing, he would blow the whistle, and "that would settle everything."[5]

Another idea was to write a round-robin letter and send it up the line, through channels, to the inspector general. That plan was rejected because all of them believed that Reber would shortstop the letter. Jones led the opposition, and his reasons for opposing the plan became representative of the group. Jones rejected going through normal channels because he thought that "if they got hold of it before we had taken the right steps, everything would be stopped."[6]

The group also decided against going through regular channels because such a move would alert Captain Cowan. They were convinced that if Cowan got wind of what was up, he and Reber would squash the complaint. They did not want any details made public until they were "reasonably sure they would not result in a fizzle."[7] And they would "go public" only if they were assured that the complaint would achieve results they wanted. What concerned them most was the possibility of being sent back to their regiments if they showed their hand too soon. They briefly revisited the idea of sending a round-robin letter to the inspector general but quickly dropped the idea again. The group opinion was that whatever steps they took, they must get results, and on that note the rebellion was born.

To get the results they wanted, they formed a plan that included a mass resignation intended to make headlines in the New York papers and the aero journals, which they believed would "stir things up in Washington." But before they committed mass career suicide by resigning from aviation, they were going to launch a clandestine investigation focusing on Cowan and Patterson that would result in charges being brought against the two officers. They hoped that the scandalous nature of the charges would attract congressional attention and result in a full investigation leading to the separation of army aviation from the Signal Corps. To protect themselves from Cowan and Reber's "curious influences" they would conduct the investigation themselves and draw up their own charges against Cowan.[8]

The group decided not to include Patterson in the charges because they believed that "charging Cowan would result in Patterson's case coming to light, and that would settle the Patterson question." But the true basis for their reluctance to go after Patterson directly might have been their decision not to include Foulois in the charges. When all this was going on, Foulois was not on flying status, but he was drawing flight pay. Drawing Foulois into the issue would only muddy the waters.[9]

The dissidents believed they were on solid ground going after Cowan for drawing flight pay, because their own positions were unassailable. After all, Cowan was not actually a pilot or a student training to become a pilot, and what little training he took was done infrequently. The legal point to which they anchored their case was Cowan's monthly affidavit that he attached to his pay voucher claiming that he was an "actual flier of heavier than air craft."

Dodd, who chaired the session, directed Jones and Willis to go to Fort Rosecrans and obtain copies of Cowan's pay vouchers and the special orders detailing him to the school. They were also directed to draw up a list of witnesses who could further verify the case against Cowan and Patterson. After the meeting ended Kirtland returned home and Dodd told him what had been decided and who had been given assignments.[10]

Two days later, Jones told Kirtland he was going to sign the charges against Cowan. Jones said he was not familiar with the format for preparing the charges, and he needed to know exactly what sort of evidence they needed to make the charges stick. The obvious source of that information was Ned Goodier's father, who was the Western Department's judge advocate. He was knowledgeable about the law, and his son was an aviator who had his own problems with Captain Cowan. Kirtland told Jones he would write a letter to Ned and include Jones's questions for Lieutenant Colonel Goodier.

On 22 March 1915 Kirtland wrote to Ned Goodier, who was still in Letterman Hospital recovering from the injuries he received in the November 1914 crash of the Martin model T. Kirtland asked his friend to "casually" find out from his father if Cowan could be tried for making a false official statement when he signed a certificate stating that he was an actual flier of heavier-than-air craft. The letter arrived in San Francisco on 25 March at a time when Ned Goodier was still in bad shape.

His father entered the room and Ned handed him the letter. "Dad, can you read this?"

The senior Goodier took the letter. "Is this a letter from Kirtland?"

Ned nodded and said, "Yes. I don't give a damn; all I want is to get well."

The senior Goodier read the letter, folded it, and shoved it into his pocket. "Boy, don't worry a bit. I'll attend to it." That same afternoon, Lieutenant Colonel Goodier wrote a reply to Kirtland.[11]

This is the point at which Lieutenant Colonel Goodier made his first mistake. The correct procedure would have been to walk into Maj. Gen. Arthur Murry's office and tell him what was brewing in San Diego. Or he could have gone to the department adjutant, Col. James B. Erwin. In either case, after giving his commanding officer a heads up, Lieutenant Colonel Goodier could have sent an independent investigator to San Diego to look into the matter. The colonel was certainly on good terms with General Murry and Colonel Erwin. So there was little chance that anyone from the Western Department headquarters would interfere with the investigation. Instead, Lieutenant Colonel Goodier chose to take an active and clandestine role in the matter under the guise of providing legal advice on procedure. Why?

The answer to that question is in his relationship with his son, and his emotional involvement in his son's situation. As a father, Lieutenant Colonel Goodier had a deep interest in what happed to his son and, by extension, his son's friends. He was fully aware that his son did not like Captain Cowan, and based on what he had seen and heard during his visits to North Island, and read in Ned's letters, he had developed a strong bias against Cowan. That bias clouded his judgment.

Lieutenant Colonel Goodier was walking in a gray area in which some of his actions were right, some were wrong, and all were questionable. The aviation school was not under General Murry's command; it belonged to the cso in Washington. And the chain of command went from Captain Cowan, through Lieutenant Colonel Reber, to the cso. But the school fell under the Western Department's authority for supply and discipline, and the latter gave Lieutenant Colonel Goodier authority to become involved in any circumstance that could lead to a court-martial. He also had authority to provide any officer with legal advice regarding procedure.

In his letter to Kirtland, Lieutenant Colonel Goodier laid out exactly what evidence was needed to prevail in a case against Captain Cowan. He also directed Kirtland to the specific army regulations governing the dissidents' actions and provided the format for the charges.[12] Kirtland turned the letter over to Jones, believing that his active participation in the plan was ended. But that was not the case.

On 28 March Kirtland wrote a letter directly to Lieutenant Colonel Goodier in which he discussed several issues, including Cowan's flight pay and the grounds for his own relief. He told the colonel,

"The idea of charges did not originate with me, but with some of the other officers." He told him that the belief at North Island was that Reber had a special arrangement with the comptroller that resulted in the comptroller's favorable opinion regarding Cowan's drawing of flight pay under the 2 March 1913 law. With regard to Cowan's inability to fly, Kirtland told Lieutenant Colonel Goodier, "Were he a student from the line of the Army, his failure to learn to fly in a reasonable time would have resulted in his relief from aviation duty."[13]

Kirtland also told Goodier that "rank favoritism and Signal Corps politics" played a major role in Lieutenant Colonel Reber's decision to relieve him. He said that army aviation was run according to Reber's "personal desires" and "not according to what was right or wrong, nor to the best interests of the service." He recounted Cowan's refusal to state the reason for his relief, and told the colonel, "If I find that any reason *has* been assigned, and that it is anything to hurt my record, I shall open things up." The letter concluded with the real issue behind the move against Cowan: "We are hoping that some means may be found to bring before Congress the knowledge of the present state of affairs, and we feel that if this ever comes to pass that we can present such an array of facts and arguments as to forever separate aviation not only from the Signal Corps, but from Colonel R. and Captain C. Not until then, can any real progress be made."[14]

That letter was not the last of Kirtland's active participation in the conspiracy, and he remained active until he left North Island on 8 May. Prior to his departure, he was busy turning in his property and making arrangements to move his wife and four-month-old daughter to Fort Douglas, Arizona. But he found time to give the dissidents advice and support, and to help type the final draft of the charges against Cowan.

He left aviation a bitter man, knowing that his replacement was "a man who not only couldn't fly, but who knows nothing about aviation work in general." It was especially galling because Kirtland firmly believed that "I could do Patterson's work and oceans more, but Patterson was wholly incapable of doing any of my work."[15]

In the meantime, Byron Jones was preparing a "Synopsis of Evidence" against Cowan. His first stop was the school headquarters, where he viewed the flight records for both Cowan and Patterson, and made notes. He did not obtain copies of the records at that time. This was the trickiest part of the investigation, because he had to be careful not to reveal his purpose. He told the enlisted clerk that he was curious to see how much flying time everyone was getting, and since there was no secrecy attached to the flight records, the clerk gave them to him. The information Jones obtained from the flight school records was accurate and damning.

Included in the school's flight records was the overblown trip out to the USS *San Diego* on 2 October 1914 that totaled twenty-five minutes and did not count as a training flight. From 11 to 21 November 1913, Cowan had made eleven straightaway hops that totaled twenty-four minutes. The next three entries in Cowan's flight record show that he flew as a passenger for a total of one hour, and while those flights were not part of his flight instruction they did count as flight time.[16]

Jones also compiled a list of witnesses that included all the instructors, civilian and army, who had worked with Cowan and Patterson at any time. After each man's name, Jones described what each witness would be able to say. Though Jones was probably correct about what evidence each man could provide, the fact is that in several instances he did not actually contact the potential witness. He inferred from the flight records what each witness might be able to say.[17]

He also did not talk to, or correspond with, his friend Ned Goodier before he included his name on the witness list. He wrote, "Captain Goodier is expected to testify that Captain Cowan is not capable of taking a heavier than air machine on an actual flight, and is incompetent to manage, control, or pilot one, and is not and never was in any sense of the word an actual flier of heavier than air aircraft."[18]

Though Goodier could and would give the testimony that Jones said he would, the fact remains that Jones was building a case without actually doing the legwork. It was an omission that would boomerang.

Jones next went to the quartermaster's office at Fort Rosecrans, where the pay records were kept. And here again his work was sloppy, incomplete, and partly fabricated. In his list of evidence against Cowan, Jones wrote, "Captain A. S. Cowan has been drawing an increase of 35% on all pay and allowances since 10 July 1913. The retained copies of his pay vouchers, in the possession of the Quartermaster at Fort Rosecrans, show this." The truth was that Jones did not see any pay vouchers that had been prepared prior to March 1914, because none were on file at Fort Rosecrans prior to that date. Jones also failed to include that several quartermasters had handled the payments over the nearly two-year period, and he failed to provide their names and the periods during which each one paid the vouchers.[19]

On 31 March 1915 Jones mailed his two-page "Synopsis of Evidence" to Lieutenant Colonel Goodier. In the cover letter, he told Goodier, "I have personally talked to the witnesses mentioned in the enclosed." As we know, that was not true in every case. He concluded his cover letter by asking for Goodier's opinion as to whether the charges against Cowan could be sustained. He also asked the colonel to give him "guidance and counsel so that I may draw them up in legal form."[20]

Lieutenant Colonel Goodier was again at a crossroads, and he made the wrong decision. It was obvious that a serious problem existed at the army's aviation school, and General Murry needed to know about it. Lieutenant Colonel Goodier was operating in a gray area because he had failed to alert his boss to the situation in San Diego before he started providing Jones with legal advice. By not keeping General Murry apprised of what was happening, advising Jones took on the appearance of conspiracy. There is no doubt that the colonel was too close to the case to be objective, and that he had an axe to grind with Cowan. His reply to Jones made those facts obvious.

The lieutenant colonel told Jones that he agreed with the dissidents on the need for secrecy, and he was taking steps to keep everything under wraps at his end. He assured Jones that once the charges were filed, Cowan would be unable to squelch them because "the strange influence he seems to have been able to wield does not extend to the officers of this Department, which has court martial jurisdiction over your school."[21]

With the letter, he enclosed a four-page document titled "Charge and Specifications preferred against Captain Arthur S. Cowan, Signal Corps, United States Army," which Jones was to use as a template to prepare his own charges against Cowan. The first charge accused Cowan of "presenting for payment to a disbursing officer of the United States a false and fraudulent claim in violation of the 60th Article of War." The charge contained five specifications, each alleging that during specific periods from 10 July 1913 to 31 March 1915, Cowan collected $113.63 flight pay for each month beginning on 1 August 1913.[22]

The 60th Article of War covered all aspects of fiscal fraud perpetrated against the government, and included fraudulent drawing of additional allowances, which included flight pay. It also covered aiding someone else to fraudulently draw extra allowances, which would apply to Cowan's actions in getting Patterson rated as a JMA. Given the circumstances of Cowan's flight pay and Patterson's JMA rating, this charge looked solid.[23]

The colonel wrote that he presumed that Jones "had verified the statement that all the vouchers had been cashed at Fort Rosecrans." He told Jones to obtain the names of the Fort Rosecrans quartermasters who had cashed the vouchers and insert them in the charges "in the proper places."[24] But Jones could not do that because none of the vouchers prior to March 1914 had been cashed at Fort Rosecrans.[25]

Lieutenant Colonel Goodier's situation was rapidly getting worse, but he did not see it. He had chosen to work secretly with a group of dissidents on a case that was politically explosive without telling his boss. He had already violated standard procedure, and now he was relying on an amateur's investigation as the basis for the charges. But that was not the end of it. Lieutenant Colonel Goodier now took it upon himself to charge Cowan under the 61st Article of War with three specifications. He might have pulled it off had he stuck to one specification, but the second and third specifications had no basis in fact. As an officer, his actions demonstrated a lack of judgment. But as a prosecutor preparing for a trial, his actions were incomprehensible.

The new charge was for conduct unbecoming an officer and a gentleman, a violation of the 61st Article of War, which said in full, "Any officer who is convicted of conduct unbecoming an officer and a gentleman shall be dismissed from the service."[26]

The first specification under the 61st Article of War dealt with Cowan's involvement in Patterson's fraudulent JMA rating. It should have gone in with the first set of charges under the 60th Article of War. The reason he put it here, in his own charges, was because the dissidents in San Diego did not want to include it in their charges. So, Lieutenant Colonel Goodier took personal responsibility for adding the charge because he felt it was warranted, even after the group, for good reasons, had rejected it.

The second and third specifications should not have been included at all, because they dealt with Cowan's 16 September 1914 seaplane flight to the USS *San Diego* and were based on typically inaccurate and incomplete press reports that made it appear he had misrepresented himself as the pilot during the flight. The dissidents had correctly dismissed the magazine and news articles as typical examples of media hype and inaccuracies.

The colonel clearly revealed that he was too passionately involved in the case when he wrote, "No decent man, not to mention an officer, or a gentleman, would sit quiet and try to reap credit for such a performance as that 16 September flying boat trip, without hastening to have the fact published that he was not entitled to any credit for that flight. It was a very raw attempt to sail under false colors, and I believe conviction of those specifications would drive him out of the service, even if he had never made false pay vouchers."[27]

In the cover letter sent to Jones, Lieutenant Colonel Goodier provided specific directions on the steps to take after the charges had been completed and retyped. The dissidents were to mail a carbon copy of the charges to General Murry with a letter stating that the charges had been handed to Captain Cowan who would forward his copy. Having mailed the carbon copy to General Murry, they were to go immediately to Captain Cowan's office and hand him his copy of the charges, and request that he forward them to the Western Department headquarters. They were told to retain a copy of the charges as well as the draft version.

Goodier assured them that when the charges arrived at Western Department headquarters, he would tell General Murry that the pilots asked him how to the prepare charges in proper form. He concluded with, "Please do not hesitate to call on me for any assistance you may feel I can render." They would.[28]

Jones received the draft of the charges on 12 April, the day before he and Milling were to leave for duty in Brownsville, Texas. Jones turned everything over to Dodd, who now learned that Jones had not actually seen all the pay vouchers that were listed in the draft charges. When Dodd and Taliaferro read the information that Jones had compiled, they found several factual errors. At the moment that did not seem to be a big problem, since Dodd believed that he could go over to Fort Rosecrans and see them himself.

That same day, Dodd, Jones, Kirtland, Milling, and Taliaferro held an impromptu meeting, during which important things were decided that affected the course of the events that followed. Initially they considered having all nine dissidents, including Kirtland, sign the charges, but decided to have just Dodd and Taliaferro sign them. They settled on two signers, to ensure that the charges would still go forward in the event that one of the signers was killed, a decision that was prophetic.[29] Dodd, Kirtland, and Taliaferro would type up the final draft after Taliaferro and Dodd had examined the pay vouchers at Fort Rosecrans and obtained the names of the other quartermasters. And all agreed that Goodier's second charge, about the uss *San Diego* flight and visit, would be eliminated from the complaint.

At one point during the discussion Dodd suggested having Foulois prefer the charges because he was the army's most senior pilot. But that idea was only a passing fantasy, and they all agreed that such an offer would "frighten him." Dodd also thought that they should inform Foulois of the charges as a courtesy to him, since he was in effect the second in command at North Island. But the

Rebellion

others, including Jones, did not trust Foulois and were sure that he would go directly to Cowan before they had time to act. Dodd and Taliaferro respected the man because, even though they felt he was a Cowan toady, he was, unlike Cowan, a pilot. As a result, Dodd continued to believe that out of respect, they should somehow bring Foulois into the loop.[30]

The others were undoubtedly right that if they informed Foulois of what they were doing, he would have gone straight to Cowan. And he should have. Actually, Foulois was not their enemy, and he agreed with several of their grievances. But in this sort of case, Foulois followed the book, and he would not have agreed with what they were doing or how they were going about it. The fact is that Foulois had a better understanding of what the army calls the Big Picture than did the dissidents.

On 13 April Dodd and Taliaferro went to Fort Rosecrans to look at the pay vouchers themselves. Capt. Franklin T. Murry, who was the quartermaster at that time, asked them on what authority they wanted to see Captain Cowan's pay vouchers. Captain Murry later told the inspector general that Dodd said they had been "instructed by a higher authority" to look at the pay vouchers. Taliaferro told the same inspector general that they had not said that, but Captain Murry "may have gotten that impression from one thing that Captain Dodd stated." According to Taliaferro, Dodd told Murry that they wanted "to see the accounts to get correct information to send to the Judge Advocate." That apparently satisfied Captain Murry, who allowed them to look at the vouchers.[31]

Dodd and Taliaferro now learned that Captain Murry had no pay vouchers prior to March 1914, but he told them that they could be found at the Western Department headquarters in San Francisco. They were also unable to locate a copy of the orders detailing Cowan to command the aviation school. The question they had to ask themselves was where did Jones find them? And the answer was, he "winged it." But they did see Cowan's pay vouchers for the year beginning in March 1914 and ending in March 1915.

On 14 April Dodd wrote a long letter to Lieutenant Colonel Goodier. He explained that he had gone to Fort Rosecrans on 13

April to "verify the vouchers," but the quartermaster told him that he had no vouchers preceding March 1914. Dodd told the colonel, "I did not have time to obtain from Jones the information as to where he learned about the earlier vouchers." He asked the colonel to locate them at the Western Department headquarters. He also asked Goodier to locate a copy of Special Order 131, dated 6 June 1913, that sent Cowan to command the school at San Diego.[32]

On 17 April Lieutenant Colonel Goodier replied to Dodd's letter and enclosed an amended set of charges that included the correct details from Cowan's pay vouchers. The colonel directed Dodd to "take off the first page from each of the sets of charges that you have and substitute the enclosed."[33] In his reply, the senior Goodier noted that the 1913 law authorizing a 35 percent increase for flight pay specified that the recipient had to have been detailed "for aviation duty" or, alternately, "on aviation duty." Cowan's 6 June orders detailed him "for duty at the Signal Corps aviation school." He assured Dodd that the first charge would stick because "it was very apparent that there was no idea in the mind of the Secretary of War or the Adjutant General that Cowan was to be on aviation duty, or that he was going to the school for aviation duty."[34]

Lieutenant Colonel Goodier was already up to his eyes in trouble. The nature of the legal advice he had provided to that point, including the preparation of the amended charge, had taken him beyond his authorized authority. Had he limited his involvement to what he had already done he would have been better off. But again he became more deeply involved in the conspiracy than he should have.

Lieutenant Colonel Goodier advised Dodd not to tell Foulois what was happening. He told Dodd that Foulois "would doubtless claim the right to investigate them and might take a lot of time and make a lot of delay." He warned that if Foulois became involved Dodd "would lose control of the situation," and would find himself "under all sorts of pressure to quit." He asked rhetorically, "Suppose he tears them up, or goes to Cowan and shows them to him without preferring them? It's a pretty good plan to go ahead without letting your action be dependent upon somebody else's."[35]

Rebellion

Goodier then shifted the focus to the charges relating to Patterson's JMA rating that he had prepared for his own signature. He had helped the dissidents prepare their case against Cowan, and now he needed their help in preparing his. He asked Dodd to locate the documents that would clearly show who was responsible for Patterson's recommendation. He told Dodd that any person who signed a statement that Patterson "had shown by tests including aerial flight that he was especially well qualified for military aviation" was "very close to the danger line."[36] Outlining his case against Cowan, he pointed out that the 18 July 1914 law provided a sixty-day window for rating a pilot as a JMA. But Patterson's rating was made on 17 September—*sixty-one days after the law became effective.*[37] It was probably a hair-splitting point, because Cowan had sent in the recommendation to Reber on 11 September. Reber sent it to General Scriven on the fifteenth, and the order was issued over the secretary of war's signature on 17 September. But the law did say that the rating had to be conferred within sixty days after the act took effect. And no matter how you count days, the sixty-day window closed at midnight on 16 September 1914.

Lieutenant Colonel Goodier was obviously intent on keeping the conspiracy a secret until it was time to hand Cowan the charges. He had typed the charges and his 10 April cover letter himself, and he had urged Dodd to keep Foulois out of the loop. Now he directed Dodd to reply with an overnight telegram, known in those days as a "night letter," sent to Goodier's residence. "There is a telegraph office a couple of blocks away on Polk Street, and I would receive it before leaving home."[38]

Dodd wrote a letter to Lieutenant Colonel Goodier on 20 April that revealed a man who was under enormous strain. The letter contained the complete details about Patterson's meager flight training and Cowan's push to have him rated before the window closed. In that same letter, Dodd told the colonel that the second charge, dealing with Cowan's 16 September 1914 flight to visit the USS *San Diego*, was "petty and might injure the case if it was retained." But the second charge also contained a specification that dealt with Cowan having recommended Patterson's JMA rating. Dodd and the others had no desire to press that issue directly, but apparently they were willing to let Lieutenant Colonel Goodier carry the ball on that one. But they were not comfortable with the second set of charges.[39]

As the time to present Captain Cowan with the charges drew closer, Dodd became increasingly aware of his precarious position. The greater the strain on him became, the less sure he was of his position. The relationship between the dissidents and the judge advocate was that of client and adviser. Officially, the dissidents were to decide which charges to bring. But Lieutenant Colonel Goodier was Dodd's only source of assurance that the action he and the others was taking was right, and though Dodd thought the second charge was a mistake, he was not sure. He wrote, "Unless I receive a telegram from you that you are very strongly in favor of keeping those items in the indictment, I will prefer only the charge of false pay vouchers." The result was that he left the decision up to Lieutenant Colonel Goodier.[40]

Dodd's fears were revealed when he told Lieutenant Colonel Goodier, "I have about reached the conclusion that I am the only one to dare the wrath of the powers to be. If I could have made a non-stop flight to San Francisco I would have felt a lot safer." He told the colonel that if the charges were not sustained, "I will gracefully have to start learning the way to handle a seacoast battery, and probably with something of a black eye as a memento of my presentation." Dodd told Goodier that he alone would sign the charges because "it will be much better for me to go back to the artillery than it will for several to leave the aviation service when it is in such a poor state of efficiency."[41]

The reference to the nonstop flight to San Francisco illustrated Dodd's concern for secrecy. He would have preferred to speak with Lieutenant Colonel Goodier personally, because the exchange of letters created a paper trail that could later be used against him. He was right on that point. He had not followed the colonel's advice to reply by night letter, probably because the letter he mailed on 20 April was too long to put in a telegram. But he obviously agreed with the colonel's suggestion that telegraphic communication was more secure. He told Goodier, "If you see fit to wire me about any-thing, send it to San Diego as the office there is not so liable to leak as the one in the Coronado Hotel."[42]

For the next two days, Dodd, Kirtland, and Taliaferro worked in shifts typing in proper form the single charge and five specifications they were going to sign. On the morning of 23 April Dodd mailed a letter to the colonel that included a copy of the charge and their thanks for the colonel's help. That evening Dodd sent a night letter to Goodier saying, "Papers signed by me and Taliaferro will be pre-sented twenty-fourth. Copy mailed Western Department, also per-sonal copy to you."[43] The order of battle was drawn up, the troops were in position, and the first volley was about to be fired. Dodd, Taliaferro, and the others believed that they had righteousness on their side. Maybe they did. But the other side had a more power-ful force on their side—powerful connections within the army.

Saturday, 24 April 1915, was a beautiful day in San Diego. Dodd and Taliaferro went together to the post office in the Coronado Hotel, where they mailed a carbon copy of the four-page charge against Captain Cowan to General Murry at the Western Depart-ment headquarters in San Francisco. That act was outside the accepted procedure. They should have simply handed the charge to Cowan, which he had to forward to the Western Department headquarters with his endorsement. Dodd and Taliaferro, act-ing on Goodier's advice, chose to send a carbon copy to Gen-eral Murry "in order to bring the matter to the attention of the Department Commander in case the original should be pigeon-holed or indefinitely held up." Despite Lieutenant Colonel Good-ier's instructions, it was the wrong thing to do.

At 1000 Dodd and Taliaferro entered Captain Cowan's office, where they found him alone, seated at his desk. Both officers reported and told the captain that they had come to see him in an official capacity. That got Cowan's attention, and an otherwise beautiful day began showing signs of becoming dismal. Dodd handed the original copy of the four-page charge to Cowan. One can only imagine the numbing shock Cowan felt as he read the charge and specifications. Dodd assured him that their action had been taken without "animus or personal feeling in the matter." Inside the tiny office, the day went from approaching dismal to utterly grim.[44]

The charge stunned Cowan, who never suspected that such a thing was brewing right under his nose. The men who had handed him the charge were men he considered his friends. They were men with whom he had enjoyed pleasant social relations and with whom his official relations had been "the very best." But he retained his composure. According to Dodd, Cowan accepted the charges "without rancor" and even "made our difficult job as easy for us as he could."

Cowan wanted to know why Dodd and Taliaferro had chosen to file a formal charge against him. Why had they not come directly to him with their concerns about his flight pay? It was a fair question, to which Dodd gave an honest answer. Dodd told him "the method of administering the flight school had made that impossible." Dodd explained, "In spite of our friendly relations, I believed that I would be relieved from aviation. If I were relieved, any charges that I might then place would be considered as due to animus caused by this relief."

Cowan read the charges again and assured Dodd and Taliaferro that he would add an endorsement to the effect that "he thought there was no animus." He also told them that he admired their backbone for acting on principle and said that he would hold the charges overnight to give them time to reconsider. He expressed his true feelings when he told them "a better procedure would have been to have reported the matter by letter for the decision of the next higher commander, and for his action."

Cowan sent for Foulois, and while they waited for him, the three officers discussed the case. Cowan told Dodd and Taliaferro that it had never been his intention to do military flying and asked if it would "satisfy our conscience in the matter if he started in and trained regularly." Cowan showed Dodd and Taliaferro the comptroller's ruling that the 1914 law did not repeal the 1913 act. "And he either read a part of a letter, or referred to it, from Mr. Hay, which was to the effect that it was not the intention of the new law to deprive Captain Cowan of his flight pay if he was flying." Dodd and Taliaferro replied that they did not see how that had any bearing on the case. Cowan said that the CSO had approved the matter of his flight pay and taken the issue to the secretary of war and Representative Hay. Cowan was sure that the charges would be quashed and added that his conscience was clear.

When Foulois arrived, Cowan handed him the charges, which Foulois read. He too was caught completely off guard. He handed the charge back to Captain Cowan with the comment that Kirtland was behind this "on account of his relief." Dodd assured the two captains that he had discussed Cowan's flight pay with "some of the other officers before it was known that Kirtland was to be relieved." Dodd assured them that Kirtland had deliberately been kept out of the loop "for fear that there would be animus suspected." That, as we know, was not the case.

Cowan again introduced the comptroller's opinion regarding his flight pay. Foulois added that the secretary of war "had passed on the thing" and concurred with Cowan that the charges would be thrown out. He "talked around the thing two or three times" and concluded that if the failure to fly once a day, week, or month was vital, they were all under the same cloud. He grumped that he felt like he too was under indictment. Dodd and Taliaferro silently agreed with him "to a certain extent, but we kept quiet." Dodd characterized Foulois's comments as "the vaporing of a not too strong personality."

The meeting broke up at noon, and Cowan's outward calm, which was the result of his genuine belief that he was justified in drawing flight pay, had an unnerving effect on Dodd and Taliaferro. It was clear to them Cowan believed that Lieutenant Colonel Reber's letters protected him, and that the CSO knew that Cowan was drawing flight pay. They left the meeting expecting Lieutenant Colonel Reber to make an appearance at North Island to "straighten things out," in which case the worst was yet to come. They were right.

15

The Reaction, 1915

Two days after Dodd and Taliaferro handed Cowan his copy of the charge and specifications, the first carbon copy arrived at Western Department headquarters in San Francisco. Lieutenant Colonel Goodier immediately added the second charge and three specifications that he had prepared in advance so that both charges would be handled together.[1] Meanwhile, Cowan wrote to Lieutenant Colonel Reber, telling him what had happened.

Reber was completely unprepared for Cowan's letter, but he quickly recovered and opened a counteroffensive. He showed Cowan's letter to General Scriven, who took it to the chief of staff, Maj. Gen. Hugh L. Scott. The CSO wanted the chief of staff to take the case away from the Western Department and bring it to Washington. But General Scott told General Scriven that he "didn't feel justified in taking the matter out of General Murry's hands."[2] Reber's first attempt to take control of the situation had failed, but he was not finished.

On 27 April Lieutenant Colonel Reber wrote to Cowan, assuring him "that this office will take care of your side of the case." But Reber was not going to limit his efforts to simply protecting Cowan, and he assured the captain that retribution would be certain. "When the thing is over this office will take Dodd's case in hand."[3]

Reber assured Cowan that he was fully justified drawing flight pay. Reber wrote, "You need not worry, as your case is perfectly clear. You have been detailed on aviation duty, and I hold that under the law you are entitled to your increase of pay because you have been an actual flier of heavier-than-air craft while so detailed."[4]

Up to this time Cowan had been sitting on his copy of the charge and was completely unaware that Dodd had mailed a second copy to General Murry in San Francisco. He hoped that his sitting on the charge would give Reber time to sidetrack it, which is exactly what the conspirators had expected and planned for. But on 30 April the Western Division adjutant, Colonel Erwin, sent a notification to Cowan that the Western Department headquarters had received a copy of the charge and specifications on 26 April, and enclosed a copy of the charge sheet. The adjutant concluded, "The Department Commander directs your prompt action in this matter."[5]

Cowan replied that same day. He forwarded his original copy of the charge with an endorsement that reflected his trust that Reber had the situation well in hand. He told the department adjutant that he had spent the past week investigating the charges. He assured the adjutant that the charges were groundless by saying, "I have in my possession, and there are also on file in Washington, copies of letters showing that the facts of my drawing this pay, and the facts of my flying status, are clearly known and authorized by my superiors." He advised the Western Department adjutant that he had asked "Lt. Col. Samuel Reber, the officer in charge of the Aviation Section, to come to this post."[6] Here again the dissidents had predicted the response.

Foulois wrote to Reber on 4 May and gave his view of the situation. Foulois, who probably had more insight into the fliers' actual grievances than Cowan did, told Reber that the whole affair was an attempt to remove aviation from the Signal Corps. He was right. To a certain degree Foulois was neutral in the matter, though his loyalties lay with the Signal Corps, including Captain Cowan. And Foulois was watching the case with considerable interest, because he knew that the flight pay issue could become a problem for him as well. Despite his common bond with the aviators, Foulois's best interests would be served if the flight pay issue just went away.

Cowan also wrote to Reber on 4 May and was almost immediately sorry that he did. He was still rattled over the letter from the Western Department adjutant, and he was worried that Reber was losing confidence in him. It was a groundless worry. He told Reber that Patterson was going to Washington, and asked Reber to "consult with Patterson to have your belief in me strengthened."[7] In another letter he closed with "Assuring you that I am not in panic and am right on the job and perfectly confident that I can handle this situation." Cowan's sagging morale got a big boost when Reber wrote to him, "I certainly have not lost confidence in you whatsoever," and closed with, "With kindest regards, believe me."[8]

Outwardly there was no indication at North Island that a serious situation was unfolding. Cowan's relations with Dodd and Taliaferro remained cordial both on and off duty, and the daily school routine remained unchanged. On 6 May Cowan commented, "Both of these officers are performing their duty in just as satisfactory a manner as they always have."[9] Cowan had known for a long time that the fliers were unhappy with the lack of progress and the equipment situation. But he had never dreamed that their discontent would be directed at him. As a result, he treated the situation like it was a bad dream that would eventually end without repercussions to him.

But in that same letter Cowan revealed the thing that troubled him the most, the one thing that he felt might be his undoing. He told Reber, "I . . . do not know whether an inspector will be sent here or not. I hope not. Because as you perhaps can realize we have done, and are doing, things here, which might be hard for someone totally unfamiliar with the conditions under which our work is carried out to understand." He justified whatever had been done on the grounds that it was in "the best interest of the service and was necessary and expedient." He assured Reber "there was nothing criminal done."

In the meantime, General Murry had assigned Capt. Dennis P. Quinlan to investigate the charges against Cowan. The general chose Captain Quinlan because he was Goodier's assistant and was already detailed to conduct two investigations in southern California. Since Quinlan was going to be in San Diego anyway, he might as well handle the Cowan matter while he was there. Quinlan was certainly qualified to conduct the investigation, and he was impartial. His impartiality stemmed from the fact that he enjoyed a close personal relationship with both Lieutenant Colonel Goodier and Captain Cowan, and he had no axe to grind with anyone.

Cowan heard about Quinlan's assignment from someone inside the Western Department headquarters, and the information gave him an uneasy feeling. Though Quinlan was a longtime friend, the fact that General Murry had assigned a judge advocate to the case seemed to give Quinlan's task a special significance. Had Cowan known at the time that Goodier had preferred a second charge, Quinlan's assignment would have caused him even greater worry, since Quinlan and Goodier shared the same office in San Francisco

While Cowan was stewing in San Diego, and Reber was pulling political strings in Washington, someone in San Diego leaked the story to the *San Francisco Chronicle*. Under the headline "Army Officer to Answer Charges," the *Chronicle* informed its readers, "Charged with falsification of pay rolls, Captain Arthur S. Cowan, Signal Corps commandant of the Army Aviation School at San Diego, and well known in San Francisco, must face a court martial, according to a dispatch from San Diego last night." The article explained that Cowan had been drawing 35 percent more pay than he was entitled to for two years, and he was not a pilot. The article also said, "It is understood that one or two other officers may have been credited by Captain Cowan with being military aviators when they were not."[10]

Someone in San Francisco sent Cowan a copy of the article, which he received on 11 May, one day after Quinlan was supposed to have arrived. The fact that the investigator had not yet shown up at North Island did little to relieve Cowan's fears. In fact, it should have. The truth was that the investigation of the charges against Cowan had no special priority and were just another investigation that Quinlan had to do. In the meantime, the newspaper article set off every alarm bell Cowan had.

He told Reber, "I am inclined to believe now that an effort

will be made to drag Foulois and Patterson into this matter, and that is the reason Foulois was not consulted before the charges were preferred. It may be that an effort will be made to show that Foulois, who has done very little flying, should not be rated as a Junior Military Aviator, and that Patterson also should not be so rated."[11] Had he known about the second charge under Article 61 of the Articles of War that Goodier had added, his anxiety would have gone off scale.

For some reason, it had not occurred to Cowan that his accusers might be vulnerable. In part, the oversight stemmed from his own sense of guilt, and no matter how much he declared his innocence in his letters to Reber, Cowan knew that his flight pay was at best questionable. Equally important was that Cowan was still unaware of a second charge, which alleged that Patterson's junior military aviator rating was fraudulent. But the main reason Cowan failed to recognize his accusers' vulnerability was that he was depending entirely on Reber to get him out of this mess. And Reber was working on it.

By 14 May Reber had recognized that the accusers were vulnerable, and he was laying the groundwork to turn things around. General Murry had forwarded copies of both charges to the adjutant general, who passed them on to the CSO. General Murry had requested certain documents related to the charges, and the entire package, at Reber's "urgent request," had ended up on his desk for reply. From his reading of the charges, Reber concluded that Taliaferro and Dodd had not instigated the charges, because they did not have access to the records that spelled out the details related to Cowan's pay vouchers. Only Lieutenant Colonel Goodier could have obtained that detailed information. Reber's conclusion was only partly correct, but it became the basis for his counterattack. Reber took the approach that Lieutenant Colonel Goodier was the chief conspirator, and Reber's goal was to have the charges against Cowan dropped and have Goodier court-martialed.

On 14 May Reber sent a long, reassuring letter to Cowan. He wrote, in part:

The Reaction

I am preparing a statement now to take to the Secretary of War, and I am convinced that the outcome will be the dropping of the charges against you and the investigation of the conspiracy, which I am confident has existed to discredit you and have you relieved. The serious part is to land the conspirators and I hope this can be done. Set your mind at rest, keep perfectly quiet, say nothing to anybody about it, and let me handle the matter to my own satisfaction. I think I am going to get one or two scalps before I get through.[12]

Reber had seen two openings in the charges that he believed he could exploit. The first had to do with whether the secretary of war had detailed Cowan for aviation duty in 1913. The dissidents based their claim on the wording in Special Order 131 dated 6 June 1913. That order sent Cowan to San Diego to take command of the flying school. Special Order 131 said that Cowan was to report to San Diego "for duty at the Signal Corps Aviation School at that place."[13] But Reber had found the earlier order that placed Cowan in command of the 1st Aero Squadron (Provisional) at Texas City on 25 March 1913. That order assigned Cowan "in addition to his other duties, to command aviation detachment, Signal Corps on relief of Captain Chandler, Signal Corps, from duty with Second Division."[14]

The wording in both orders was subject to interpretation when it came to deciding if the secretary of war had, or had not, detailed Cowan to aviation, but Reber believed that he had found the winning document. He told Cowan, "Had the people who are involved in this conspiracy known of the telegram of 25 March 1913, which put you in command of the aviation detachment at Texas City, or had they read paragraph 1269 of the Army Regulations, they certainly would not have exposed themselves to counterattack."[15]

The second opening Reber found was in the first specification of the second charge. In that specification, Goodier alleged that Cowan had "willfully, corruptly, and fraudulently represented . . . that 1st Lt. William Lay Patterson . . . had shown by practical tests, including aerial flights, that he was especially well qualified for military aviation." On this point Reber was on solid ground, because Cowan had not used those words when he recommended that Patterson be rated a junior military aviator. What Cowan wrote was: "recommend 1st Lt. William Lay Patterson be detailed a Junior Military Aviator."[16] Reber absolved Cowan of any responsibility, saying, "This office recommended Patterson's detail and stated he was qualified. You did not state he was qualified (see your telegram, 11 September 1914)."[17]

It was all hair-splitting, but Reber had found the weakness in the dissidents' assault—an incomplete investigation and sloppiness in preparing the charges. And there would be more hair-splitting as the case against Lieutenant Colonel Goodier developed. But the hair-splitting would have been worthless had Reber not backed it up with astute political maneuvering. And that was the dissidents' greatest weakness—they were in California and Reber was in Washington.

Reber sounded confident in his letters to Cowan, but he was paranoid as evidenced by his 17 May letter to Cowan, in which he provided a complicated cipher to be used when they exchanged telegrams. He also provided an indecipherable explanation of how to use the cipher and included several examples of how to use it and the key. To top it off, his example was incorrectly enciphered so that the message was unreadable even with a key. Cowan never used the code, but the letter would come back as a powerful weapon against Reber.[18]

Reber was also aware that, despite his connections, he might not be able to protect Cowan and Patterson. Patterson was especially hard to defend because of his inability to fly and his, by any realistic standard, fraudulent junior military aviator rating. Making matters worse were the progress reports coming in from California. The most recent had been written on 12 May and said, "The civilian instructors report that in their opinion Captain Patterson will never make a flyer of sufficient flying ability to do military flying."[19] And now Patterson was in Washington on a three-month sick leave, which meant that he would not be taking any lessons until sometime in July or August.[20]

Patterson's favored status was highlighted six days later when Reber told Cowan, "I don't want you to waste any more time than necessary on any students who cannot make good." He directed Cowan to fully document the reasons for washing out a student and suggested that four months was long enough to form an opinion about the student's potential to be a military aviator.[21] That same day Reber met with Patterson, who after fourteen months still could not fly and of whom the civilian instructors said lacked the ability to become a military aviator. Seated across from Reber was a man who according to any reasonable standard, including the one he had just sent to Cowan, should have been washed out long ago. Yet Reber was about to hand him a field command.

Reber told Patterson that "after a consideration of all personnel," he had selected him to command the 2nd Company of the soon-to-be-formed 2nd Aero Squadron. His duty station would be in the Philippines. He admonished Patterson "you must learn to fly," and told him that he was to organize his company and be ready to sail for Manila in January 1916.[22]

On 18 May Reber had identified whose scalps he was after when he wrote, "Push the instruction of your student officers as much as possible as you are very likely to lose three Junior Military Aviators in the near future," meaning Goodier, Dodd, and Taliaferro. He ended the letter with a statement that left no doubt about his intent to crush the rebellion.

> I want your outfit to get this idea clearly in their heads. The Aviation Section of the Signal Corps is a military organization, and that the commanding officer of the Signal Corps Aviation School is in fact a military commanding officer. The Aviation Section of the Signal Corps will be reduced to zero before any insubordination or unmilitary conduct on the part of its members will be tolerated. If your bunch thinks that it can scare this office by a threat to quit the game and leave the office in the lurch, they have misunderstood its position. It's about time for us to clean up the situation in such a way that it will never repeat itself.[23]

Shortly after his conversation with Patterson, Reber scored a major political success when he got the judge advocate general, Brig. Gen. Enoch H. Crowder, to replace Captain Quinlan with

Col. David C. Shanks to investigate the charges against Cowan. In a single stroke Reber had effectively removed the case from General Murry's control and had transferred it to Washington. Colonel Shanks met with Quinlan before the captain went to North Island and received from him the case file that had been prepared in San Francisco. On 30 May Colonel Shanks arrived at the school and began his investigation.

This was the second time that Colonel Shanks had inspected the school. The first had been from 22 to 26 January, when he conducted the second annual inspector general's inspection, and on that occasion, Shanks had given the school a good report. On the basis of the favorable report and the fact that Reber knew Shanks well enough to call him "Davy," Reber had lobbied to have Shanks assigned to the case. As Reber had expected, Shanks was on Cowan's side.

Colonel Shanks arrived in San Diego on Thursday, 30 May 1915, and took a room in the U. S. Grant Hotel. That evening, before he started his investigation, he invited Cowan to an informal meeting in his room at the Grant. The meeting lasted from 2030 to 0030, and Cowan was relieved to find that Colonel Shanks was "friendly disposed toward me." Cowan believed that Shanks's warm feeling for him stemmed from Cowan having known the colonel "for quite a-while," and the fact that Shanks knew "a great many people who have known me intimately." More important, Shanks made it evident that he was "not on particularly friendly terms" with Lieutenant Colonel Goodier and gave Cowan the impression that "Lieutenant Colonel Goodier has overstepped himself very decidedly."[24]

The inspector general spent all day Friday and Saturday taking depositions and reviewing the school's records, conducting a whirlwind investigation that put the school "out of commission" for two days. The only negative criticism he made with regard to Cowan was that Cowan and Reber were corresponding privately about official matters. He referred to it as "this official personal correspondence." Cowan told Reber, "He seemed to take a very decided exception to it and will probably make a point of it." Cowan suggested that "it might be well for us to stop now."[25]

When Reber found out that Cowan had shown Colonel Shanks all their correspondence, he was not pleased. He fired off a letter to Cowan in which he made it clear that their correspondence was to be considered private and not official. He told Cowan that unless his letters were "signed officially" they were to be considered private and not shown to anyone. "There are a great many subjects which I deem it more advisable to take up in an informal way."[26]

While Shanks's attitude reassured Cowan and raised his morale, Shanks's questioning during the dissidents' depositions had a distinct prosecutorial tone. It was apparent that Colonel Shanks was building a case showing Lieutenant Colonel Goodier to be the chief conspirator and instigator of the charges against Cowan. He was not able to actually establish that, but his line of questioning, and the sometimes muddled answers that Dodd and Taliaferro gave, produced a sense that Lieutenant Colonel Goodier had orchestrated and directed the gathering of evidence against Cowan.

In addition to building a case against Lieutenant Colonel Goodier, Shanks was clearly building Cowan's defense. When he took Taliaferro's deposition, he started with the issue of Cowan's flight pay, peppering Taliaferro with questions designed to produce answers that justified Cowan drawing flight pay. He then established that Taliaferro was a Curtiss pilot, and his first flight had been in the same Curtiss flightless grass-cutter that Cowan used. And if that justified Taliaferro drawing flight pay under the 2 March 1913 act, why was Cowan not justified in doing the same thing?

The weakness of that attack would seem to be that Taliaferro's flight training was regular and continuous, whereas Cowan's was not. But paragraph 1269 did not say anything about regular and continuous training. It just said that an aviator was considered a flier of heavier-than-air craft on the date of his first flight, which by common practice was equated with his first flight lesson.

In the meantime, Reber was becoming annoyed with Patterson's antics in Washington. Patterson was apparently not listening to what Reber had told him about the importance of learning to fly as soon as possible. On 7 June, three weeks after Reber had warned Patterson that he was in danger of being relieved unless he learned to fly, Patterson was still in Washington. Reber was clearly exasperated with Patterson's lax attitude. "I told him that the matter is in his hands and he will have to abide by his own action." Patterson, still lackadaisical about learning to fly, told Reber that he would try to get back to San Diego by the end of the month.[27]

In fact, it was late July before Patterson returned to North Island, but on 27 July he did start a fairly regular training program that would bring his flight time up to thirty-one hours and forty-four minutes.[28] He finally soloed on 27 September, but his instructors held out little hope for him. Taliaferro reported on 30 September 1915 that the civilian instructors believed he would never be a qualified military pilot "on account of his lack of feel of the machine and his inability to cope with various emergencies that may, and often do, arise in the air." Taliaferro agreed with their assessment and added, "I would not fly with him acting as pilot in a machine with single controls."[29]

In the meantime, the charges against Cowan remained on hold. In early August Colonel Shank's report on his investigation went to the judge advocate general, and a copy ended up on Reber's desk. Out in California it was business as usual at the school, and there were no outward signs of any trouble. Cowan had been busy getting the 1st Aero Squadron up to strength so that Foulois could take it to Fort Sill, Oklahoma, in July. The most remarkable thing was that while Reber was out to "get scalps," Cowan maintained cordial relations with the pilots and was planning to send Jones to the Massachusetts Institute of Technology to take an aeronautical engineering course.[30]

But while he remained on cordial terms with the dissidents, Cowan was eager to make a fresh start with new blood. He was planning to send most of the dissidents to Fort Sill with the 1st Aero Squadron. He told Reber, "I am particularly anxious to clean out all of the old regime and start in here with a new slate made up entirely of youngsters who have not been contaminated by association with the old regime, which still bears some of the taint of Texas City."[31]

For a time during July and into August, Reber was the acting cso during General Scriven's absence, and he used the opportunity to lobby the judge advocate general and the adjutant general to have the charges against Cowan dropped. On 10 August he personally delivered the case file to the adjutant general. The following day he wrote to Cowan, telling him, "I am glad that I had a chance to handle this case in person as acting Chief Signal Officer. The General will probably be back tonight, and I thought it best for me, being familiar with everything, to handle it." He closed with the hope that "when the smoke of battle clears . . . we will have completely ended the old state of affairs."[32] On 14 August he got what he wanted.

16

The Turnaround, 1915

There is no doubt that Reber wanted the case against Cowan dismissed, and he used all his connections to make it happen. There is little, if any, doubt that the secretary of war, the adjutant general of the army, and the CSO would also welcome the charges being dismissed simply to head off any embarrassment to the army.

On 19 May 1915 Reber wrote the twelfth endorsement to the charges. He listed Patterson's poor health and the school's shortage of airplanes as the reasons for the delays in Patterson's flight training, which, while alibis, were at least plausible excuses, and he provided names of flight instructors whom he claimed rated Patterson's progress as "good," which was not true. He included a reference to the 25 April 1913 order directing Cowan to relieve Captain Chandler at Texas City and assume command of the provisional aero squadron there.[1] This was something new that he had found on his own, and he wrote that its discovery rendered the charges groundless. He sent the endorsed copy of the charges up the line to the next stop, which was the Office of the Judge Advocate General of the Army, where Brig. Gen. Enoch H. Crowder added the thirteenth endorsement on 14 August 1915. From there the charges and all the endorsements went to the secretary of war, Lindley M. Garrison.[2]

The secretary of war undoubtedly read the endorsements to the charges against Cowan before asking the judge advocate general to provide his legal opinion of the charges. It appears that General Crowder used Reber's endorsement as a guide to write his 4 August legal opinion, starting with Reber's discovery of a 25 April 1913 order for Cowan to relieve Captain Chandler at Texas City and assume command of the provisional aero squadron there. Both men treated the order as though it were the Holy Grail and built their case from there. Another indication that the general used Reber's endorsement as a guide is that his legal opinion contains errors dealing with Cowan's flight records that only Reber could have provided, since none of the other endorsements contained comments about the school's flight records. Even with Reber's endorsement as a guide, the judge advocate general had his work cut out.

General Crowder first addressed the issue of Cowan drawing flight pay. He started by asking two questions: "Was Captain Cowan regularly detailed on aviation duty?" And "Was he, while so detailed, under the law and regulations, an actual flyer of heavier-than-air craft?" To answer the first question, he cited the 2 March 1913 act that said that "this increase of pay and allowances shall only be given to such officers only as are actual fliers of heavier-than-air craft, and while so detailed." He then cited Army Regulations paragraph 1269, which said, "An officer shall be considered an actual flyer of heavier-than-air craft from the date of his first flight after reporting by order of the Secretary of War for duty at the aviation station . . . and until relieved of such duty."

Next, he argued that since the 2 March 1913 act was not repealed with the passage of the 18 July 1914 act, the language used in the 2 March 1913 act was still valid and applicable. He was on solid ground at this point, but then he cited the 25 March 1913 telegram directing Maj. Gen. William H. Carter, commanding the Second Division at Texas City, to "assign Capt. Arthur S. Cowan, Signal Corps, in addition to his other duties, to command the aviation detachment, Signal Corps on relief of Captain Chandler, Signal Corps from duty with the Second Division." Based on the telegram, Major General Crowder concluded,

When this order was issued, Captain Chandler was in command of the aviation school and detachment of the Signal Corps then on duty with the Second Division at Texas City, Texas; that he (Chandler) was on duty and an actual flyer of heavier-than-air machines and had been rated a military aviator in G. O. 54, WD, 1914; and that he was drawing the 35 percent increase in pay authorized by the Act of March 2, 1913. It further appears that the telegraphic order was issued *with the intention that Captain Cowan should replace Captain Chandler in all* his (Chandler's) duties and relations to the aviation work, and therefore, that he (Cowan) should qualify as an actual flier of heavier-than-air craft.[3] (emphasis in the original)

The conclusion can be challenged on two points, the first being that on 25 March 1913, Cowan was not a pilot, had not yet started his flying training, and had not even ridden in an airplane as a passenger, though he did make three flights as a passenger *after* he relieved Chandler.[4] The second point is arguing that because Cowan relieved Chandler, who *was* a pilot, Cowan, who was not a pilot, should therefore qualify as an "actual flier of heavier-than-air craft."

Under the subheading "Was Captain Cowan regularly detailed on aviation," the general addressed the language used to assign Cowan to relieve Chandler, and here he had a bigger problem. The issue was whether Cowan had been given a flying assignment or an administrative one. In the subheading, the general used the language regularly employed to assign an officer to a flying assignment, which was "detailed *on* aviation or detailed *for* aviation." But Cowan's orders to relieve Chandler said, "Assign Captain Arthur S. Cowan, Signal Corps, in addition to his other assignments, to command aviation detachment, Signal Corps, on relief of Captain Chandler, Signal Corps, from duty with Second Division. By Order Secretary of War." The order actually came from Lt. Col. Eugene F. Ladd, the Second Division adjutant general who made the order official by including, "By order of the Secretary of War" in closing.[5]

Since Lieutenant Colonel Ladd's order did not detail Cowan "on aviation or for aviation" but said "assign," General Crowder had to come up with an argument that made "assign" mean "detailed on, or detailed for." He wrote:

While the orders detailing line officers for aviation work specified particularly that they were detailed for aviation duty, whereas the telegraphic order in the case of Captain Cowan specified that he was to *assume command* of the aviation detachment, and the order of June 6, 1913 (Para. 13, S. O. 131, W. D. 1913) that he was to proceed to San Diego, California *for duty at the Signal Corps Aviation School* [emphasis added]. There appears to be no variation between the language of the orders assigning him to aviation duty and those issued in the case of other Signal Corps officers on aviation duty and having in view the fact that it was the intention to have him replace Captain Chandler and qualify for aviation work, and that he was detailed for duty at an aviation station as specified in the regulations. I think it must be held that he was regularly detailed on aviation duty, and under detail to such duty at an aviation station, except briefly from between April 25, 1914 and May 19, 1914 during which period he was relieved from aviation duty at the aviation school. Even assuming the orders issued in the case of Captain Cowan were lacking in explicit direction that he was detailed for aviation duty, it is clear that he accepted them in this sense and the Department has ratified the interpretation he placed on them so that the regularity of his detail for aviation duty may not now be raised.[6]

The judge advocate general's argument is seriously flawed by the fact that the 25 March 1913 order did not use the words "*assume command* of the aviation detachment" (emphasis added) that he wrote in his argument. The order said, "*Assign* Captain Arthur S. Cowan, Signal Corps . . . to command aviation detachment . . ." (emphasis added). Even if the order had said "assume command," it is absurd to suggest that Cowan "sensed" that he was detailed for aviation duty. He knew his assignment was a stopgap measure when he relieved Captain Chandler in Texas City, leaving no grounds for him to "sense" that his orders meant anything other than that. The following August he heard the cso tell a congressional committee that his position at the school was administrative, which should have settled the issue, but the next month he asked Reber if he could learn to fly, knowing that he was not in a flying assignment at the school. Given that he had been drawing flight pay since the end of July, his desire to have some authority for taking lessons was clearly motivated by the need to protect himself should his drawing of flight pay be questioned.

The judge advocate general now turned to the question: Was Cowan an actual flyer of heavier-than-air craft? Here he noted, "After reporting for duty pursuant to the telegraphic order of 25 March 1913, he made two or three instructional flights with Milling as pilot: but did not claim extra pay while in Texas for the reason, as stated to the Inspector General, that he had not determined the matter in his mind." The truth was Cowan made three flights while he was in Texas.[7] He flew with Kirtland once and with Milling twice, but they were nothing more than orientation or "joy" rides. There was no instruction involved, but they might have set Cowan's mental gears to turning about flight pay, which had been authorized just over three weeks earlier. That might explain the bit about having not then "determined the matter in his mind." Based on the foregoing, the general now asserted that Cowan had "acquired the status of an actual flier of heavier-than-air craft."

He disposed of the fact that Cowan's flying lessons were not regular and frequent as required by the 18 July 1914 act. He acknowledged that the statute "contemplated progressive instruction by flights leading up to skill in aviation; and therefore, the duties of an actual flyer should be in a proper sense continuous: but the Regulation on this matter prescribes that the status as an actual flier continues *until the officer is relieved from such duty*" (emphasis in the original). What he was talking about here was the assumption that Cowan had started his flying lessons in Texas with the "two or three flights with Lieutenant Milling," but those lessons were interrupted by Cowan being sent to San Diego three months later, in June 1913. Even if one accepts the general's claim that Cowan had started his flight training in March 1913, a three-month gap in his flight-training was not "progressive instruction."

General Crowder listed all the "reasons" why Cowan's flying instruction was not regular and continuous in San Diego. It all boiled down to this: with too many students and not enough airplanes, Cowan's sense of duty kept him on the ground so as to not interfere with the training of the student pilots. During the Goodier court-martial, on 15 December 1915, testimony was given showing that Cowan's flight training was not regular and there were long periods between flights. First Lt. Edgar S. Gorrell, the school secretary who was responsible for the school's training records, was asked, "Was there anything, so far as you know, that would have prevented him [Cowan] from going in a machine and flying?" He answered, "I know of no reason why he should not have flown."[8] Additionally, weekly reports listing the names of everyone who had taken flight training, that is, actually flew, during the reported week were sent to the cso. Cowan's name was conspicuously absent from many of those lists.[9]

The judge advocate general wrapped up his legal opinion regarding the charges against Cowan by including something that was never an issue, which was that Cowan had not learned to fly in over two years of sporadic flight lessons and should have been relieved "as contemplated in the regulation." One hesitates to question General Crowder's professional competency, but Cowan was a signal officer and the regulation pertained only to detailed officers. But the important thing was that he exonerated Cowan completely by writing,

> His weekly reports of flights to the Chief signal officer of the Army apprised that official of the fact that he was not flying, and the responsibility for his relief by reason of his discontinuance of progressive instruction, as contemplated in the regulation, devolved on his superior officers. Without expressing an opinion as to whether the circumstances required his relief, I am clearly of the opinion that Captain Cowan is not criminally responsible for his receipt of increased pay during the period or periods of his detail to the Aviation School. It follows, therefore, that the charges against Captain Cowan based on his increased of pay during such periods cannot be sustained.[10]

There remained only the charge that Cowan had "falsely represented that 1st Lt. William Lay Patterson, 7th Infantry, then on aviation duty, had shown by practical tests, including aerial flights, that he was well qualified for military aviation service." The general could have effortlessly dismissed this charge on the grounds that Cowan did not actually make that statement.[11]

What happened was that on 10 September, General Scriven sent a night telegram to Cowan reminding him that the act approved on 18 July allowed sixty days to rate officers below the rank of captain as junior military aviators (JMAS).[12] The deadline was midnight on 16 September 1915. Cowan, knowing that Patterson was not qualified for the rating, sent a telegram to Scriven that said, "Recommend First Lieut. Wm. Lay Patterson seventh infantry be detailed in aviation section signal corps as junior military aviator and on flying status."[13] Scriven turned the telegram into a memorandum and sent it to the adjutant general of the army, Maj. Gen. Henry P. McCain, who turned it over to the army personnel office. A clerk from that office brought the memorandum back to Scriven's office with direction from the personnel chief to have the memorandum amended using the proper language as required in section 2 of the 18 July 1914 act.[14] The memorandum, now dated 15 September, was amended to read: "It is recommended that under the provisions of Sections 2 and 3 of the Act to Increase the Efficiency of the Aviation Service of the Army, and Other Purposes, Approved July 18, 1914, 1st Lieut. William Lay Patterson, 7th Infantry, now on aviation duty, who has shown that he is especially proficient in military aviation, be detailed in the Aviation Section of the Signal Corps, be rated as a Junior Military Aviator, and be given the rank of Captain."[15] Brig. Gen. George P. Scriven, CSO, signed the amended memorandum, and everyone in that room, other than the personnel clerk who took it back to the adjutant general for action, knew it was a fraud.[16]

Patterson was rated a JMA on 17 September 1914 at a time when he could not fly and had received only fifty-four minutes of instruction.[17] When General Crowder addressed this issue in his legal opinion, he noted that following his rating, Patterson "performed practically no flying until March 13, 1915." Given the facts of how that rating came about, how was the judge advocate able to justify it?

He first noted that in a 15 May 1915 letter Reber reminded Cowan that Cowan had not stated Patterson was qualified, "knowing full well at the time that Patterson's full record was on file in the office of the Chief Signal Officer of the Army and left the matter entirely in the hands of that office," which resulted in the CSO submitting the memorandum that resulted in Patterson's rating as a JMA. On that basis, the judge advocate general wrote, "I am compelled to conclude that the order rating Captain Patterson as a Junior Military Aviator was issued on an erroneous certificate, inserted in the office of the Chief Signal Officer in the request for such rating; that Captain Patterson had not shown by practical tests, including aerial flights, that he was especially well qualified for military aviation service; and that the action making the rating should be revoked, as the result of *an apparent error*" (emphasis added).[18]

Crowder recommended that Patterson's JMA rating be revoked and that he be made to "refund any extra pay he has received by reason of such erroneous ratting." He mitigated that recommendation by adding that the amount Patterson should refund should be the difference in pay between the 50 percent he received for being a JMA and the 30 percent he received as a student pilot under the 2 March 1913 act. He then turned to Captain Cowan's role in the affair.

General Crowder safely noted that "Cowan did not make the certificate alleged in the charges; he merely recommended the detail, leaving the question of his [Patterson's] qualifications for the determination for higher authority, full information of Patterson's qualifications being on file in the office of the Chief Signal Officer," but added that Cowan "was not without blame" with regard to Patterson's fraudulent rating. And then he got to the reason he was writing this legal opinion. Nevertheless, his closing statement ended with "but, I do not think he could be convicted of any criminal offense and I do not, therefore, think that any disciplinary action is called for under this charge."

Cowan was off the hook, and Reber had what he wanted.

Though the judge advocate general's opinion was never tested in court, it had the effect of law in Washington. The secretary of war dismissed the charges against Cowan, and General Crowder drew up charges against Colonel Goodier for violations of the 62nd Article of War, "Conduct to the prejudice of good order and military discipline." On 7 September 1915 Special Orders no. 209, War Department, was issued. The order said, "By direction of the President, a general court martial is appointed to meet at San Francisco, California at 10 o'clock a.m., on 1 October 1915, or as soon thereafter as practicable, for the trial of such officers as may be brought before it." As things worked out, the Washington brass might have been better off to have let the sleeping dog lie.

In the meantime, a bewildering sequence of events concluded with General Crowder issuing an even more bewildering review of Patterson's JMA rating. On 27 August 1915, in response to General Crowder's 14 August legal opinion, the War Department revoked Patterson's JMA rating.[19] Four days later, without explanation, the War Department reinstated his rating.[20] Then, a week after the secretary of war had reinstated Patterson's JMA rating and flight pay, General Crowder wrote a memorandum to the secretary of war saying that Patterson should retain his rating and his extra pay even though they were based on "erroneous" information.

In his 7 September memorandum, General Crower acknowledged that the CSO had told him the amended 15 September 1914 memorandum on which Patterson was rated a JMA was not true and that the claim that Patterson was on aviation duty requiring him to participate regularly and frequently in aerial flights was also not true. The judge advocate general further acknowledged that at the time Patterson was rated a JMA, he was not qualified for that rating and was not on aviation duty that required him to participate regularly and frequently in aerial flight. In short, it was all a fraud. But that is not the way General Crowder saw it.

My view, however . . . is that the matter is one of fact found and acted upon by the Secretary of War in due course of administration, and that such action cannot now be declared to have been invalid. This seems to be established on general principles. What the Secretary of War does in obedience to the statute, deliberately and advisedly, induced and effected by no fraud, cannot in my judgement, in view of subsequent evidence, be declared to have been invalid. If the rating were valid, though upon, information now proved to be unreliable or erroneous, whatever action the Department may be moved to take by reason of recent disclosures, should be prospective in its operation.[21] The qualification for the rating was established in the usual administrative way and presumably as the statute intended. The finding was made upon the certificate advice and recommendation of the head of the Bureau to whose domain the subject belonged and whose recommendation the statute expressly required. The facts were regularly found and the detail on its face regularly made; subsequent investigation tending to show that the information furnished the Secretary of War was unreliable or wrong or such as would have caused him, had he known the truth, to reach a different conclusion, cannot, in the absence of fraud, serve to change the rating there made. The rating may have been erroneous in fact but cannot be said to be invalid in law. The same reasoning applies to the announcement made by the Secretary of War as to the character of this officer's duty.[22]

Put in simpler terms, though it may have all been built on lies, the proper procedure was followed, so the rating was valid. But at least on 3 June 1916 the conditions under which flight pay was authorized were tightened to eliminate a repeat performance.

Exactly one week before the trial opened, a tragedy apparently validated Dodd and Taliaferro's decision to have two signers on Cowan's charges. On 11 October 1915 Taliaferro was attempting to loop a Curtiss Model J at two thousand feet. As the airplane was inverted at the top of the loop, it fell off on the right wing, and spun into San Diego Bay, crashing in fifty feet of water. Navy divers recovered Taliaferro's body from the wreckage twenty-four hours later.[23]

17

Court-Martial, 1915

Round I, 18–19 October 1915

The trial opened at ten o'clock on the morning of Monday, 18 October 1915, at 216 Pine Street in San Francisco. The court originally consisted of thirteen officers: Brig. Gen. William L. Sibert as the court president and twelve field grade officers. Capt. John T. Geary, Coast Artillery Corps, was the judge advocate, which in a military trial is the prosecutor. The defense objected to one member of the court, Col. Even Swift, on the grounds that he had prior knowledge of the case, and Colonel Swift withdrew.

Lieutenant Colonel Goodier had two legal counsels: Capt. Allen J. Greer, Infantry, and William P. Humphreys, a civilian attorney whose practice was in San Francisco. Captain Greer's primary role was to advise Humphreys on military law and procedure, and he asked few questions during the trial. William Humphreys was an experienced trial lawyer who early in the trial grabbed an opportunity to shift the focus from his client to Cowan and Reber, turning the trial into a national exposé of implied corruption and Signal Corps mismanagement of aviation.

The single charge against Goodier had three specifications, which Captain Geary read to the court. The charge was made under the catchall article 62 of the Articles of War, which dealt with "Conduct prejudice of good order and military discipline."[1] The first specification alleged that Goodier's 17 April letter to Dodd showed that Goodier was not impartial in the matter, and the act of writing the letter was a contravention of his official duty as judge advocate of the Western Department. In support of the specification, Captain Geary included a copy of Goodier's 17 April letter to Dodd. Of the three specifications, this one was the easiest to prove, and the least serious.

In the second specification, the prosecutor alleged that Goodier acted maliciously with intent to "incite, promote, and foment discord in the official and personal relations" between Cowan and the seven dissenters, whom the specification named. The specification also alleged that Goodier's intent was to make the seven dissenters disrespectful in their feelings and conduct toward Cowan. And last, the specification alleged that Goodier had concealed his actions from military authority and urged the others to do the same. To support this specification, Geary included a copy of Goodier's 10 April letter to Jones. This was the most serious of the three specifications, and the easiest against which to mount a defense.

The third specification, which also included malice as the motive, alleged that Goodier had "sought to induce and persuade" the seven officers to "take concerted action against" Cowan. The specification referred to Goodier's 17 April letter, and provided excerpts from it to support the specification. In seriousness this specification fell somewhere between the first and second specifications and presented both the defense and the prosecution with an equal challenge.

There were the usual defense motions to strike all or part of the charges and the prosecution's arguments to keep the charges intact. The court let the charges stand, and Captain Geary opened his case. Geary's strategy was to show that Lieutenant Colonel Goodier took a poorly organized group of dissenters and gave them leadership and direction. If he could show that Goodier already harbored a dislike for Cowan before the dissenters contacted him, then he could make the argument that the colonel manipulated the situation to achieve his personal goal.

Humphreys's defense strategy was to show that the intent to file charges against Cowan was already well developed before the dissenters made contact with Colonel Goodier. He wanted the court to accept the argument that the colonel was acting within his authority when he gave them the legal advice for which they asked. Humphreys would hammer on the argument that his client did not solicit the contact, and he did not do any more than the dissenters asked of him.

But as the trial unfolded, Humphreys immediately recognized the emergence of a new dynamic, which he turned to his advantage. To make his case Captain Geary allowed his witnesses to tell their stories in full without directing their testimony. In the process of carrying out that strategy, he opened the door for Humphreys to make the case against Cowan that the judge advocate general had dismissed. If Humphreys had not arrived in court with the intent to shift the focus from Colonel Goodier to Captain Cowan and Lieutenant Colonel Reber, he certainly capitalized on the opportunity that arose when Roy Kirtland took the stand.

After asking Kirtland to give the court a brief summary of his army service, Captain Geary asked him why he had been relieved. Kirtland answered, "Upon Captain Cowan's recommendation to Colonel Reber regarding over-obligation of the school funds." Geary asked Kirtland if he had a conversation with Cowan about the over-obligation, and when Kirtland affirmed that he had, Geary said, "Please state to the court all of the facts connected with it, what you said to him and what he said to you."

Humphreys looked up in surprise, unable to believe that the prosecution was going to give Kirtland a free run. Kirtland grabbed the ball and ran with it for thirty minutes, giving a detailed, uninterrupted, blow-by-blow account of how Cowan had ordered expenditures for which there was no money. He described how Cowan had ignored Sam Reber's decision not to buy the machine shop equipment until the next fiscal year and recounted how Cowan had dodged his responsibility by relieving Kirtland. He was even allowed to describe the bald threat that Cowan made if Kirtland pushed to have an explanation attached to the recommendation for his relief.[2]

Apparently unaware of what was happening, Geary asked Kirtland, "Did this relief of yours, coming as you stated in an unexpected way, cause you to feel hostile or beget any ill will towards Captain Cowan?" Kirtland answered, "Well, as anyone could understand, I did not feel in the most pleasant way," and launched into a five-minute speech describing how Cowan ducked responsibility for the over-obligation. He concluded, "I did not think I had a square deal, and under the circumstances I did not feel as pleasant toward the captain as I had."

Geary then introduced copies of correspondence between Kirtland and Goodier. The purpose was to show that Goodier was a prime mover in the plot to get Cowan. Under questioning Kirtland made it clear that the effort to get Cowan had started before Colonel Goodier had written to him. Time and again Geary asked Kirtland questions that allowed Kirtland to expand on the theme that Cowan was widely disliked. Finally, Geary moved to show that there was something significant about Kirtland having gone to Goodier for legal advice.

He asked Kirtland why he had not gone to the senior officer at Fort Rosecrans, which was just three miles away. On its face the question was a good one, but Kirtland turned it around when he patiently explained that the commanding officer at Fort Rosecrans was not an attorney, whereas Colonel Goodier was. He told Geary, "As a general rule, if you want advice you think of who is qualified to give it."[3] Geary recovered some of the lost ground when he got Kirtland to admit that the dissenters went to Colonel Goodier not simply because he was the best source of legal advice. They had gone to him because they knew him and his son.

Geary asked Kirtland about Cowan's flight pay and read an excerpt from a letter in which Kirtland wrote, "To my mind he could be convicted by proof that he has not been a bona fide student for a period of at least one year."[4] Geary asked Kirtland how he concluded that Cowan had broken the law. The question proved to be a tactical mistake because it took the trial down a path that Geary did not want to go, and he lost control of it.

Geary expected Kirtland to say something that would show that Goodier had influenced him in arriving at that conclusion. Instead, Kirtland delivered a lengthy and uninterrupted answer, in which he told the court how he had learned about Cowan drawing flight pay, that Cowan rarely flew, and that he had no intention of learning to fly. His tone was matter-of-fact and firm. In a deep, resonant voice, he made it clear to everyone in the room that his own values had brought him to the conclusion that Cowan was guilty of deliberate fraud. He ended his answer by saying, "So, in my mind, knowing when he had ceased taking instruction, knowing that he could not fly, had never qualified as a flier, I would think, and do think, that he could be convicted of it. I cannot conceive of the law being written any other way than to cover a real, bona fide student or a qualified aviator. It certainly was not intended to be that way."[5]

By noon, the focus of the trial had gone from Colonel Goodier to Captain Cowan. Humphreys could not have orchestrated the shift any better than Geary already had. All Humphreys had to do was keep the focus on Cowan. When the court reconvened after lunch, Humphreys opened his cross-examination, and an unknowledgeable observer would have thought that Kirtland was Humphreys's witness.

Under Humphreys's direction, Kirtland spent nearly two hours detailing Cowan's sins. He described an officer who became progressively petty and unreasonable as the months went by. He told about the growing dissent among the pilots and their growing support for separating aviation from the Signal Corps. He was even allowed to talk about Chandler's lack of leadership at College Park in 1912, and the blowup at Texas City in 1913. Humphreys led Kirtland into a discussion of Patterson's fraudulent rating as a JMA. Throughout the questioning the prosecution did not once object to the direction the testimony was going.[6] Finally, toward the end of the cross-examination, Humphreys asked a question that applied directly to the charge against Colonel Goodier.

"Did he in any way urge the preparation of charges against Captain Cowan in his letter to you?"

"No, sir."

But Geary was able to blunt some of the damage during his redirect examination. During the redirect, both the judge advocate and the court president asked Kirtland why he had not taken his grievances to the inspector general, which would have been the proper procedure. It was a damaging question because it highlighted the thin ice the dissenters were on, and Kirtland could offer only a lame answer. By going not to the inspector general but instead to Lieutenant Colonel Goodier, Kirtland had not followed army procedure. It was a point scored for the prosecution. The court placed enormous weight on operating within official channels. The fact that Kirtland had gone outside official channels indicated to the court that there was more to the matter than a junior officer's casual request for legal advice.

Geary called Byron Q. Jones as his second witness. Geary established that Jones had done the initial fact gathering in the case against Cowan and asked him where he went to get the information. Jones described his activities, making the point over and over that neither Kirtland nor Colonel Goodier had anything to do with his investigation of Cowan's flight pay. He told the court that, like Kirtland, he never doubted Cowan's guilt. His concern was that without expert help in preparing the charges, he would not do it right and the charges would "fizzle." When asked why he thought it was up to him to sign the charges against Cowan, Jones told the court, "I thought it was up to anybody who had any sense of duty, or when anything was going on that they considered rotten graft, it should be stopped."[7]

Geary had made an opening when he asked Kirtland why he had not gone to the inspector general with his suspicions, and now he widened it with Jones. All the apparently extraneous talk about Cowan and his flight pay might be made to work in Geary's favor if he could show that the dissenters deliberately operated outside official channels.

The judge advocate asked Jones, "Well, if you considered that there was some rotten graft on the part of Captain Cowan in drawing his flying pay, why did you think it necessary to correspond with the Judge Advocate of the Department on an official matter outside official channels?"

Jones gave a rambling answer that included his desire to get the best legal advice available, and then he said, "And I wanted to correspond with a man I had met there, rather than with a stranger." It was the answer Geary wanted.[8]

The picture beginning to emerge was that of several disgruntled young officers conspiring to bring charges against their commanding officer. To be sure, they had grounds for suspicion, but they were ignorant about what the law really was in the matter. And the implication was that despite their suspicions about Cowan's flight pay, there might not have been a crime at all. Their uncertainty caused them to operate outside official channels, since doing otherwise would expose their activities and bring about their relief from aviation. Geary pushed ahead with this line of attack, apparently heedless of the damage it was doing to the Signal Corps and the army.

He asked Jones whether he or any of the others had consulted with Captain Foulois about the matter. Jones told the court he had not consulted Foulois: "I consider Captain Foulois to be a very wishy-washy man. I consider him to be a man afraid of responsibility and afraid of the Signal Corps. . . . If I discussed the matter with him he would undoubtedly be frightened of such an idea and would probably report the matter at once to the commanding officer. And that would settle everything."[9] Again, Geary had gotten the kind of answer he wanted.

The judge advocate had established that not only did the dissenters not go to the inspector general, they also did not talk to the next most senior officer at the school, who was also a pilot. Not only that, Geary had created the picture of junior officers going behind their commanding officer's back. The court certainly heard the charges against Cowan, but they were there to hear the evidence against Goodier, and they were listening.

The prosecution's next move was to show that Cowan disliked Ned Goodier, and that the senior Goodier took up his son's cause. Kirtland had already said that Cowan was down on Ned Goodier, and Jones underscored that opinion when Geary gave him a free hand in describing a run-in Cowan had with Ned Goodier. Jones recounted an incident in which Tom Milling very nearly landed on top of Goodier's airplane. Jones told the court that Cowan's allegations that Goodier was responsible for the near crash were "unfair" and added, "Captain Cowan's attitude was decidedly antagonistic to Lieutenant Goodier."[10]

Geary had already scored a strong point by showing that the dissenters had not followed army procedure, and now he had successfully raised the possibility that Lieutenant Colonel Goodier had acted maliciously in bringing charges against Cowan. During his cross-examination Humphreys opened a line of questioning intended to cast doubt on Cowan's actions as a commanding officer. The cross-examination did not seem to be going anywhere until, from out of the blue, Jones dropped a bomb. He was telling the court about a search he had made of the school's records when he told the court: "I saw a letter in the official files. It was to Colonel Reber from Captain Cowan in which he states, you have to knock some of these youngsters in the head once in a while, so as to keep down the rest, so that they don't get to feeling that the Signal Corps owes them something."[11]

In one of the rare times that Captain Greer addressed the court, he rose and said, "I may state to the court that before the trial is concluded we shall ask for all the records at the aviation school at San Diego, and among these we expect to produce this letter which has just been mentioned." Jones had lifted the lid on a Pandora's box, and the defense wanted a peek inside.[12]

Before the court ended the first day at 1645, Brigadier General Sibert asked Jones if he was drawing flight pay. Jones told him he had stopped drawing flight pay on the date he left San Diego to attend the Massachusetts Institute of Technology. The court president asked if Jones had considered filing charges against any of the other officers at San Diego who were fraudulently drawing flight pay. The court president probably knew something about the Patterson issue, and his question implies that he was buying Geary's argument that the dissidents had maliciously singled out Cowan with Goodier's help. Jones told him that he felt that if Cowan were brought to trial "the Patterson question" would be settled.[13]

The court reconvened at 1000 on Tuesday, 19 October. The first two witnesses on the second day were Maj. Gen. Arthur Murry, commanding officer of the Western Department, and his adjutant, Col. James B. Erwin. Captain Geary used them to establish that Lieutenant Colonel Goodier had not followed proper procedure and had operated outside the normal channels. Insofar as the officers sitting on the court were concerned, this was the heart of the case. Both officers told the court what everyone knew, that Lieutenant Colonel Goodier should have gone to either Murry or Erwin to obtain authorization to investigate the charges against Cowan. The message was crystal clear: senior officers who hold command positions do not like surprises, especially embarrassing surprises. It was a message that every member of the court understood and agreed with. Lieutenant Colonel Goodier had surprised his commanding officer, General Murry, and that was a mistake. But Humphreys was about to surprise everyone, right up to President Woodrow Wilson. And that was a smart move.[14]

Humphreys requested that he be provided with all correspondence between Reber and Cowan. Geary strongly objected. Following a short recess, the court president ordered Geary to "take the necessary steps to have such correspondence by telegraphing for it." The lid to Pandora's box popped open.

The remaining testimony that day got bogged down in minutiae that had the effect of blurring the focus of the trail. While questioning Lt. Townsend Dodd, Geary introduced testimony that allowed Dodd to further castigate Cowan and raise issues of mismanagement by the Signal Corps.[15]

The questioning also exposed the conspirators' sloppy investigation. Nevertheless, when the court recessed at 1605, round one was over, and it had gone to Captain Geary. He had managed to create an image in the court members' minds of junior officers behaving disrespectfully toward their commanding officer and conspiring to discredit their commanding officer under the tutelage of the department judge advocate, who had a personal axe to grind with Cowan. Given that the court was composed almost entirely of field grade officers, Geary had a sympathetic audience.

But the audience outside the courtroom was anything but sympathetic, and the direction the trial was going was starting to look like a case of losing the battle but winning the war. The Wednesday, 20 October 1915 front-page headline in the *San Francisco Chronicle* was, "AVIATORS OF ARMY TELL OFFICERS OF PAY GRAFT," and below that came, "HEARING MAY LEAD TO INQUIRY BY CONGRESS." The following morning headline was, "AVIATOR CHIEF UNABLE TO FLY." Alerted by the leaked news story in May, the press was eager to follow up on the scandal and was predicting "a sweeping investigation of the Army aviation school" before the trial even started.

During the first two days of testimony the press focused on allegations that Cowan was a nagging officer who, together with Sam Reber, ran the school as though it were Reber's personal fiefdom. The press detailed the scandalous circumstances of Cowan's fraudulent flight pay and Patterson's equally fraudulent rating as a JMA. The coverage was exactly what Humphreys wanted, and the members of the court must have been aware of what was being said outside the courtroom. Though sensational in tone, there was much truth in the press reports. And the astounding fact was that the testimony the press reported came almost exclusively from the prosecution's witnesses.

There were two trials under way at 216 Pine Street. In one, a military court was hearing the case against Lieutenant Colonel Goodier. In the other, the public was hearing the original charges against Arthur Cowan, which now included the lurid details of Reber's involvement and Patterson's fraudulent rating. The charges against Goodier received scant attention from the press and the public, while the charges against Cowan became national headline news. The dissenters had believed that if they brought charges against Cowan, their cause to separate army aviation from the Signal Corps would attract attention in Washington. And they were right.

Round II, 26–27 October 1915

When the court reconvened on Tuesday, 26 October, Geary had already made his case against Goodier, at least enough to assure a conviction, and there was little doubt among the army observers in the courtroom that the court would find Goodier guilty.

Many felt that Geary should rest his case, but Geary wanted Goodier convicted on *all* counts and that meant carrying the prosecution forward.

He now knew that Humphreys would continue diverting attention from Goodier by trying the case against Cowan, Reber, and the Signal Corps' mismanagement of aviation. Humphreys's strategy sidetracked Geary's effort to keep the focus on Goodier by forcing Geary to defend Cowan—a man who was not on trial. Reluctantly, Geary called Cowan to the stand.[16]

Geary was on dangerous ground. Sitting on the other side of the rail was a courtroom filled with reporters whose interest was in selling newspapers. A story about a colorless army attorney who had not followed proper procedure was dull stuff compared to one about corruption and junior officers putting their careers on the line to expose it. But when Cowan told the court about the junior officers' separation movement, he was talking to senior army officers who took a dim view of junior officers who rocked the boat. The court members listened to Cowan, but Congress and the public read the papers.

Humphreys approached Cowan with a full understanding of the audience to which he was playing. The issue was Cowan's alleged unauthorized pilot training and his flight pay. Under Humphreys's closely focused questioning, Cowan admitted the decision to learn to fly had been his own, and Reber had supported the decisions with limitations. The tactic was very effective with the press, but it worked less well on the court. Nevertheless, the court members were practical men who did not tolerate questionable behavior, especially when it bordered on criminal fraud—or sounded like it did. Though Humphreys's approach was not entirely effective on the court, it did get their attention.

Humphreys now entered the Cowan-Reber correspondence into evidence. In the court of public opinion, the effect was devastating. In the media, the focus shifted from Cowan to Reber and by extension to the Signal Corps. As Humphreys read one letter after another to the court, Reber was shown to be an autocrat who was not above pulling the wool over his chief's eyes.

The following morning, 27 October 1915, Captain Geary struck back. He introduced the judge advocate general's opinion and told the court, "This decision, approved by the Secretary of War, shows that all the actions of Captain Cowan with respect to drawing this pay were legal and proper, and within the law." A heated argument ensued over whether the judge advocate general's legal opinion had the force of law or not, and Humphreys lost.[17] The court allowed the judge advocate general's legal opinion to be admitted. Geary then told the court that he was going to put Reber on the stand, and the court recessed until Reber could arrive from Washington.

Round two was over, and though there was some question about how the testimony had affected the court, there was no doubt about its impact on the press and the public. The headlines said it all. In the eyes of the press, Cowan and Reber were as guilty as sin, and Goodier was a victim of dirty politics. Humphreys was enormously pleased, and the War Department was already circling the wagons. Reber was right about some scalps being taken, but now the question was, Whose scalps?

Round III, 2–4 November 1915

By the time Lt. Col. Samuel Reber took the stand on 2 November 1915 his image was already badly tarnished, and his testimony did nothing to improve it. On the stand he came across as an officer who acted on the belief that his opinion had the weight of absolute authority, whose actions were unassailable, and for whom duplicity was routine. The press had already painted him as the puppeteer who pulled Cowan's strings, and his testimony confirmed that.

Captain Geary's direct examination was a disaster, because he reintroduced the letters that Humphreys had already placed in evidence and asked Reber to explain some of his statements from those letters. Reber's answers were long-winded and peppered with self-importance. One is astounded at the way Reber repeatedly admitted his complicity in Patterson's fraudulent rating and Cowan's fraudulent flight pay. One had the impression that Reber saw no wrong in how he ran the Aviation Section because things were done the way he wanted them done.

That attitude was clearly apparent when he told the court how he would answer anyone who asked about Patterson's inability to fly but was rated a military aviator. "If people on the outside would ask questions as to why he had not any hours in the air, why, it was none of their concern." In a letter dated 15 December 1914 he told Cowan that if people asked how often Patterson was flying, "they will not be answered."[18]

The explanations that Reber provided for some of his letters made sense. When he was asked about his statement, "The fewer things that are done in Washington during my absence, the better I am pleased," he answered, "You can readily appreciate when you go away and leave a man, who doesn't know anything at all about your work, in charge of your desk, the fewer things that he might do to disarrange your already existing program, the better it is for you when you come back."[19]

Reber told the court that matters such as Cowan's flight pay were "considered a question of routine administrative financial adjustment of accounts." But when Dodd and Taliaferro made Cowan's flight pay a question of criminal fraud, Reber was "naturally led to believe that these two officers were no longer of use to the aviation service. They certainly lost their usefulness if they conspired against their commanding officer." Humphreys objected on the grounds that Reber was "going into argument, and not a statement of facts."[20]

Reber, apparently believing that he was an officer of the court responded, "I withdraw that remark."[21]

It was also evident that Reber came to the court with an agenda, which was to aid the prosecution in convicting Lieutenant Colonel Goodier. When Geary asked Reber to explain the purport of his vow to "take one or two scalps,"[22] Reber said:

I found this state of affairs: The commanding officer at San Diego had been charged under the 61st Article of War with conduct unbecoming an officer and a gentleman, the gravest charge which can be brought against an officer. Knowing Captain Cowan's real personality and his service and knowing also that these charges had been drawn by a man of years of experience, versed in the law, and the legal adviser to the Department Commander, I could naturally infer that there must be some reason and some malice. I was further convinced, confirmed in this view of mine, when the consideration of certain actions was called into question. He said that he didn't care whether his actions were regular or not, he was going to force that son-of-a-bitch out of the service—referring to Cowan.[23]

Reber's duplicity was demonstrated in how he handled two personnel matters. The first example stemmed from General Scriven's plan to put Signal Corps officers in the aviation command slots. There was a possibility that Capt. George S. Gibbs, who was senior to Cowan, would replace Cowan under Scriven's plan. To prevent that, Reber planned to propose that officers in command of schools and squadrons be given the temporary rank of major. Geary asked Reber to explain that proposition, and Reber righteously told the court, "I felt that a man who did the work should get the appointment."[24]

But where were his lofty principals when he placed Patterson, an officer who could not fly, in command of the soon to be formed 1st Company, 2nd Aero Squadron? Questioned on that point, he told the court, "As far as ability was concerned, not only from the standpoint of command, but administrative ability, Captain Patterson was the man most qualified for that position." Many of the courtroom observers were quick to note that Capt. Townsend Dodd, a former military aviator and a junior military aviator since 18 July 1914, was not only a fully qualified pilot, but his captaincy predated Patterson's by two months. Reber never mentioned him.[25]

Despite the effect that Reber's testimony was having on the reporters and civilian observers, it did not damage the case against Goodier. The court certainly did not agree with Reber's attitude toward Cowan and Patterson's flight pay, and the members certainly did not approve of Patterson's fraudulent JMA rating. But they were all field grade officers who understood how to handle unruly subalterns.

The court reconvened at 1000 on 3 November, and Reber retook the stand. Geary quickly wrapped up his direct examination and turned over the witness to Humphreys for cross-examination. The cross-examination lasted only fifteen minutes and covered six points that left the spectators with the impression that Reber was manipulative, secretive, and dishonest. Reber stepped down from the stand and walked out of the room, followed by a horde of reporters.

The defense got off to a slow start with its first witness, Dodd. Through his testimony, Humphreys hoped to reinforce the previous testimony that Cowan mismanaged the school almost to the point of criminal negligence. Humphreys opened by asking Dodd about the dangerous "peculiarities" of the Curtiss JN-2 that the 1st Aero Squadron was flying at Brownsville. The basis for the questioning was that Cowan had in his possession a technical report detailing the airplane's faults but that it had been withheld from the pilots who were flying the plane. The testimony became a technical explanation of what causes a stall, which no one in the courtroom understood. Following a brief questioning by Brigadier General Sibert about wing design and angle of attack, the answer to which again no one in the room understood, Dodd was allowed to step down.[26]

The next defense witness, Col. James B. Erwin, the Western Department adjutant, retook the stand. The important part of his testimony for the defense came at the end of the questioning, when Colonel Erwin explained that there were circumstances in which an officer could "obtain information through interviews, and not by official communication," and added, "I know it to be the custom that the heads of departments would handle business in exactly the same way."[27]

The next defense witness, Ned Goodier, offered no testimony that materially aided the defense. Humphreys led him through a recitation of his aviation career, including two serious injury crashes. Humphreys apparently hoped to show that Goodier, who had been retired due to his injuries, was a victim of Cowan and Reber's dislike for him. He wanted the court to see Ned Goodier as an injured flier who would eventually recover and be capable of flying again. The problem with that plan was that Ned Goodier was still in terrible condition when he appeared in the courtroom. The court probably sympathized with him, but the man they saw on the stand was far from well, and there was nothing in his testimony to suggest that he had been a victim of "company politics." Geary did not cross-examine him.[28]

First Lt. Robert H. Willis, the officer who had run afoul of Cowan over his riding attire, followed Ned Goodier to the stand. One might say that Willis had a uniform problem, because when he took the stand, he was in civilian clothes, and his appearance drew an immediate reaction from Brigadier General Sibert, who demanded to know why Willis was out of uniform. Willis replied that when he left Brownsville his uniforms were en route from Fort Sill. No one thought to ask what happened to the uniform he was supposed to be wearing when he left Fort Sill for Brownsville. Needless to say, Willis did not impress the court.[29]

When the court reconvened on 4 November at 1000 the first witness was Lieutenant Colonel Goodier. The room was packed with reporters who were sure that the defendant would provide the crushing blow to the prosecution. Surely Humphreys would use his client to reveal even more slanderous details about the graft and corruption in army aviation. That revelation did not happen.

Goodier's testimony in response to Humphreys's questions was long-winded and boring, and offered nothing new. Goodier gave a lengthy description of his close relationship with Ned and described what he believed was negligence in the way the Signal Corps managed the army's aviation, using examples from Ned's time on aviation duty. The tactic misfired because it weakened his defense against the charge of not maintaining "the quality of impartiality."

When the court reconvened after lunch, Goodier ran into a major problem trying to explain why he had told Dodd, "I doubt the wisdom of presenting the charges to Foulois." Army protocol required Dodd and Taliaferro to at least discuss the issue with Foulois, because Foulois was the senior officer at the school after Cowan. Not doing so made it appear that Dodd and Taliaferro had gone behind the backs of their superior officers and made their undertaking look like a conspiracy. At least that is how the court saw it. And Goodier's recommendation to Dodd to bypass Foulois made it appear that Goodier was an active participant in the conspiracy.

The cross-examination was a disaster for Goodier, and it underscores why many attorneys urge their clients not to take the stand. Goodier undoubtedly believed strongly in the righteousness of his case, but from the beginning of the cross-examination until the end, Captain Geary took Goodier apart piece by piece. Geary's attack had three goals: to create the impression that Goodier was not as competent an attorney as was believed, to establish that Goodier had malice toward Cowan, and to show that his actions had been outside the chain of command and were improper.

The questioning started with a reading of Army Regulations paragraph 1269, which covered flight pay. Geary asked if the regulation entitled an officer to flying pay until he is relieved from aviation duty. The question demanded a yes or no answer. Instead, Goodier fell into a discourse filled with legal double talk and hairsplitting that did not answer the question. In fact, he sounded like a man who was deliberately evading the question.

Goodier responded to further questioning with nitpicky and long-winded answers that often had little to do with the question. His nonanswers may have been a good tactic from a lawyer's point of view, but they did not play well with the court, whose members wanted direct answers to what they thought were straightforward questions.

At one point, Goodier launched into an account of his having to repay an overpayment for a commutation of quarters. The digression gave Geary an unexpected opening, and the judge advocate used it with devastating efficiency. At the end of Goodier's digression, Geary asked, "The thing known in the United States Army as commutation of quarters, is that not an extra allowance and is it not prescribed by law?" Goodier dodged the question by saying, "I will have to consult the law before I know which." Geary's riposte was immediate and damaging. He asked, "You mean to say you have been a Department Judge Advocate and have been in the Army for a number of years, and you don't know whether or not commutation of quarters is an extra allowance?"[30] Goodier, who was becoming visibly irritated, resorted to stonewalling. Finally, after three painful hours, Goodier left the stand and the court adjourned.

Round three had ended with the prosecution clearly in the lead. But though it was clear that Geary had swayed the court to the prosecution's view, the press had an entirely different take on what had been said in the courtroom at 216 Pine Street. Regardless of how the court received the testimony, the press saw it as an open-and-shut case that the Signal Corps, represented by Cowan, Reber, and Scriven, was guilty of corruption, mismanagement, and a careless attitude toward the safety of the aviators. And it was going to get worse.

Round IV, 15–18 November 1915

First Lt. Edgar S. Gorrell took the stand at 1000 on Monday, 15 November. Humphreys had called him there to rebut Cowan and Reber's testimony that "Cowan was flying in a satisfactory manner." He also wanted to rebut Cowan's testimony that his "judgment in appointing Patterson a Junior Military Aviator was justified by the results." Reading from the records, Gorrell testified Cowan had flown a total of seventy-three minutes when Dodd and Taliaferro handed him the charges. The records were much less kind to Patterson, showing that he had been rated as a JMA after just fifty-four minutes in the air as a passenger.[31]

Geary did not cross-examine Gorrell, but he did recall Cowan to the stand to rebut earlier allegations that Cowan had withheld a report written by the navy's aeronautical engineer, Lt. Jerome Hunsaker, describing the JN-2's unsafe features.[32] Geary apparently had not done his homework before he questioned Cowan about the report. Geary asked him if, on reading the Hunsaker report, he had sent a telegram to Reber asking that the plane be withdrawn from service. Cowan told the court that he did not send a telegram. Geary asked him why he did not send the telegram, and Cowan answered, "In the first place, there is a tendency among younger officers to get rather panicky when questions of safety are brought out. In the second place, that equipment was not under my jurisdiction. I had nothing to do with the 1st Aero Squadron, and I did not feel that it was my business to interfere in any way with their work."[33]

The courtroom observers were astounded, shocked, and outraged. Here was a commanding officer who was not a qualified pilot, had almost no mechanical aptitude, and did not fully understand the technology of flight, disparaging pilots for being concerned about their safety. Even the court was taken back by Cowan's statement. Brigadier General Sibert asked why Cowan had not told Foulois about the Hunsaker report, since Foulois commanded the 1st Aero Squadron, which was using the JN-2s. Cowan told the court president, "I could hardly deal directly with Captain Foulois. I would have to send that information through the Chief Signal Officer. Captain Foulois was not under my command."[34]

Cowan stepped down and left the room, and both the prosecution and the defense told the court that they had no more testimony to offer. General Sibert adjourned the court at 1230, directing everyone to return to the courtroom on Thursday, 18 November, at 1000 for the closing arguments.

In the press the decision was all but in, and Lieutenant Colonel Goodier was as good as exonerated. But for a reporter on the *San Francisco Chronicle* the decision was not that certain. In a tone that indicated he had been listening to the questions General Sibert asked throughout the trial, the reporter wrote, "It is possible that Colonel Goodier may get a reprimand for preferring charges against Captain Cowan, and airing the troubles at the aviation school, without first consulting with General Murry, Department Commander."[35]

During the two days the court was adjourned, the press focused on Patterson's fraudulent JMA rating, reminding readers time and again that he had been in the air for only fifty-four minutes before he was awarded the rating. His automatic advancement in rank, coupled with increased pay that was compounded with 50 percent flight pay, and his reward with a coveted command at the expense of deserving pilots who could fly, became the trial's showcase scandal. Not even Cowan's flight pay could match Patterson's fraudulent rating for pure reader appeal. The fact that Patterson had just recently soloed did nothing to mitigate the scandal.

The defense presented its closing arguments in two parts with Captain Greer leading off. He presented a legal argument for acquittal that was at times strong but which also addressed issues not included in the three specifications and sometimes taken up out of order. Greer's arguments were strongest when he was attacking Reber, whose testimony he described as careless, malicious, and "flatly shown to be incorrect."[36]

William Humphreys rose to deliver his closing argument, telling the court, "I shall confine myself to a general sketch of the whole situation, commenting on such matters as seem pertinent." His "general sketch" took nearly an hour and a half to deliver, during which he pilloried Cowan, Patterson, and Reber unmercifully. The performance, aimed as much at the press as it was at the court, was emotionally powerful. And to be sure that every word was correctly recorded, he provided the court and the press with a typed copy of his argument.[37]

Showmanship, organization, and delivery made Humphreys a tough act to follow, but Captain Geary was up to the task. Geary's delivery was much less bombastic, much more directed at the issues before the court, and much shorter. From the moment he opened his closing arguments, Geary aimed his remarks directly at the values and priorities that each court member embraced. His remarks were narrowly focused on the issues contained in the three specifications, and he closed his argument by telling the court, "If ever a man was maligned and misrepresented, that man was Captain Cowan."[38]

It was over, and all that remained was for the court to reach a verdict and hand down a sentence. The court retired to consider a verdict at 1520 and returned ninety minutes later. But when the court reconvened at 1650, the verdict was sealed.

The press, with nothing specific to report, resorted to citing legal experts, headquarters officers, and anyone else who had an opinion about what the verdict probably was. The consensus was that Goodier was innocent, and the headlines reflected the conventional

wisdom of the many experts. In America, three things make news—
sex, scandal, and violence. And it has always been that way. The
Goodier court-martial, especially Humphreys's closing argument,
had provided the press with more scandalous material than they
could use, and the press made the most of it. Curiously, the order
of attack in the press was Reber, then Patterson, and then Cowan,
with Reber getting the most ink and taking the hardest beating.

Brigadier General Sibert and Captain Geary signed the verdict,
which was handwritten on two sheets of legal-size paper. The court
found Lieutenant Colonel Goodier guilty on all three specifications but found him not guilty of specific parts within each specification and sentenced him to be reprimanded. The sealed verdict
went to the judge advocate general, who recommended that the
sentence be "carried into execution." Attached to the memorandum was a prepared two-page executive order for President Woodrow Wilson's signature.

18

The Garlington Board and the Kennedy Committee, 1916

Goodier had been convicted, but the trial had gotten the desired result of attracting congressional attention to the separation movement. During the five months following the trial, the future of army aviation was a hot topic in Washington. On 5 January 1916 Senator Joseph T. Robinson introduced Senate Resolution 65, which called for an investigation of the Aviation Section of the Signal Corps.

The Goodier court-martial had ended at the same time the Preparedness Movement was gaining strength. This organized effort was wrapped up in the national debate between people who wanted to keep America out of the war in Europe and those who believed we should intervene on behalf of the British and French. And there were supporters of the Preparedness Movement who had their own agendas, notably the industrialists who saw the prospects of major government contracts, and the Aero Club of America. Both of those special interest groups were powerful backers of building a bigger, more effective air service, which for the ACA included a major expansion of National Guard aviation.

While the Preparedness Movement gathered strength and captured headlines from January to June 1916, the army took action to deal with the scandal that the Goodier trial had made public. In the short term, the army's move to lay the Goodier trial scandal to rest meant more trouble for Scriven, Reber, and Cowan. The long-term effects, which would be felt after the 1916 National Defense

Act became law, spelled more trouble for the Signal Corps. The army started its action on 1 January 1916.

On that date, Col. David C. Shanks made the annual inspector general's visit to the school at North Island. His report reflected many of the problems that had come out during the trial. Among the problems he cited was the lack of a properly equipped aviation center "where men and apparatus can be properly cared for and where flying instruction can be carried on under favorable conditions. He also noted a shortage of airplanes and "everything pertaining to them." He wrote that there was a need for stronger administration of the aviation school and an improvement of discipline in the Aviation Section. Closely related to discipline was the fact that there was an "unbalance as to grades" among the pilots, adding that the problem was exacerbated by the fact that they were "young in years and service." He also said that the pilots were not well grounded in the customs of the service and the duties of an officer. But his sharpest criticisms were directed at the behavior and practices of the men themselves, including Reber and Cowan.

Without naming anyone, he criticized those who drew flight pay "for periods of more or less length while making no flights during those periods." But he did name those who carried on "improper correspondence concerning official matters through the medium of so-called personal letters." Here he named the culprits whose correspondence was "in violation of Army Regulations" and who "made disrespectful references to other officers." He named Reber, Cowan, Kirtland, Dodd, and Jones. He was particularly harsh about the pilots' attempt to remove aviation from the Signal Corps and "form a new organization." That was the work of "officers who have therein resorted to unmilitary, insubordinate, and disloyal acts to further their own ambition to form a new and independent organization."[1]

Brigadier General Scriven wrote his endorsement to the report on 9 February. He took note of the administrative problems and said that while some were already being worked on, implementing some of the other changes would take more money than was currently available. He enthusiastically agreed with Colonel Shanks's

The Garlington Board

description of the pilots. The CSO described the separation effort as a "selfish, unscrupulous, drive for personal aggrandizement on the part of the officers." He accused the officers of having "tainted and obstructed many efforts to obtain beneficial changes in conditions in the Army." He even harked back to the August 1913 congressional hearings in connection with H5304, describing Beck's testimony as "unmilitary utterances," and attributed the officers' behavior to "underlying jealousies and personal ambitions."

He recommended that the only action necessary, based on the serious deficiencies that Colonel Shanks had described, was simply that the "administration of the Aviation Section be supported by the War department."

On 9 February Brigadier General Scriven probably thought he had the situation well in hand. Colonel Shanks had been particularly harsh with regard to the pilots, and the other matters, such as unlawful flight pay and private correspondence, could be easily handled within the office of the chief signal officer. To ensure that the pilots, and not the administrators, shouldered the blame, Scriven lauded Cowan and Reber for their selfless efforts to develop military aviation. He said, "That so much progress had been made has been due in great part to the energy and ability of Lieutenant Colonel Reber and Captain Cowan." He then recommended that Cowan be sent to Manila to relieve Patterson and take command of the 1st Company, 2nd Aero Squadron. Reber was to be retained as head of aviation and to additionally assume command of the school at San Diego. He sent his endorsement up the line to the adjutant general.[2]

Ten days later, Senator Joseph T. Robinson introduced Senate Joint Resolution 65, calling for a congressional investigation of the Aviation Section. In his Senate report, Robinson described the Aviation Section as "hopelessly inefficient" and charged that Scriven, Reber, and Cowan concealed that fact from the War Department and Congress. The senator pointed to the fact that since 1909 only twenty-four officers had qualified as military aviators and few of them had ever done any "military work or even seen from an aeroplane a field gun fired." Only one or two of the pilots had flown a bomb-equipped airplane, and the army still did not have any bombs, or a bomb-dropping device, and had no way of mounting a gun in an airplane.

Robinson denounced the poor quality of the airplanes that the Signal Corps had bought over the years, citing the high percentage of deaths, just under half of which had occurred in a ten-month period. He ascribed the death rate to the fact that the aviators had to fly "antiquated biplanes known to be defective and dangerous." He charged that incompetence and indifference had added to the "dangers inherent in aviation" that resulted from unskilled, unscientific, negligent, and corrupt control." The senator then entered into the record copies of letters between Reber and Cowan. Most of the letters had been made public during the trial, but that did not lessen their impact.[3]

On 15 February, three days before Senator Robinson introduced his resolution for a congressional investigation of the Aviation Section, the adjutant general, at the direction of the secretary of war, formed a board of officers consisting of Brig. Gen. Ernest A. Garlington, inspector general of the army; Brig. Gen. Montgomery M. Macomb, chief of the War College; and Brig. Gen. Henry P. McCain, adjutant general of the army. The board, known as the Garlington Board, was directed to "examine into the conditions respecting the administration of the Aviation Section of the Signal Corps, with special reference to the disclosures of the record of the trial of Lieutenant Colonel Lewis E. Goodier." The board was empowered to "call for additional papers and take additional testimony." The secretary of war directed that the board "report its recommendations as to the further action to be taken by the War Department."[4]

The Garlington Board met from 17 February to 29 March 1916, during which time the three members spent twelve days reading reams of Signal Corps records. On 3 March the board called Brigadier General Scriven.[5] During his testimony Scriven told them he exercised "a very slight supervision" over Reber or the Aviation Section. He described himself as the "supervisory head, and tended to the signing of papers, handling money, and so on." He told the board that Reber had an absolutely free hand and "rarely consulted me about details" and that he (Scriven) looked upon the Aviation Section as an "independent section under Reber's charge." He allowed Reber to run the Aviation Section "as he saw fit." The rest of his testimony underscored his lax supervisory style, giving one the impression that Scriven had little interest in the Aviation Section.

Reber testified the following day, and he was as arrogant before the Garlington Board as he was during the Goodier trial. When asked if he was aware that "seventy-one percent of the fatal accidents occurred in Wright C machines," he answered that he did not think that was true. When a member of the board reminded him that a board of experienced pilots had determined that the Wright Model C had an "inherent tendency" to nose down on the application of power, he replied, "I do not concur with the board."

He was equally arrogant when being grilled about Cowan's flight pay, Patterson's fraudulent JMA rating, and Ned Goodier's relief from aviation. Reber told the board that it was his opinion that after a man made his first flight, he was entitled to flight pay even if he did not fly again. A board member asked, "Do you mean that a man can go on duty and fly for ten minutes and draw flight pay until he is relieved?" Reber answered, "I would say so, until he is relieved." He admitted that Patterson was not actually qualified to be rated a JMA, had never taken the JMA qualification test, and had never been before a board. But he defended the fraudulent rating, giving his opinion that the detail was legal. He held that opinion even after the board members had read the army regulations to him. It was apparent to the board that Reber's opinion was all that mattered to him.

The board read the letter that Reber had written to Cowan on 9 December 1914, dealing with his intent to have Ned Goodier relieved from aviation. In the letter Reber wrote that he was going to urge the doctors to recommend Ned Goodier's relief. Asked why he did not relieve Ned Goodier himself, Reber answered, "If a man is relieved on account of physical disability, it isn't nearly as much against his record as if relief came from this office."

It was obvious to the board that Reber ran the Aviation Section as he saw fit to do, rarely consulting Scriven about his decisions, withholding information from the cso, and frequently bypassing his commanding officer when dealing with higher authority. He actively worked to thwart Scriven's plan to bring other Signal Corps officers into the Aviation Section and, in one case, to prevent Cowan from being replaced as the school commandant. In a letter to Cowan, Reber assured him, "I will take care of your interest and see that you remain in command of the school." He explained his actions to the board, saying, "I felt that Captain Cowan ought not to be displaced in command of the school."

In its conclusions, the Garlington Board found Brigadier General Scriven censurable for "very slight supervision," culpable in Cowan's unlawful flight pay and Patterson's fraudulent JMA rating. The board recommended that Scriven be censured.

The board found that Lieutenant Colonel Reber was censurable for failing to report to the cso an instance in which Lieutenant Carberry and his enlisted subordinates failed in their assigned duty. Reber was found culpable for "failing to inform himself of the actual condition of the airplanes in use at the Signal Corps Aviation School" and in failing to tell the cso that Patterson's fraudulent JMA rating "was not based upon an accurate statement of fact under the law." The board wrote that in failing to keep Scriven fully informed, Reber had "failed in his manifest duty." Turning to the correspondence that Reber carried on with Cowan, the board said that he "had no proper sense of proportion and disregarded the fundamental rules that govern written intercourse concerning official matters between officers of the Army." But the hardest blow came when the board determined that "Lt. Col. Samuel S. Reber has not the qualifications best suited to inaugurate and develop the aeronautical service of the U.S. Army." The board recommended that he be relieved.

The board found that Cowan and Patterson had unlawfully drawn flight pay when in fact they were not flying. They also found that Foulois had drawn flight pay unlawfully but did not hold any of them censurable, blamable, or culpable for that. They did, however, recommend that they be made to return the money and that Patterson be relieved from aviation duty. The board did determine that Cowan's indiscretions, unlawful drawing of flight pay, and his administration of the flight school "indicate that he does not possess strength of purpose and adequate professional equipment for the duty of commandant of the Signal Corps Aviation School." They recommended that he be relieved.

In the final conclusion, the board wrote, "Notwithstanding the deficiencies and irregularities in administration . . . considerable progress has been accomplished since April 1913 in training pilots." But the board added, "There has been little progress in training observers or in the aeronautical art in the way of improved engine and a satisfactory type of military aeroplane."[6]

Three weeks before the Garlington Board completed its investigation, an international crisis developed in Columbus, New Mexico, that brought the United States and Mexico to the brink of war and underscored the sorry shape of army aviation. In the early morning hours of 9 March 1916, Francisco "Poncho" Villa and about five hundred men raided the town of Columbus and attacked Camp Furlong, headquarters of the 13th Cavalry. During the raid, Villa's men killed ten soldiers and eight civilians, burned some buildings, and stole horses and a small amount of money.

Taken out of context, Villa's raid was nothing more than a bandit attack. In fact, it was Villa's strategic maneuver to get the United States to send troops into Mexico. Villa, who was fighting against the current Mexican president, Venustiano Carranza, wanted to engineer an armed confrontation between Carranza's soldiers and U.S. troops, and his plan worked. On 14 March 1916 Brig. Gen. John J. Pershing left Columbus with the Punitive Expedition Forces to pursue Villa in Mexico.

The deployment of the 1st Aero Squadron was the first time that the War Department had sent a full squadron to operate with an expedition in the field. Much has been written about the hardships and problems that the 1st Aero Squadron faced during its operations from 15 March to 15 August 1916. But more important was the experience that the officers and men of the 1st Aero Squadron gained under actual field conditions.

Those experiences revealed that little had changed since the

Goodier trial. The airplanes the 1st Aero Squadron was flying were underpowered, poorly designed, and shoddily constructed. They were utterly unsuited for field service, a condition that the pilots under Foulois attributed to the nonflying Signal Corps officers, who at the time were Scriven, Reber, and Cowan. The aviators' solution was to remove aviation from the Signal Corps, and now Foulois was in agreement with the dissidents.

The pilots' poor opinions of their Signal Corps leaders and of their airplanes created a tempest in the War Department when those opinions appeared in the nation's newspapers in April 1916. It looked for a short time that there would be another Garlington Board–type investigation with the 1st Aero squadron pilots the focus of the inquiry. In fact, the whole affair passed quickly, and the War Department took no action against Foulois and his men. But the episode was a public reminder that conditions in the Aviation Section had not improved, and the separation issue was very much alive.

On 3 April 1916 the secretary of war, Newton D. Baker, censured Scriven and Reber. The adjutant general relieved Reber and recalled Col. George S. Squier from England to replace him. In the interim, Capt. William "Billy" Mitchell became the acting chief of the Aeronautical Division, which put him in charge of the Aviation Section. On the same day, the adjutant general relieved Cowan and appointed Col. William A. Glassford to command the aviation school. The public announcement of the shakeup appeared in the nation's newspapers on 18 April.

The announcement closed the Goodier affair. Brig. Gen. Enoch A. Crowder's smoke-and-mirrors justification for Cowan's unlawful flight pay and Patterson's fraudulent JMA rating was effectively squashed, and the North Island dissidents were vindicated. But their goal of establishing an independent air force was not realized, nor was their goal of getting Congress involved. They had gotten the attention of the Congress, but on 4 May 1916, the resolution to investigate the Aviation Section was passed over, and nothing more was heard of it.

Even though Congress had stepped back from the fray, the dissidents' hopes were raised when Secretary of War Baker directed four officers to convene a committee on 24 April to "immediately take up and complete a thorough study of the present organization, methods of administration, etc., of the Aviation Section of the Signal Corps and make specific recommendations as to any reorganization and changes in methods which are desirable."[7]

The separation movement that Paul Beck started in 1912 with his *Infantry Journal* article was definitely alive, and the revelations that came out of the Goodier trial had brought the issue into the open. But the secretary of war was not yet ready to create a separate air arm. The reason was that there were no field or general grade officers qualified to command and administer an air corps. More time for development was needed, and for that reason Baker's directions to what became known as the Kennedy Committee were, "The study will be based on the assumption of the retention of the Aviation Section in the Signal Corps."

The four general staff officers who made up the committee were Col. Chase W. Kennedy, Maj. P. D. Lochridge, Maj. Paul M. Palmer, and Capt. Dan T. Moore. The Kennedy Committee sat from 24 April to 30 June 1916, and during that time they "examined and considered official reports regarding military aviation in the present war and consulted military and civilian experts." The principal players in the Goodier affair and Benjamin Foulois, who now supported separation, were among the experts who testified before the committee. This was the last time that the dissidents from Texas City and North Island would play a direct role in separating aviation from the Signal Corps.

The CSO immediately assigned Tom Milling to represent the Signal Corps as a consulting member of the committee, a choice that Foulois did not like. Foulois and the 1st Aero Squadron were still with the Punitive Expedition, where the squadron had spent six weeks operating under harsh field conditions with inadequate airplanes and a critical shortage of supplies. By 20 April all of the original Curtiss planes that the squadron had taken to the border were gone. At that time, Foulois and the pilots of the 1st Aero Squadron were the only aviators in the army who had any field service experience, and Foulois felt strongly that he and his pilots were the only ones qualified to discuss the needs of an aviation unit on field service.

On 30 April Foulois wrote a personal letter to committee member Major Palmer. Foulois opened his letter with three points that he believed the committee needed to know. The first point was that of the twenty-three aviators then on duty, only two—Milling and Patterson—favored keeping aviation in the Signal Corps. Of the twenty-one aviators who favored separation, "not one of them was present in Washington to submit or explain their views." His third point was that there was no officer on duty in Washington "who has had one single day on active field duty with aeroplanes or an aero squadron." And then he turned to Milling.

> I have also learned that Lieutenant Milling is to act in an advisory capacity to your committee. I have a very high regard for many of Lieutenant Milling's views as regard the technical side of aviation, but he has no active field service with aeroplanes or an aero squadron; nor has he had the hard, practical experience that the officers of the First Aero Squadron have had in connection with the innumerable details of building up, organizing, and maintaining a field flying unit. His entire aviation service has been limited almost entirely to the technical side of aviation and not to the military side. His views on questions of organization or reorganization cannot be based on practical experience. From a technical point of view there are several aviators on duty with my command equally as efficient. From a military standpoint, the majority of the military aviators in my command are superior to him in the knowledge of the needs of field flying units, particularly as regards questions of equipment, organization, and maintenance of field units for field service.[8]

Foulois correctly believed that one of his officers should either be on the committee or appear before the committee as an expert.

Major Palmer replied that the committee had already interviewed Virginius Clark, Byron Jones, and Tom Milling, who comprised the Aviation Section's Technical Aero Advisory and Inspection

Board. Clark and Jones were solidly in the separation camp and had already written to Foulois, telling him to review and comment on their detailed proposal for an aviation organization that was separate from the Signal Corps. In closing, Palmer told Foulois, "While there are many very powerful arguments for a separate Aviation Corps, it may not be the policy of the War Department to recommend such a separation at this time. In that event, it is important to get as good an organization as you can under the circumstances. In order to meet this possible contingency, it would be well for you also to state what changes in organization there should be, assuming that for the present the Aviation Section is to remain under control of the Signal Corps."[9]

By the time Palmer's reply reached Foulois, the latter had already convened a board made up of the pilots who were in the 1st Aero squadron at Columbus, New Mexico. On 2 May they submitted a detailed reply to the recommendations that Clark and Jones had sent to the 1st Aero Squadron, which included a draft proposal for legislation establishing a separate flying corps.[10] Foulois sent Herbert Dargue to Washington with the reply, and as the 1st Aero Squadron's personal representative to the board.

It is evident from reading the Kennedy report that the twenty-three pilots who favored separation were in touch with one another. On 26 May Roy Kirtland, who was stationed at Douglas, Arizona, with the 22nd Infantry, wrote to the committee. He included a proposal for a tactical organization and a legislative bill for a separate aviation corps. Though much less detailed than what had already been produced, Kirtland's proposals were very similar. He assured the committee, "The officers now flying are almost unanimously in favor of the organization as set forth herein, and its provisions have come from the practical work of the flyers in the field and garrison."[11]

The committee listened to or corresponded with several civilian experts, including representatives of the National Advisory Committee for Aeronautics, the ACA, the Aeronautical Engineers Society, and the Aeronautical Society of America. They also heard from the CSO and received reports on military aviation in Britain,

France, and Germany from the air attachés in the U.S. embassies. But Clark, Jones, Milling, and the pilots of the 1st Aero Squadron clearly dominated the committee's time.

During the time that the Kennedy Committee was in session, the National Defense Act of 1916 was moving through Congress on the road to acceptance. The committee shared the aviation provision with the four pilots who were in Washington—Clark, Dargue, Jones, and Milling. The committee asked them for their opinions and for any suggested changes they might suggest. During the session on 23 May, during which Dargue, Jones, and Milling argued their case, Milling had shifted to the separation viewpoint. The three of them made so many suggestions for changes that committee member Capt. Dan Moore said, "Your criticism of this bill comes back to the fact that you would sooner have the bill that you propose to adopt in place of this one. I mean you are going through this bill paragraph by paragraph and changing it so as to make it conform to the bill that you have already drawn up and submitted to us."[12]

The part of the impending legislation that they did not like was that aviation remained under the Signal Corps. That status could not be changed, but Dargue argued that "since it seems evident that a separation of the Aviation Section from the Signal Corps is bound to come, it seems quite in place at this time to suggest a law which will separate aviation from the Signal Corps on some future date." He told the four committee members that "it would be the desire of all the flyers, and I include Lieutenant Milling in this, to simply affix to this bill . . . a clause setting the date for separation." He believed that separation could occur "not more than six or eight months from the passage of the bill."[13]

By 31 May the committee had arrived at the conclusion that establishing a "new and separate arm of the service" was needed to fully develop an effective air arm. On that date, the committee asked the chief of staff for direction on how to proceed, inasmuch as their findings were not in accord with the directive that they proceed under the assumption aviation would remain under the Signal Corps. On 3 June Maj. Gen. Tasker Bliss, assistant chief of staff, gave his opinion to the chief of staff, Maj. Gen Hugh L.

Scott. He wrote, "I see no reason why, as a committee of the General Staff, it should not make its recommendation to that effect to the Chief of Staff."

On 3 June the National Defense Act of 1916 became law and increased the number of officers in the Aviation Section from sixty to 148, the increase was to be made in increments over the next five years, with an immediate increase of seventeen officers. The act also increased opportunities for promotion, though none happened immediately. But the real benefit with regard to expansion was the creation of an Officers' Reserve Corps and an Enlisted Reserve Corps.[14] But army aviation was still part of the Signal Corps.

19

Separation Achieved, 1917–1918

The total separation of army aviation from Signal Corps control grew out of the aircraft production scandal that began developing in November 1917 and erupted into a full-scale witch hunt in the spring of 1918. Like most scandals, there was more hyperbole and hysteria than solid facts. The basic problem was that Americans, from the president down, expected too much from America's infant aviation industry, and when it failed to deliver on the civilian leadership's overzealous promises of mass-produced airplanes, the public, the press, and politicians demanded someone's head.

The United States' entry into the war created an immediate demand for thousands of airplanes, but there were only twelve companies that had produced even ten airplanes a year. What there was of the American aircraft industry was a few piecework shops that barely survived from year to year, because there had been no meaningful civilian market for airplanes and virtually no government orders. Without guaranteed government orders for substantial numbers of airplanes, the few American manufacturers had been unwilling to make large prewar capital investments to expand their facilities and preorder materials.

Another factor was that airplanes were hand-built by craftsmen skilled in woodworking, especially cabinetmakers, which meant that airplane manufacturing did not lend itself to the production-line methods associated with the mass production of cars. Equally important, the aircraft industry lacked standardization of basic materials used in aircraft production, such as fasteners, engine parts, and metal fittings. An even more serious hindrance was that most of the important aircraft patents were held by the Wrights and Curtiss, and until a cross-licensing agreement could be reached, there could be no quantity production of airplanes. A cross-licensing agreement was not reached until July 1917.

When the U.S. government began placing large wartime contracts in July 1917, after the Aircraft Manufacturers Association had brokered a patent agreement, the manufacturers undertook a rapid expansion program. But the other problems remained in place and new problems were added. The aircraft industry largely met the demand for building training planes, but its failure to produce warplanes was almost complete.

Since all of the warplanes that American companies were asked to build were based on foreign designs, time was lost converting metric measurements and specifications, a task made more difficult by the lack of standardization in the industry. Time was also needed to redraw all the foreign drawings to conform to American manufacturing practices, and more time was needed to make tools, dies, and jigs. Another major problem with regard to building the foreign-designed airplanes was the frequent cancelation of orders and the substitution of new orders requiring new drawings, tools, dies, and jigs.

But the aircraft industry was not entirely responsible for the production shortfalls and delays. Bearing the greatest burden were the president's civilian appointees to the Aircraft Production Board and the Signal Corps' Engineering Division, the two agencies making the day-to-day production decisions. But there were no aviation industry people on that board or in that division. The majority of the top positions were held by men from the automobile industry who had little or no understanding of airplane manufacturing. The chairman of the Aircraft Production Board, Howard Coffin, had been the vice president of Hudson Motor Company before the war, and Edward Deeds, who headed the Signal Corps Equipment Division, was the founder of Delco.

A valid criticism is that the automobile men were ignorant of what was required in an aviation program. An example is a conversation that Hap Arnold had with Howard Coffin. Coffin told Arnold that forty thousand airplanes were on order, causing Arnold to ask how many spare parts were on order. Coffin replied by asking, "What do you need spare parts for?"—apparently unaware of the critical importance of spare parts in aviation.[1]

The automobile men did much better with respect to engine design and manufacturing, except they failed to recognize that the horsepower available in existing American-built engines was too low for military airplanes. The problem stemmed not so much from incompetence as it did from inexperience. In fact, the single most significant reason for the apparent failure of America's aircraft production program was inexperience at all levels.

Inexperience was a major cause of errors in planning, organization, and direction of effort. Inexperience also played a major role on the shop floor, where men from the automobile industry were adapting to the manufacture of aircraft engines, air frames, and parts. Inexperience also featured in the necessity, caused by rapid expansion, of hiring thousands of inexperienced laborers to fill jobs requiring precision work skills. Even before 6 April 1917, when the United States declared war on Germany, there was a severe shortage of tool-and-die makers and a shortage of tool room space nationwide. The problem got worse as the few tool-and-die makers were drafted into the army.[2]

The absence of a single command authority to direct the aviation program resulted in lack of coordination and uniform direction. The civilian administration that managed the aircraft production program was not efficiently organized to handle the job, working through committees rather than having one man in charge. During the congressional hearings in June 1918, the manufacturers were unanimous in denouncing "too many experts" whose frequent changes caused delays. Henry Ford said the problems encountered in getting the Liberty Engine into production resulted from "one committee after another trying to produce improvements in it." There was a single overall plan, but the daily coordination of that plan was absent.[3]

Bad decisions and outright blunders were frequent, though probably to be expected, given the newness, size, and complexity of the undertaking. There was no institutional memory or knowledge even for the building of training airplanes. And no one in the Signal Corps, the civilian administration, or among the manufacturers had any knowledge of what the aviation requirements for modern war were. No one knew the requirements for airplanes, engines, instruments, ordnance, or armament. No American-built airplane had ever carried a machine gun or been equipped with any but the simplest instruments. In fact, very few American airmen had ever seen a warplane.[4]

Many of the most vexing problems that caused delays had to do with the day-to-day minutiae of such a huge production program. One of the most vexing was the inherent army bureaucracy and red tape, as illustrated by a single example having to do with a requisition for ninety-seven spare parts, specifically, thrust bearings. The requisition was created in the Construction Division on 3 December 1917. From there it went to the Air Division, where the requisition was approved and forwarded to the Supply Division for another rubber stamp and then on to the Equipment Division, where it arrived on 11 December. From there the requisition passed through eight more offices before contracts were issued for the thrust bearings, and the individual orders were placed. By 24 January 1918, fifty-two days after the requisition was initially submitted, only six thrust bearings had been shipped. The rest of the items on order were still waiting on the acceptance of bids.[5]

Another bottleneck was the distribution of drawings and blueprints to the manufacturers. All the design work and drawings were done in the Equipment Division and then sent to the manufacturers, but due to a shortage of draftsmen there was an ongoing backlog of drawings to be made. The result was the frequent complaint from manufacturers that they were idle because drawings had not been provided.

The American Expeditionary Forces (AEF) played a role in that delay too. It was the responsibility of the AEF to send complete specifications and drawings for every foreign-built airplane they sent to the United States to be copied and put into production. But since such coordination rarely happened, much time was lost in waiting to convert European designs to American specifications.

Two parallel factors laid the foundation for the scandal that abruptly erupted in the spring of 1918. The first was that despite the aviation industry's weakness, the U.S. government adopted an unrealistic aircraft production program. The reason was an eagerness to demonstrate to the Allies that American industry was capable of meeting their demands for war material. The other factor was that Howard Coffin had overly optimistic production expectations for aviation based on the capabilities of the automobile industry.

On 29 March 1917 Dr. Charles D. Walcott, chairman of the National Advisory Committee for Aeronautics, wrote to the secretaries of war and the navy and to the Council of National Defense, telling them that "at present the industry may be divided into two parts, the Curtiss Aeroplane and Motor Corporation and the others." At that time only twelve companies were capable of government work, and except for Curtiss, most of them had produced fewer than ten planes a year.[6]

Following the declaration of war, the government's plan called for production of 3,500 training planes to be delivered by 31 December 1917, a goal that the Aircraft Manufacturers Association felt the airplane manufacturers could meet. But even that modest goal was unattainable, as shown by the fact that the army had placed orders for only 336 airplanes from nine factories in October 1916, but only sixty-four had been delivered by 6 April 1917, six months later.[7]

On 26 May 1917 a telegram from the French premier, Alexandre Ribot, arrived at the White House. The French wanted the United States to have 4,500 planes, complete with personnel, spare parts, and materials, in France by the spring of 1918. In addition, they wanted the American airplane manufacturers to immediately start production of 2,000 planes and 2,000 engines per month, and they wanted 16,500 planes and 30,000 engines of all types

Separation Achieved

produced during the first six months of 1918. The numbers were beyond reach, but without hesitation the government adopted the French figures as the production goal for the American aviation industry. That is where the trouble started.

Howard Coffin led a well-coordinated and tightly focused public relations campaign to get Congress to appropriate $640 million for aviation. The campaign was so successful that he was able to steamroller the legislation through both houses in just over seven weeks. During his campaign he, and those he worked with, made exaggerated claims that appealed to American nationalism, among them the promise to "secure to the Allies next year the permanent supremacy of the air and with that we hope to become an immediate deciding factor in ending the war." Brigadier General Squier seconded him when he told reporters, "There is no reason why we should not be able to produce in a comparatively short space of time an absolutely overwhelming aerial fleet."[8]

The most undeliverable promise was Coffin's assurance that American airplanes would "sweep the Germans from the sky, blind the Prussian cannons, and the time will be ripe to release an enormous number of flying fighters to raid and destroy military camps, ammunition depots, military establishments of all kinds." Commenting on a dispatch reportedly received from France on 14 June that the Germans would add 3,500 planes to the front by the spring of 1918, Coffin said, "Our plan contemplates nothing less than driving German fliers out of the air and maintaining a constant raiding patrol over the territory for fifty miles back of the fighting lines."[9]

It became quickly evident to those inside the aviation industry, as well as to the members of the Aircraft Production Board and the Signal Corps Equipment Division, that the dreamed-of production figures were a fantasy and that reality would be only a fraction of those numbers. Production delays caused by the problems already described started on the first day, and the shortfall in production steadily grew. Despite the airplane manufacturers' obvious shortcomings, the men running the program continued to put out glowing reports of production successes. Nevertheless, by December 1917 clues that things were not going as claimed began appearing in the press.

It was inevitable that revelation of the shortfalls in production, in light of the grand promises, would cause a hostile public reaction. But that reaction, and the ensuing scandal, would not have been so fierce had the aircraft production program's organization not lent itself to suspicion of fraud and corruption.

The Aircraft Production Board, which became the Aircraft Board on 1 October 1917, was at the heart of the perceived scandal, because all the members were associated with the automobile industry. Two of them, Coffin and Deeds, held the top positions, Coffin as chairman of the Aircraft Board and Deeds as chief of the Signal Corps Equipment Division. The Aircraft Board made recommendations for production to the Signal Corps, and the Signal Corps placed the production orders, which meant that Coffin and Deeds were the principal players in the arrangement. Both were Dayton businessmen, and the fact that the automotive industry received the lion's share of the contracts was cause for suspicion, especially when a large percentage of the contracts went to automotive interests in and around Dayton. Dayton-Wright Airplane Company, a new concern that Deeds had founded and incorporated on 9 April 1917, alone received a contract for four thousand DH4s.

The makeup of the Signal Corps Equipment Division, which was responsible for aircraft procurement, also lent itself to suspicion. The division chief was Edward Deeds; the chief of engine production was Harold H. Emmons, an attorney and the secretary and treasurer of the Regal Motor Company since May 1913; the chief of instrument production was Leonard S. Horner, of the Acme Wire Company; the chief of inspection was George W. Mixter, vice president of John Deere; the chief of airplane production was Harry L. Shepler, product manager for Willys Overland; and the chief of engine design was J. G. Vincent, a Packard Motor Car Company vice president and one of the Liberty Engine designers. His assistant was Sidney D. Waldon, vice president and general manager of Packard Motor Car Company.

Unfulfilled promises and expectations, combined with an apparently cozy relationship between the Aircraft Board and the Equipment Division, was enough to create a scandal, real or imagined.

Separation Achieved

But one man, Gutzon Borglum, turned the scandal into a witch hunt and cast Col. Edward Deeds as the scandal's archvillain. Borglum was a famous sculptor who had many well-placed friends and acquaintances, among them Wilbur Wright and President Wilson. Even without his connections, his name alone would open many doors. Borglum had been an ACA member since 1906 and had represented the club at the army acceptance trials for the Wright airplane in 1908. Though he never flew, and his technical knowledge about airplanes was sketchy, he styled himself an expert on flying and all aviation matters.[10]

He had tried designing propellers and even considered opening a propeller factory. He also drew fanciful designs for airplanes and once sent a letter to the Smithsonian explaining why airplanes should be shaped like fish. His designs were based on his artistic talent rather than his technical knowledge. In September 1917 he told Brigadier General Squier that he had invented and successfully tested an "air brake" that could be attached to any airplane. He described the device as a "speed regulator," which also "acted as a stabilizer" and accomplished the "long coveted feat of hovering." He also told the CSO that he could build eighty "tube airplanes" capable of remaining aloft for one thousand hours and could deliver them in six months.[11]

For reasons unknown, Borglum visited the Dayton-Wright plant in November 1917, but the visit might have been maliciously motivated. Howard Coffin had been a member of a committee that in 1912 commissioned Borglum to create a memorial to the Wright brothers on Huffman Prairie, near Dayton. The 1913 Dayton flood canceled the project, and Borglum was only partially paid. Whatever his reason for being in Dayton, on 22 November Borglum wrote a letter to Joseph P. Tumulty, President Wilson's secretary, about corruption and graft in the aircraft production program. Tumulty passed the letter on to the president, who responded on 5 December, asking Borglum for more details.[12]

Deeds and Charles F. Kettering, inventor of the electric starter, founded Dayton Engineering Laboratories (Delco) in 1909. In 1915 United Motors bought Delco, paying with stock and cash. Both

Deeds and Kettering held stock in United Motors, and Kettering became the president of Delco. That same year, Deeds and Kettering, together with Harold E. Talbott Sr. and Talbott Jr., founded Domestic Engineering Company, which built a 540,000-square-foot plant on property Deeds owned. Three days after the United States declared war on Germany, the Dayton-Wright Airplane Company was incorporated and bought the newly built plant from Domestic Engineering.

Deeds held 40 percent of Domestic Engineering's stock and was a signer of the Dayton-Wright incorporation papers. In June he was both a member of the Aircraft Production Board and the head of the Equipment Division, and during that month the Signal Corps issued a contract to Dayton-Wright for four hundred training planes and in August a contract for four hundred De Havilland DH4s. At about the same time Delco became the sole supplier of ignition systems for the Liberty Engine program.[13]

When Borglum submitted his report to the president, the Senate had been holding hearings about shortfalls and delays in the Quartermaster Corps and the Ordnance Department production programs since December 1917. Two lines of inquiry took shape during the January and February hearings. One focused on the general breakdown of the war administration with regard to concentrating war contracts in one area and failing to coordinate the many war work programs. The other dealt with questionable contract practices. But neither line of inquiry touched on aviation, and the congressional focus remained on the Quartermaster Corps and the Ordnance Department.

In December 1917 the press had hinted that things were not right in the aircraft program. On 13 December the *New York Times* ran a story quoting from an article that had appeared in the French magazine *Revue Hebdomadaire*. Whitney Warren, an American living in Paris, wrote the article, titled "America's Role in Aerial Warfare," in which he said, "As for the 1,000 planes mentioned in sensational dispatches, I am not aware that a single one has yet crossed the sea."[14]

An even bigger hint appeared in the *Times* on 23 December in an article titled "Our Army's Work." The article focused on the ongoing scandal concerning the Quartermaster Corps and the Ordnance Department in which charges of graft and profiteering held center stage. Aviation received just a single paragraph: "Now we are going through the preliminary phases with respect to aircraft production. Nearly a billion dollars was appropriated at the last session of Congress. Somebody said that America would have 10,000 airplanes and win the war in the air, and the public still takes that part of the program for granted, something as already well under way. But not so much as ten percent of that promise of aircraft is even in sight of fulfillment."[15]

On 10 January 1918 Howard Coffin told the press that the aircraft program was doing well, a claim that seemed to be confirmed when the Senate, which opened an aviation inquiry in January 1918, said that the initial reports on the situation were "very gratifying." Statements that Coffin and Deeds made about aircraft production being forty-five to sixty days behind schedule did not arouse much interest, even in the press. Nevertheless, in January the president appointed William C. Potter to replace Deeds as the chief of the Signal Corps Equipment Division. Whether Wilson made the change on the basis of Borglum's January report is not known, but the change certainly occurred within a short time of the report.[16]

On 6 February Senator Lee Slater Overman, at Wilson's urging, introduced a bill to give the president sweeping powers to reorganize government agencies and departments for the duration of the war. The opposition to the Overman Act was so strong that it appeared initially the bill would not even reach the floor, and on 13 February Wilson met with Senate leaders to reach a compromise.[17]

On 21 February the nation was assured that the airplane production program was proceeding according to plan. That afternoon Secretary of War Baker told reporters that the first American-built warplanes were then en route to France and the shipment was "nearly five months ahead of schedule." The statement proved to be a major public relations blunder by whoever wrote the press release. The truth was that only a single DH4 was crated and waiting to be put aboard a freighter at Hoboken, New York. That same day, the *New York Times* ran a story headlined "Foe Come and Go at Will," in which a reporter, who was with American troops at the front, told readers that the German air force owned the sky over the American lines. He wrote, "American troops holding the sector are endangered because there are no American airplanes with them."[18]

By the end of February, when the Senate Committee on Military Affairs had finished its investigation into the production scandals involving the Quartermaster Corps and the Ordnance Department, the initial satisfaction with the aviation program had vanished. On 1 March the Senate Committee on Military Affairs met to discuss new information that had recently come to light regarding aircraft production and decided that the situation was so serious that "the matter ought to be laid before President Wilson." Reportedly one senator, on hearing the details, "put his head on the committee table and wept from disappointment and chagrin."[19]

One week after the Senate Military Affairs Committee sent its report to the president, the editors of the *Providence Journal* met with Secretary of War Baker on 8 March and told him about an investigation they had made at the Curtiss plant in Buffalo. The information they gave to Baker appeared in the *Journal* and the *New York Times* on 20 March. The editors described the situation in the Curtiss plant as "chaos" and said that a standing joke among workers there was that they spent most of their time "making tool boxes and handles for their tools." The editors also described delays in receiving needed supplies and told the secretary that "whole sets of drawings have been recalled time after time, that an inconsequential change might be made, such as shifting a bolt hole one inch one way or the other." The result was that as of 8 March only one warplane had been shipped to Europe and it was still at sea. The editors said that the conditions at Curtiss were repeated throughout the industry and that quantity production was "many months behind."[20]

The *Journal*'s brief investigation had identified the main problems in the airplane production program, and significantly said nothing about corruption and profiteering. Assistant Secretary of War Benedict Crowell sent the *Journal*'s information to the president. Acting at the president's direction, Crowell appointed H.

Snowden Marshall to head a three-man committee to make "a broad survey of the Government's aeronautical program, with particular reference to industrial phases of the work." In announcing the creation of the Marshall Committee, Crowell's representative told reporters the survey was a routine matter intended to keep the secretary of war "thoroughly advised of the detail workings of the various departments."[21]

About the time the Marshall Committee was being formed, Borglum was growing testy because there was no public sign that the president had taken action on his 21 January report. On 11 March he wrote to Wilson, asking what was being done. On 15 March Wilson replied, apologizing for "writing in great haste," and assuring him that the aircraft matter was undergoing "a very thorough review." He did not tell Borglum that the Marshall Committee would not be dealing with the charges of corruption and profiteering that Borglum had made.[22]

Dissatisfied with the president's answer, Borglum gave the *New York World* a story about his investigation and the charges, but without naming names. The *World* published the lengthy account in two installments between 12 and 16 March, and the scandal was born. The *New York Times* followed the *World*'s lead by printing stories about the charges on 17 and 19 March.[23]

Borglum's charges did not provoke the reaction he wanted. At the time, there was an ongoing Senate investigation into the production delays and the Marshall Committee was conducting its inquiry, and the press seemed to be content to wait until those reports were made public. There was little or no mention of scandal in the airplane production program for nearly a month following the publication of Borglum's charges. One of the reasons that his charges received relatively little attention was because he had not named anyone, making his charges general and vague.

Angry that the White House was not giving his charges top billing, Borglum sent the president telegrams and letters over an eight-day period from 28 March to 4 April, demanding action against Deeds and wanting to know why he had been left out of the investigation. Then, on 11 April, Borglum again got his name in the paper and added more fuel to the fire. Still avoiding naming anyone, and still casting himself in the role of President Wilson's official investigator, he told the press that the automobile men running the aviation program should be removed for the government to "have planes and engines in place of promises." He still did not name anyone, but it did not take much effort to recognize whom Borglum was talking about.[24]

The Senate Committee on Military Affairs completed its investigation of the War Department in March and on 10 April released its report on the aircraft industry. The committee majority said that while "engineering and manufacturing errors" accounted for part of the "gravely disappointing situation," much of the delay in producing combat aircraft was due to "ignorance of the art and a failure to organize the effort in such a way as to centralize authority and bring about quick decision." The committee gave three contributing causes, all pointing to the automobile industry clique in charge of the aviation program:

1. A certain aloofness in dealing with persons possessing information based upon experiences

2. An apparent intention of confining the actual production to a restricted number of concerns

3. A failure of the officials in charge of the work to grasp the situation in a broader way and seize upon the best approved foreign engines and planes and proceed promptly to build as many as possible for the campaign of 1918

The committee concluded, "It is greatly to be regretted that statements of Government officials have misrepresented the progress of the aviation program." In a less bombastic way, and without naming anyone, the committee had given support to Borglum's charges.[25]

On 12 April 1918 the Marshall Committee submitted its report to the president, and two days later the White House released the committee's recommendations: the president should appoint one man to head the entire aviation production program, aviation should be entirely separated from the Signal Corps, and legislation should place the responsibility for issuing contracts with an agency other than the Signal Corps. Again, there were no specific allegations of corruption or profiteering, but the Senate and Marshall committees had essentially reached the same conclusions.[26]

Fed up with Borglum's grandstanding and increasingly scurrilous attacks on the aircraft production administration, President Wilson wrote him a letter on 15 April in which he said:

> I never at any time constituted you an official investigator. I merely gave you the right to look into the matter of your own motion, and I am sure that in the letter which the Secretary of War provided you with he gave you the same purpose and idea. We have wished at every point to assist you and to make possible for you what you wished to do, but we have at no time regarded you as an official representative of the Administration. If I had so regarded you, I would, of course, have supplied you with such assistance as you feel you have lacked.

The president assured Borglum that he said this "in the most cordial way."[27]

On 24 April 1918, one month before the Overman Act became law, the president replaced Coffin with John D. Ryan as chairman of the Aircraft Board and placed him in charge of a newly created Bureau of Aircraft Production. Ryan, who was the president of the Anaconda Copper Company, had absolutely no affiliation with the automobile or aircraft industries, which lent some weight to Borglum's charges. William Potter remained in charge of the Signal Corps Equipment Division, a significant decision, since he was an investment banker closely associated with the tobacco industry.[28] At the same time, Wilson appointed Brig. Gen. William L. Kenly to the newly created post of director of military aeronautics. Squier was no longer associated with aviation, his authority being limited to strictly Signal Corps matters. For the moment, the reorganized structure remained in the Aviation Section of the Signal Corps, but in name only.

The following day the *New York Times* ran an editorial savagely attacking Squier. The editorial opened, "A long-suffering people will applaud the War Department's detail of Gen. George O. Squier to devote his attention to the administration of signals. The editorial said that as the "genius of Army aviation he had been a lamentable and exasperating failure," and had "no recognizable fitness" for the job of directing army aviation. The editor commented snidely that "it is not of record that he was in any degree an authority on practical aeronautics" other than "he had been the military attaché at London and danced well." The editorial concluded that "his failure was cause for jubilation in Germany."[29]

Three days after the president appointed Ryan and General Kenly, Borglum demanded criminal charges be brought against "members of the Aircraft Board, of men under Squier, and a ring of aircraft contractors." Borglum did not name any of the men he wanted charged, but it was obvious that he was after Deeds and Coffin. He called Squier "the official rubber stamp for a group of American Junkers," and charged that Squier was imposed on America's aviation production program by "a ring of aircraft manufactures who were guilty of colossal profiteering."[30]

On Monday, 29 April, Senator Frank B. Brandegee opened a debate in the Senate by demanding that the Wilson administration start an investigation of Borglum's charges. During the one-hour debate, Senator James D. Phelan questioned Borglum's qualifications as an expert on aviation matters, adding, "A great artist, such as Mr. Borglum, is principally distinguished for his flights of imagination and no other flights." Senator Gilbert H. Hitchcock, a member of the Military Affairs Committee, told the Senate that the committee had asked Borglum to "lay his facts before the Committee," but he failed to do so, leading the committee members to believe that Borglum was unable to substantiate his allegations. Senator Gilbert H. Hitchcock said that he had spoken to Borglum on several occasions and had come to the conclusion that the sculptor was not "dependable."[31]

Borglum's credibility was further questioned when Senator Duncan U. Fletcher asked Brandegee if he could definitely say that the president had picked Borglum to investigate the aircraft production program. Brandegee answered that he had only repeated what he had read in the *Times*. Fletcher asked Brandegee if he knew that Borglum had "applied to the President," offering information and the President had merely given him a letter authorizing him to make an investigation. He concluded, "That would be a different thing from the President selecting him to make this investigation."

It was becoming apparent that there was a growing doubt about Borglum and his investigation. That doubt was strengthened when Senator Norris asked Brandegee if Borglum was affiliated with an "aircraft organization." Brandegee admitted that he had heard something about Borglum being "interested in aircraft production." His source had "intimated" that an unidentified aircraft association or board had made "some sort of charge against Borglum on the grounds that he may possibly be interested in aircraft production." There was even a hint that Newton D. Baker's brother might be involved.[32]

Despite doubts about Borglum's motives and qualifications, his charges had provoked a major public reaction. A *New York Times* editorial demanded a federal grand jury be convened to look into the charges, and the House announced that it would start an "aviation inquiry." Attached to that report was a paragraph saying that Senator Jacob H. Gallinger, a Republican member of the Committee of Expenditures, was demanding that the "Borglum charges be sifted."[33]

Alarmed at the rising clamor, Coffin sent Wilson a telegram asking that the president order a special inquiry into Borglum's charges. Coffin asked for the inquiry "in order that the reputation of innocent men may not be ruined." Equally alarmed, Squier requested a military court of inquiry. The president passed Coffin's request on to the secretary of war, who declined to convene boards for Coffin and Squier at that time.[34]

Borglum must have believed that his demands were being met when on the afternoon of 6 May, President Wilson directed the U.S. attorney general, Thomas W. Gregory, to conduct a criminal investigation of the aviation production program. Gregory turned the case over to Assistant Attorney General William L. Frierson, and on 16 May Wilson appointed former Supreme Court justice Charles E. Hughes to "assist" the Justice Department in the investigation. Though the two groups of investigators did cooperate, the Hughes investigation overshadowed the Justice Department effort and garnered all the publicity. In the end, the Justice Department produced its own report and Hughes produced his.

While the Hughes investigation was getting under way, the Overman Act passed and became law on 20 May 1918. Four days later the president issued an executive order separating the Aviation Section from the Signal Corps and creating a directorship of military aeronautics and a Bureau of Aircraft Production. He placed both under the secretary of war. John D. Ryan headed the Bureau of Aircraft Production, which had "full and exclusive jurisdiction and control over production of aeroplanes, engines, and aircraft equipment." The cso retained control of all Signal Corps duties "which are not connected with the Aviation Section of the Signal Corps, or with the purchase, manufacturer, maintenance and production of aircraft."[35]

On 29 May 1918 the adjutant general of the army, Frederick W. Lewis, acting at the direction of the secretary of war, completed the separation by abolishing the Aviation Section of the Signal Corps and establishing the Air Service of the National Army.[36] On that same day, the U.S. Senate launched its own investigation of the Aircraft Production Program failures. At the same time, a subcommittee of the Senate Committee on Military Affairs opened its investigation of the aircraft production scandal. Senator Charles Thomas chaired the five-member subcommittee, which had agreed not to interfere with Charles Hughes's criminal investigation. The subcommittee would be plowing the same ground that the full committee had done two months earlier. But with allegations of graft and profiteering rife, the opportunity for political grandstanding and publicity was too much to resist.

When the separation occurred, the aircraft production scandal was at its peak, and the appointments of Ryan and Kenly did little to dampen it. The scandal, which had started as a failure in organization and administration, had become an ugly witch hunt, largely through Borglum's efforts. The two highly publicized investigations were concluded in August and October 1918, but the scandal remained a witch hunt until the end of the war. The newly created Air Service was spared further association with the scandal, due largely to reports from France of American aviation successes in battle. The focus shifted from the absence of American-built aircraft in France to the exploits of American airmen in France.

With America's entry into World War I, the separation of army aviation from the Signal Corps became inevitable. In September 1917 Gen. John Pershing separated the AEF air service from the Signal Corps on the basis that "aviation was in no sense a logical branch of the Signal Corps."[37] Townsend Dodd's presence on his staff probably influenced Pershing's decision, since he thought highly of Dodd and must have heard his views on aviation organization. Pershing's action was an important step in effecting the separation of army aviation from the Signal Corps that Beck had set in motion in 1912 and the Goodier trial had brought to the public's attention. Beck had been right when he said that there was no justification for combat aircraft being under Signal Corps control, and Foulois had been equally right when he told the congressional committee that it would be only a matter of time until the separation took place. Curiously, it was Billy Mitchell who told the congressional committee that "the Signal Corps will itself be aviation."[38]

The Goodier court-martial, and the subsequent events that finally separated army aviation from the Signal Corps, created Billy Mitchell. Mitchell went on to lead the second effort to create a separate air force and brought about his own court-martial in November 1925, ten years to the month after the Goodier court-martial opened in San Francisco. But that is another story, and it has been well covered.

Epilogue

With the end of the war, Gutzon Borglum, the man who created the scandal, lost interest in it. He had bigger fish to fry. Already a famous artist and millionaire, he went on to greater fame and fortune, culminating in his greatest undertaking, the sculpture on Mount Rushmore. Borglum died on 6 March 1941, nineteen days before his seventy-forth birthday.

What became of the men who had played important roles in the turbulent separation movement? Second Lt. Frederick E. Humphreys was the first army officer to solo but was returned to the Corps of Engineers before he could qualify for the FAI pilot's certificate. His relief from aviation, despite the fact that his orders assigning him to aviation limited his detached status to six months, so disgusted him that he resigned his commission on 1 August 1910 and became an engineer in the New York National Guard. He returned to aviation as a major during World War I and returned to the National Guard after he was released from active service in 1919. He retired from the National Guard as a brigadier general in 1936 and moved to Florida, where he died on 20 January 1941 at the age of fifty-seven.[1]

Paul Beck, the man who started the separation movement with his 1912 *Infantry Journal* article, served as an infantry officer in the Philippines and in the United States throughout World War I. On 1 July 1920 he returned to the Air Service as a lieutenant colonel and went through the JMA pilot training program from 30 September 1920 to 31 March 1921 at Carlstrom Field, Florida. On 14 April 1921 he took command of Post Field, near Oklahoma City.

Beck had not lost his knack for cultivating influential people, and after his wife died in August 1921, he became a frequent participant in Oklahoma City's social whirl. He befriended retired judge Jean Day and his wife Audrey, and Beck had an affair with Audrey. On the evening of 3 April 1922, Judge Day, his wife Audrey, and Beck had dinner in a trendy restaurant and then went to the judge's house at 411 West Nineteenth Street. An impromptu party was attended by half a dozen people, and a considerable amount of alcohol was consumed. Sometime after midnight the party broke up, and Judge Day offered to drive some of his guests home, even though they lived less than a block away.

Judge Day probably suspected there was something between Beck and Audrey, and he deliberately left them alone to create a situation in which he could confirm his suspicions. Returning after forty minutes, he looked through the front window into the living room, where Beck and Audrey were embracing on the couch. When the judge entered the house through the front door, the couple quickly separated and Beck stood up. Judge Day crossed the living room without saying a word and went upstairs to get his pistol.

When the judge returned to the living room and did not see Beck, Audrey told her husband that Beck was in the dining room. The judge confronted Beck there, and when Beck turned away the judge shot him in the back of the head, killing him instantly.

The coroner's jury predictably returned a no-bill verdict in the judge's favor, since in 1922 Oklahoma, husbands who shot their wives' lovers were not considered guilty of a crime. In fact, the coroner's jury declared that Judge Day was "protecting his home and his wife's honor," which made it a case of justifiable homicide. A board of army officers who also heard the case ruled that Beck "died in the line of duty." Shortly after the killing, Audrey and Judge Day divorced.[2]

Capt. Arthur S. Cowan's military career was not seriously damaged as a result of the Goodier trial, though he was relieved of his command at North Island. In October 1916 he was assigned to a Signal Corps post in the Panama Canal Zone and was not again involved in aviation, except for helping Hap Arnold locate suitable landing field sites in 1917. During World War I he was a Signal Corps major in the AEF's general headquarters in France, and he commanded the Signal Corps school at Fort Leavenworth from 1929 to 1937. He retired as a colonel two years later, at the age of sixty-four. The War Department called him up in 1940 for service in World War II, but age and health problems forced his second retirement eighteen months later. He died in Washington DC on 22 June 1957 at the age of eighty-two.[3]

The man who took over from Jones as the dissident leader, Capt. Townsend F. Dodd, served with Benjamin Foulois in the 1st Aero Squadron in Mexico, where he came to General Pershing's attention. When Pershing went to France in 1917 he appointed Major Dodd the aviation officer, American Expeditionary Forces, and placed Dodd on his staff, where Dodd's views apparently found a receptive ear. Dodd held what at the time was the highest aviation post in the AEF until Lieutenant Colonel Mitchell relieved him when Pershing and his staff arrived in France in June. Mitchell's rank forced Pershing to relieve Dodd. But Dodd's influence continued after he left Pershing's headquarters, as evidenced by the fact that in September 1917 Pershing separated aviation from the Signal Corps in the AEF, noting that "aviation was in no sense a logical branch of the Signal Corps." Dodd remained on staff duty in France throughout the war, and in August 1918 he was the information officer in Colonel Mitchell's First Army Air Service headquarters as a lieutenant colonel, and in 1919 he commanded Langley Field in Hampton, Virginia.

Dodd was killed in a crash on 5 October 1919 while preparing for the 1919 Transcontinental Endurance and Reliability Test. He and his mechanic, S.Sgt. George E. Hess, took off from Langley Field and arrived over Bustleton Field near Philadelphia shortly after 1600, when they encountered heavy fog. Low on fuel, Dodd try to land through the fog and was just twenty feet off the ground when he hit a tree. The impact drove the engine back into the pilot's cockpit, crushing Dodd. Sergeant Hess, in the rear cockpit, escaped from the crash unhurt.[4]

Though he was not part of the separation movement, Benjamin Foulois was an important player who figured prominently in the events. He went to France during World War I and for a time was the chief of the Air Service, AEF. While in France he and Mitchell clashed, but Foulois finally recognized Mitchell's superior combat command skills and stepped aside. The feud lasted, however, until the day Foulois died. Between the wars, he held several administrative and command positions, among them military attaché in Berlin and command of Mitchel Field at Long Island, New York. He was promoted to major general and made chief of the Army Air Corps from 1931 to 1935, and he retired as a major general on 31 December 1935. In retirement he was a frequent speaker on aviation matters and ran for Congress in 1941 but was defeated. He died on 25 April 1967 at the age of eighty-seven, the longest living of the army's first pilots.[5]

Lieutenant Colonel Goodier's presidential reprimand was not as damaging as it appeared to be. The fraud and mismanagement that the trial exposed had overshadowed his actions to the degree that when the reprimand was announced, the report was buried in the back pages of the nation's newspapers. Goodier continued to be the judge advocate for the Western Department until 1920, when he was assigned to the Northeastern Department, headquartered in Boston. He retired in 1921 at the age of sixty-four and lived in San Bruno, California, a few miles south of San Francisco.[6]

First Lt. Byron Q. Jones emerged from the ordeal without any disciplinary action being taken against him. After his testimony in San Francisco he returned to MIT, where he completed his aerodynamics course. During World War I he commanded Selfridge Field, Michigan, and after the war he held a series of commands, including command of the 8th Pursuit Group. As a major in 1934 he commanded the army's air mail operations in the Eastern Zone along with Lt. Col. Horace M. Hickam (Central Zone), and Lt. Col. Hap Arnold (Western Zone). In 1935 he was a lieutenant colonel in command of the 2nd Wing during the 1935 tests to determine if a wing could operate as a self-contained unit in the field during wartime conditions. He retired on disability as a colonel in 1944 and died on 30 March 1959.[7]

Roy C. Kirtland returned to aviation in 1917 and was given the nonflying assignment of organizing the Motor Mechanics' Regiment, which had the task of training aircraft mechanics for World War I. Later he held a nonflying assignment in the AEF in France. Following the war, he commanded several aviation depots, and in 1920 he entered the School of the Line and General Staff College at Leavenworth. He graduated from the Army War College in 1926 and became the Air Corps personnel representative on the general staff. In 1930 he received the assignment to command Langley Field, which included nominal command of the 2nd Bombardment Wing and the Air Corps Tactical School.

In 1931 he was at the top of the list to become the assistant chief of the Air Corps under Benjamin Foulois, and promotion to brigadier general. But his role in the Goodier court-martial came back to haunt him, and Foulois rejected him in favor of Oscar Westover, who was younger. Colonel Kirtland retired in 1938.

He was recalled in 1940 and took command of the West Coast Army Air Forces Training Center at Moffett Field, California. He died there of a heart attack on 2 May 1941, twelve days short of his sixty-seventh birthday. On 13 January 1948 the Albuquerque Army Air Base was renamed Kirtland Army Air Field, and it later became Kirtland Air Force Base. It is one of the largest bases in the Air Force Material Command.[8]

Capt. William Lay Patterson was allowed to retain his junior military aviator rating, along with the advance in rank and the flight pay, which proves that justice is illusionary. On 1 December 1915 the 1st Company, 2nd Aero Squadron, was organized at San Diego, and the squadron departed San Francisco on 5 January 1916 with Patterson in command. He finally passed his FAI tests in January 1916, after arriving in the Philippines, and received FAI certificate no. 390. He never took the junior military aviator tests. After World War I, Colonel Patterson was involved in establishing a string of Air Service coastal defense stations in conjunction with the Coast Artillery. After that he faded into obscurity.[9]

Lt. Col. Samuel Reber went on a four-month leave of absence in July 1916, and in October the War Department assigned him as the CSO to the Central Department. He was not again associated with aviation. But the negative publicity that he had received did not seriously damage his career, and did not prevent the army from promoting him to colonel during World War I. He was fifty-four years old when he retired as a colonel in 1919 and became the general foreign representative for Radio Corporation of America (RCA). In 1922 he became the vice president of RCA, a job he held until his death at age sixty-eight on 16 April 1933.[10]

Brig. Gen. George P. Scriven remained CSO until Brig. Gen. George O. Squire relieved him on 14 February 1917, when Scriven retired. The War Department reactivated him after the United States entered World War I, and he saw duty in Italy in 1917 and 1918. He died on 7 March 1940 at the age of eighty-six.[11]

Though involved to a lesser degree than Dodd and Jones, 1st Lt. Thomas S. Bowen was named in the charges against Lieutenant Colonel Goodier and was thus an identified dissident. He served with the 1st Aero Squadron on the Mexican border in 1916 and went to France in 1917 as a major in charge of the ground personnel assigned to the 28th Aero Squadron. After Col. Raynold C. Bolling was killed on 27 March 1918, Bowen was appointed the Air Service liaison to the British Expeditionary Forces, but the assignment lasted only until mid-May.

On 29 May Major Bowen took command of the Second Corps Aeronautical School at Chatillon-sur-Seine and held the command until early September, when he was relieved before a replacement had been selected. In late September he took command of the 1st Day Bombardment Group, but that proved to be a one-month assignment. Bowen's problem seems to have been that he was too stringent a disciplinarian—the same sort of behavior of which he had accused Cowan. The British did not like him, and the Americans who served under him shared the feeling. He retired on a disability in 1920 as a major and died in Washington DC on 17 July 1927 at the age of forty-two.[12]

Charles DeForest Chandler remained associated with aviation

after he left Texas. While he was the assistant CSO, Philippine Division, he flew with Frank Lahm at Lahm's seasonal flying school. When he returned to the United States, he became the director of the Signal Corps School at Fort Leavenworth until November 1916, when he went to Washington. He was active in the balloon aspect of army aviation, establishing the Signal Corps Balloon School at Fort Omaha in 1916 and serving on the Joint Army-Navy Airship Board. He went to France with Foulois in November 1917 and was given command of the Balloon Section, AEF. Chandler retired in 1920 and became the aeronautical editor for Roland Press, the house that published *How Our Army Grew Wings* in 1943. He remained active in sport ballooning until his death on 18 May 1939 at the age of sixty.[13]

Another dissenter who attended the 16 March 1915 meeting in Dodd's living room was Carlton G. Chapman. He served with Foulois in the 1st Aero Squadron in 1916 and remained on aviation duty until he retired in 1922. He was an air observer in London during 1916 and 1917, was the chief disbursing officer for the AEF in France during 1917 and 1918, and was assigned to Mitchell's command, Air Service, First Army, in 1918. He retired in 1922 at the age of thirty-six. The War Department recalled him to active duty in 1940, and he remained on active duty until 1946. He died a lieutenant colonel on 11 November 1971.[14]

Another peripheral character was Harold Geiger, who had run afoul of Cowan and Reber shortly after he returned from Hawaii in 1914. Geiger returned to aviation in March 1917 as a student at the balloon school at Fort Omaha, Nebraska, but did not qualify as an aeronaut, which was the name for balloon pilots in 1917. He did, however, remain on aviation duty and served in France as a lieutenant colonel. After the war he reverted to his permanent rank of captain and took the assignment as the U.S. air attaché in Berlin. In October 1924 he flew home on the dirigible ZR3, which was being delivered to the U.S. Navy to be commissioned as the USS *Los Angeles*.

In 1927 he was a major in command of Phillips Field at Aberdeen, Maryland. On 18 May he and a Lieutenant Steele flew from

Phillips Field to Olmstead Field, Maryland, where Steele was to pick up a repaired DH-4 and fly it back to Phillips. Geiger took off on his return flight, and as his DH-4 lifted off, the engine sputtered, coughed, and quit. The DH-4 stalled, fell off on its left wing, and crashed. Geiger managed to unstrap and leap out as the plane hit the ground. He was still sprawled on the ground when the gas tank ruptured and spewed flaming gasoline over the wreck. Geiger crawled and attempted to run from the crash but was engulfed in flaming gasoline before he could get clear. His body was recovered near the tail of the burned airplane. He was forty-two when he died. In 1941 the War Department bought Sunset Field near Spokane, Washington, and renamed it Geiger Field. Today the former army air field is the Spokane International Airport.[15]

Though not directly involved in the attack on Cowan, Ned Goodier was an early casualty. He was still in Letterman Hospital when he was relieved from aviation by Special Order 150, 1 July 1915. The immediate effect was that he reverted to first lieutenant, which meant a cut in pay. Goodier left the hospital on disability leave on 1 January 1916, hoping to return to aviation when he was fully recovered. Though not actually involved in what was then known as the Goodier Affair, his name, and the fact that his relationship with Cowan surfaced frequently during the trial, implicated him. That Kirtland had written to him first about bringing charges against Cowan cemented the connection. The War Department retired him on 1 July 1916.

In June 1916 Henry Souther, the civilian consulting engineer to the Aviation Section's newly established Technical Aero Advisory and Inspection Board, asked Ned Goodier to assist him. Brigadier General Scriven was not pleased to have him, but by that time the Garlington Board had completed its investigation. The War Department had relieved Cowan and Reber for their roles in the Goodier Affair, and the secretary of war had censured Scriven. Scriven did not like having Ned Goodier in his office, but there was nothing he could do about it.

Ned worked with Souther as a civilian assistant until the War Department called him to active duty on 22 April 1917. In May the

Technical Aero Advisory and Inspection Board became the Aircraft Engineering Division under Maj. Henry Souther with Capt. Ned Goodier his second in command. Goodier worked for Souther until August 1917, when the name was again changed, this time to the Equipment Division, and Col. Edward Deeds took charge. Goodier, now a major, took command of Chandler Field at Essington, Pennsylvania, and later moved to Gerstner Field at Lake Charles, Louisiana. From April 1917 to the end of the war he was back in Washington. The War Department recalled him in 1942 as a lieutenant colonel and assigned him as the chief of staff to the headquarters at Camp San Luis Obispo in California. Ned Goodier died on 29 December 1961 in Santa Barbara, California.[16]

First Lt. Thomas DeWitt Milling was one of the few early aviators to reach general grade rank, though he never served on active duty at that rank. In April 1916 he, together with Capt. Virginius Clark and 1st Lt. Byron Q. Jones, was appointed to an aviation board charged with responsibility for specifications and technical inspections for new airplanes. On 31 July 1916 he advanced to captain, and in August 1917 he was promoted to lieutenant colonel and took charge of Air Service training in the AEF. He later became Billy Mitchell's chief of staff, Air Service, First Army, AEF, and advanced to lieutenant colonel. He ended the war as a colonel commanding the Air Service, First Army.

Milling returned to the United States in 1919 and became the second in command in the Training and Operations Group of the newly established Army Air Service. He held various staff and command positions until he was admitted to Fitzsimmons General Hospital in September 1931, where he remained hospitalized until July 1933, when he was retired on disability as a colonel. He was recalled to active duty as a major on 16 March 1942 and was promoted, again, to colonel on 24 September 1942, which rank he held until he reverted to retired status in 1946. Milling never served as a brigadier general, but he was advanced on the retired list to that rank, backdated to 13 June 1940. He died at Walter Reed Hospital on 26 November 1960 at the age of seventy-three.[17]

Among the pilots who played a peripheral role in the event leading up to the Goodier court-martial was 1st Lt. Robert H. Willis, another veteran of the 1st Aero Squadron's operations in Mexico. Following duty in Mexico, Willis became the chief instructor for the Field Officers' Course in Aeronautics at San Diego. Shortly after the United States entered the war, Willis was promoted to lieutenant colonel and held various staff positions in Washington and in France, his last assignment being in the operations division of the AEF Air Service, First Army Air, under Brigadier General Mitchell. He was shot and killed accidentally on 13 September 1918 at the front near Remiremont, Voseges, France.[18]

George O. Squire survived the 1918 airplane production scandal with his reputation intact and served as the CSO until his retirement as a major general in 1923. By the time he retired he held sixty-five patents, one of which was for his invention of "multiplexing," which allowed multiple signals to be transmitted along a single telephone wire. In 1922, while still CSO, he sold the multiplexing rights to the North American Company, which used the system to establish the Wired Radio Company. Wired Radio, which became Muzac in 1934, provided piped-in music to businesses and subscribers. Following his retirement, he was elected to the National Academy of Sciences. He died in Washington DC on 24 March 1934 at the age of sixty-nine.[19]

The man Reber relieved in September 1913 following the Texas City "incipient mutiny," Maj. Edgar Russel, missed the fallout from the Goodier court-martial and went back to being a Signal Corps officer. He was a colonel during World War I and the CSO of the AEF, for which he received the Distinguished Service Medal. He had a brief connection with aviation while he was in France as the chairman of a board of officers convened on 19 June 1917 to make recommendations on various aviation matters in the AEF. On the board with him were Billy Mitchell, Townsend Dodd, and Joseph Carberry. Russel retired from the army on disability as a colonel in 1922 and died in New York City on 26 April 1925.[20]

NOTES

Introduction

1. U.S. War Department, *Field Service Regulations, United States Army, 1905*, paragraphs 59–91.

2. Brig. Gen. Enoch Crowder, "Conditions at the Aviation School, San Diego, California, and in the Aviation Section of the Signal Corps," PT14, General Court-Martial, no. 95565, Lt. Col. Lewis E. Goodier, 18 October–15 November 1915, trial transcript, Records of the Office of the Judge Advocate General (Army), RG153, National Archives at College Park, Maryland (hereafter cited as General Court-Martial, no. 95565, Lt. Col. Lewis E. Goodier).

3. Allen, *Report of the Chief Signal Officer to the Secretary of War, 1909*, 28.

4. Allen, *Report of the Chief Signal Officer to the Secretary of War, 1910*, 24–25.

5. U.S. War Department, *Regulations for the Army of the United States, 1904*, article 6, paragraph 40.

6. Allen, *Report of the Chief Signal Officer, U.S. Army, to the Secretary of War, 1911*, 24–25, 23.

7. Milling, "Early Flying Experiences," 98.

8. Neumann, *Die deutschen Luftstreitkräfte im Weltkrieg*, 5.

9. Arnold, *Global Mission*, 31.

10. Chandler and Lahm, *How Our Army Grew Wings*, 80–81; Holley, *Ideas and Weapons*, 27; Tretler, "Opportunity Missed," 6; and Nalty, *Winged Shield, Winged Sword*, 10.

11. Raines, *Getting the Message Through*, 120.

12. *Aeronautics in the Army: Hearings before the Committee on Military Affairs in Connection with H.R. 5304*, 63rd Cong., 1st Sess., 8 (1913; hereafter cited as HR 5304 Hearings).

13. Col. John L. Chamberlain, "Report of Annual Inspection of First Aero Squadron and of Signal Corps Aviation School, San Diego, 19 March 1914," Records of the Inspector General (Army), 1814–1962, RG159, National Archives at College Park, Maryland (hereafter cited as Chamberlain IG Report, 19 March 1914).

14. Senator Joseph T. Robinson speaking to the committee, *Army and Navy Register*, 26 February 1916, 721.

15. Mixter and Emmons, writing about the status of U.S. army aviation in June 1917, two months *after* the United States entered World War I, in *United States Army Aircraft Production Facts*, 41.

1. The Army's Balloons

1. Raines, *Getting the Message Through*, 12–13.

2. Raines, *Getting the Message Through*, 35, note 48; Chandler and Lahm, *How Our Army Grew Wings*, 34.

3. Chandler and Lahm, *How Our Army Grew Wings*, 34, 43; Hennessy, *United States Army Air Arm*, 11.

4. Raines, *Getting the Message Through*, 44.

5. Raines, *Getting the Message Through*, 41–43.

6. Raines, *Getting the Message Through*, 46.

7. Grice, "Beginning of the National Weather Service," 11.

8. Grice, "Beginning of the National Weather Service," 11.

9. Cooper, *William Babcock Hazen: The Best Hated Man*, 314.

10. Grice, "Beginning of the National Weather Service," 12.

11. "An Act to Increase the Efficiency and Reduce the Expenses of the Signal Corps of the Army, and to Transfer the Weather Service to the Department of Agriculture," 51st Cong., 1st sess., section 2 (1890).

12. Greely, "Balloons for Military Purposes," 48, appendix 1 in *Report of the Chief Signal Officer of the Army for the Fiscal Year Ending 1889*, Records of the Office of the Chief Signal Officer, 1860–1982, RG 111, National Archives at College Park, Maryland.

13. Chandler and Lahm, *How Our Army Grew Wings*, 42–43.

14. Maj. Gen. Enoch H. Crowder to the Secretary of War, "Conditions at the Aviation School, San Diego, California, and in the Aviation Section of the Signal Corps," PT 19, 27 April 1916, General Court-Martial, no. 95565, Lt. Col. Lewis E. Goodier; U.S. War Department, *Regulations for the United States Army*, 1895–1901; and U.S. War Department, *Field Service Regulations*, 1897–1901.

15. Hennessy, *United States Army Air Arm*, 13.

16. Hennessy, *United States Army Air Arm*, 14.

17. Hennessy, *United States Army Air Arm*, 15.

18. Chandler and Lahm, *How Our Army Grew Wings*, 42.

19. Allen, *Report of the Chief Signal Officer, for the Fiscal Year 1906*, 26.

20. Chandler and Lahm, *How Our Army Grew Wings*, 80–81.

21. Crowder, PT 14, General Court-Martial, no. 95565, Lt. Col. Lewis E. Goodier.

22. Chandler and Lahm, *How Our Army Grew Wings*, 148; Hennessy, *United States Army Air Arm*, 15.

23. HR 5304 Hearings.

24. Chandler and Lahm, *How Our Army Grew Wings*, 80–81.

25. "Rules and Regulations of the International Aeronautic Federation Governing the Issue of Pilots' Certificates," in Aero Club of America, *Aero Club of America, 1912*, 49–50.

26. Chandler and Lahm, *How Our Army Grew Wings*, 71.

27. Aero Club of America, *Aero Club of America, 1912*, 3–12.

2. Benjamin D. Foulois

1. Foulois, *From the Wright Brothers to the Astronauts*, 7–44. All the biographical material about Foulois was taken from this source.

2. Chandler and Lahm, *How Our Army Grew Wings*, 287–90, 295–98.

3. Chandler and Lahm, *How Our Army Grew Wings*, 113, 161; Turnbull and Lord, *History of United States Naval Aviation*, 6.

4. Chandler and Lahm, *How Our Army Grew Wings*, 160–61.

5. Chandler and Lahm, *How Our Army Grew Wings*, 162–63, 303–4; Foulois, *From the Wright Brothers to the Astronauts*, 66–70.

6. Chandler and Lahm, *How Our Army Grew Wings*, 303–4; Hennessy, *United States Army Air Arm*, 42.

7. Foulois, *From the Wright Brothers to the Astronauts*, 70.

8. Foulois, "Early Flying Experiences," Part I, 29.

9. Miller, "Kept Alive by the Postman," 41–44; Hennessy, *United States Army Air Arm*, 42.

10. Foulois, *From the Wright Brothers to the Astronauts*, 75.

11. "The Aerial Market Place," *Aeronautics*, August 1909, 32; "The Aerial Market Place," *Aeronautics*, October 1910, 185; "The Aerial Market Place," *Aeronautics*, December 1910, 234, "Training School Begins Activity," *Aero*, April 1911, 4; "The Aerial Market Place," *Aeronautics*, 1911, 168.

3. Paul Ward Beck

1. Hon. Finis E. Downing to Secretary of War, 20 April 1896, and Paul W. Beck to Adjutant General, U.S.A., 7 July 1896, in Beck, Military Records, Records of the Adjutant General, 1783–1928, RG94, National Archives at College Park, Maryland (hereafter cited as RG94).

2. Paul W. Beck to Adjutant General, U.S. Army, 10 January 1897; Paul W. Beck to Adjutant General, U.S. Army, 11 January 1897; and Adjutant General to Paul W. Beck, 13 January 1897, RG94.

3. U.S. War Department, *Regulations for the Army of the United States, 1910, corrected to 20 June 1913*, article 5, paragraph 28.

4. Recruiting Officer, Ft. Duchesne, to Adjutant General, telegram, 7 August 1897; Assistant Adjutant General to Commanding Officer, Ft. Duchesne, telegram, 9 August 1897; William H. Beck to Col. J. C. Gilmore, 11 August 1897; Assistant Adjutant General to Captain Beck, telegram, 20 August 1897, RG94.

5. Direct commissions were available to civilians on a very limited basis and were made only after West Point graduates and enlisted candidates had been commissioned. If there were any vacancies left, civilians could be commissioned to fill them. Until 1913, authority for commissioning civilians was found in article 5 of the U.S. War Department's *Regulations for the Army of the United States*, though the specific paragraph number might change from one edition to another. The basic requirements up to 1913 were that a civilian had to be an unmarried U.S. citizen between twenty-one and twenty-seven years of age. The testing and physical examination process was the same as for enlisted men. U.S. War Department, *Regulations for the Army of the United States, 1910, corrected to 20 June 1913*, article 5, paragraphs 27 and 34.

6. William H. Beck to Adjutant General, 24 April 1898; William H. Beck to Adjutant General, 5 May 1898; Paul W. Beck to Honorable Russell A. Alger, Secretary

of War, 9 August 1898; Rachel Longate Beck to William McKinley, President of the United States, 28 December 1898, RG94.

7. "Wedding Announcement," *Denver Post*, 20 April 1898.

8. Brig. Gen. E. V. Sumner to Secretary of War, 14 December 1898, RG94.

9. Paul W. Beck to Adjutant General, 1 July 1898; and Paul W. Beck to Adjutant General, 17 August 1898, RG94.

10. Adjutant General to General Schwan, memorandum, 9 May 1899, RG94.

11. Paul Beck to Brig. Gen. J. Schwan, 12 May 1899; Mr. Chew to Assistant Adjutant General, typed note, 27 May 1899, RG94.

12. Maj. Charles Richards, MD, physical examination of Paul W. Beck, 15 June 1899; and Proceedings of a Board of Officers Convened at Fort Monroe, VA, 15 June 1899, RG94.

13. Paul W. Beck to Chief Clerk, M & R Division, 21 June 1899; Paul W. Beck to Chief Clerk, Adjutant General's Office, 22 July 1899; and Assistant Adjutant General to Paul Ward Beck, 16 August 1899, RG94.

14. Proceedings of a Board of Officers Convened at Washington Barracks, DC, 5 September 1899; and Oath of Office, 18 September 1899, RG94.

15. Paul W. Beck to Adjutant General, 18 April 1900; Form of Medical Certificate, 5 June 1900, RG94.

16. Dr. C. W. Flock, handwritten certification, 3 May 1900; and Form of Medical Certificate, 5 June 1900, RG94.

17. Paul W. Beck to Adjutant General, 7 July 1900; second endorsement, 14 July 1901; Efficiency Report of 2nd Lt. Paul W. Beck for the period 30 June 1900 to 30 June 1901; and Adjutant General to 1st Lt. Paul Beck, Commission of First Lieutenant of Infantry, 25 July 1902, RG94.

18. Chief of Artillery to Secretary of War, memorandum, undated; 2nd Lt. Paul W. Beck to Adjutant General, letter with enclosure, 9 June 1902; Adjutant General to 1st Lt. Paul W Beck, 11 August 1902; Paul W. Beck to Adjutant General, 6 November 1902; and Efficiency Report of 1st Lt. Paul W. Beck, 30 June 1902 to 30 June 1903, 1 July 1903, RG94.

19. Efficiency Report of 1st Lt. Paul W. Beck, 30 June 1903 to 30 June 1904, 30 June 1904; and Efficiency Report of 1st Lt. Paul W. Beck, 30 June 1904 to 30 June 1905, 30 June 1905, RG94.

20. Efficiency Report of 1st Lt. Paul W. Beck, 30 June 1905 to 30 June 1906, 30 June 1906, RG94.

21. William H. Beck to Maj. Gen. Fred C Ainsworth, 16 February 1906; and Military Secretary, United States Army, to Brig. Gen. William H. Beck, 21 February 1906, RG94.

22. Foulois, *From the Wright Brothers to the Astronauts*, 43.

23. Individual Service Report of 1st Lt. Paul W. Beck, 30 June 1907, RG94.

24. Glen Curtiss to Secretary of War, 19 November 1909; U.S. War Department, Special Orders no. 298, 23 December 1909, RG94.

25. Individual Service Report of 1st Lt. Paul W. Beck, 30 June 1907, RG94.

26. Beck's bomb-dropping activities are taken from Beck, "Flying Men-O-War," 253–57 and 345–46.

27. HR 5304 Hearings, 37.

28. The claim that Beck designed the radio is found in Chandler and Lahm, *How Our Army Grew Wings*, 89; the history of the radio's design and testing is found in Ennis, "Wireless Telegraphy from an Aeroplane."

29. Ennis, "Wireless Telegraphy from an Aeroplane," 38; Chandler and Lahm, *How Our Army Grew Wings*, 88; Hennessy, *United States Army Air Arm*, 45; Arnold, *Global Mission*, 24–25; and John W. Mitchell, "San Francisco Air Meet Draws National Attention," *Aero*, 28 January 1910, 68–69.

30. Beck, "Doves of War," 295.

31. Special Orders no. 8, 11 January 1911, Records of the Army Staff, 1903–1996, RG319, National Archives at College Park, Maryland; Paul W. Beck to Adjutant General, 24 January 1911, with endorsements; Special Orders no. 31, 7 February 1911, RG94.

32. Paul W. Beck to Adjutant General, 5 June 1911; Oath of Office, 5 June 1911; and Brig. General James Allen to Adjutant General, 12 June 1911, RG94.

33. Paul W. Beck to Adjutant General, telegram, 25 March 1911; and Adjutant General to Capt. Paul W. Beck, telegram, 25 March 1911, RG94.

4. The Foulois-Beck Feud

1. "New Features of the Army Curtiss," *Aero*, April 1911, 9–10.

2. Hennessy, *United States Army Air Arm*, 42.

3. Foulois, "Early Flying Experiences," Part II, 56; Casey, *Curtiss*, 76; Hennessy, *United States Army Air Arm*, 42; Chandler and Lahm, *How Our Army Grew Wings*, 188, and Jakab, "Eugene Ely and the Birth of Naval Aviation."

4. Foulois, *From the Wright Brothers to the Astronauts*, 91–92.

5. Chandler and Lahm, *How Our Army Grew Wings*, 190; Foulois, "Early Flying Experiences," Part II, 55.

6. The damage Beck did to the airplane, and Foulois's criticisms of its repair that follow, are from Foulois, "Early Flying Experiences," Part II, 55–57; Foulois, *From the Wright Brothers to the Astronauts*, 92; and Arnold, *Global Mission*, 24.

7. The details of the accident that follow are from Chief Signal Officer, "Accident No. 2," published as "Mortality in Army Aviation," *American Aviation Historical Society Journal* 9, no. 2 (Summer 1964); "How Lieutenant Kelly Lost His Life," *Aero*, May 1917, 157–58; and "Death of Lieutenant Kelly, Army Aviator," *Aeronautics*, June 1911, 203. Foulois, *From the Wright Brothers to the Astronauts*, 92–93; and Foulois, "Early Flying Experiences," Part II, 56.

8. Foulois, "Early Flying Experiences," Part II, 56–57; and Foulois, *From the Wright Brothers to the Astronauts*, 92–93.

9. "How Lieutenant Kelly Lost his Life," *Aero*, May 1917, 157–58.

10. Foulois, *From the Wright Brothers to the Astronauts*, 93.

11. "Death of Lieutenant Kelly, Army Aviator," *Aeronautics*, June 1911, 203.

5. The Flying Club

1. Chandler and Lahm, *How Our Army Grew Wings*, 195.

2. Loening, *Our Wings Grow Faster*, 19.

3. Loening, *Our Wings Grow Faster*, 49.

4. Loening, *Our Wings Grow Faster*, 53.

5. Arnold, *Global Mission*, 31.

6. Milling, "Early Flying Experiences," 97.

7. "Army Navy Members," in Aero Club of America, *Aero Club of America, 1912*, 49–50.

8. Arnold, *Global Mission*, 34–35.

9. "The Chicago Meet," *Aeronautics*, September 1911, 91.

10. "The Chicago Meet," 86, 136.

11. Hennessy, *United States Army Air Arm*, 54; New York World, *World Almanac and Encyclopedia, 1912*, 435; and "Ovington Won 160-mile Tri-State Race," *Aeronautics*, October 1911, 136.

12. "Ovington Won," 132.

13. Arnold, *Global Mission*, 35; and "The Nassau Meet," *Aeronautics*, October 1911, 134.

14. Arnold, *Global Mission*, 35.

15. U.S. Patent Office, *Annual Report of the Commissioner of Patents, 1912*, 877.

16. Hennessy, *United States Army Air Arm*, 126.

17. Air Force Systems Command (AFSC), "Early Optical Bombsight Development," chapter 1 in *Development of Airborne Armament, 1910–1961*, vol. 1, *Bombing Systems*, n.p.

18. Allen, *Report of the Chief Signal Officer, for the Fiscal Year 1908*, 37.

19. Scriven, *Report of the Chief Signal Officer to the Secretary of War, 1914*, 4.

20. Scriven, *Report of the Chief Signal Officer to the Secretary of War, 1914*, 5–7.

21. "In Congress: Army Aeronautics," *Army and Navy Register*, 4 May 1912, 4.

22. Crozier, *Ordnance and the World War*, 75–78.

23. Crozier, *Ordnance and the World War*, 185–86.

24. Crozier, *Ordnance and the World War*, 183–84.

25. Arnold, *Global Mission*, 38.

6. The First Signs of Trouble

1. The details regarding the content of Chandler's article, including the quotes, are taken from Chandler, "Army Aviation: Its Needs."

2. General Court-Martial, no. 95565, Lt. Col. Lewis E. Goodier, Kirtland's testimony, 23.

3. Chandler and Lahm, *How Our Army Grew Wings*, 248.

4. Chief Signal Officer, "Accident No. 2," 110. Arthur L. Welsh's original name was Laibel Welcher until he changed it in 1903. "Welsh" is often misspelled "Welch."

5. Foulois, *From the Wright Brothers to the Astronauts*, 82–84; and "Round Table Discussion with Generals Benjamin Foulois, Frank Lahm, and Thomas Milling," Air Force Historical Foundation, Maxwell Air Force Base, Alabama, 66–67 (hereafter cited as "Round Table Discussion").

6. Paul Beck, "Military Aviation in America: Its Needs," *Flying*, October 1912, 30–34; *Flying*, November 1912, 30–33; and *Leslie's Weekly*, 14 November 1912, 18–22.

7. HR 5304 Hearings, 97.

8. Foulois, *From the Wright Brothers to the Astronauts*, 103; and Foulois, "Early Flying Experiences," Part II, 64.

9. U.S. War Department, *Regulations for the Army of the United States, 1913, Corrected to 10 June 1918*, article 6, paragraph 39, C.A.R. 20.

10. Foulois, "Early Flying Experiences," Part III, 115–16.

11. Foulois, "Early Flying Experiences," Part III, 117.

7. Upheavals

1. Aero Club of America, *Aero Club of America, 1913*, 60–61, 72.

2. Aero Club of America, *Aero Club of America, 1913*, 60–61, 72.

3. Delano to Geiger, 28 January 1913, Reference: "FAI Certificate Tests," Records of the Office of the Chief Signal Officer, 1912–1916, RG111, National Archives at College Park, Maryland. Hereafter all sources from this record group will be cited as RG111.

4. Aero Club of America, *Aero Club of America, 1913*, 63.

5. Chandler and Lahm, *How Our Army Grew Wings*, 219.

6. Geiger to Secretary, Aero Club of America, 4 February 1913, RG111.

7. Aero Club of America, *Aero Club of America, 1913*, 6–13, 43.

8. Reber to Russel, 12 February 1913, Reference: "FAI Certificate Tests," RG111.

9. Chandler to Scriven, memorandum, 23 February 1913, RG111.

10. "Rules and Regulations of the International Aeronautic Federation Governing the Issue of Pilot's Certificates," in Aero Club of America, *Aero Club of America, 1913*, 52–54.

11. Scriven to Geiger, order to comply via Russel, RG111.

12. Geiger to Scriven, first endorsement, 17 March 1913, Reference: "FAI Pilots' License Status," RG111.

13. Russel to Geiger, second endorsement, 24 March 1913, Reference: "FAI Pilots' License Status"; and Geiger to CSO, third endorsement, 1 April 1913, Reference: "FAI Pilots' License Status," RG111.

14. Chandler and Lahm, *How Our Army Grew Wings*, 242, 253–54.

15. The details of the letter that Foulois wrote to the CSO, including the quotes used below, are found in Foulois, "Early Flying Experiences," Part III, 119–24.

16. Hennessy, *United States Army Air Arm*, 94.

17. Foulois "Early Flying Experiences," Part III, 120.

18. Foulois "Early Flying Experiences," Part III, 124.

19. Hennessy, *United States Army Air Arm*, 109.

20. The details of Foulois's lobbying efforts, including the quotes used below, are found in Foulois "Early Flying Experiences," Part III, 122–24.

8. An Incipient Mutiny

1. Arnold, *Global Mission*, 41–42; and General Court-Martial, no. 95565, Lt. Col. Lewis E. Goodier, Cowan's testimony, 222–23. The author has been unable to locate the letter, which is believed to have been deliberately destroyed in 1913 to protect the men who were involved in the incident. This opinion is drawn from the author's telephone conversations with and email messages from Air Force historians Juliette A.

Hennessy, Roger Miller, Alfred Goldberg, Dan Hagadorn, and Dick Dasso between 11 November 2001 and 5 July 2002.

2. Brig. Gen. Ernest A. Garlington et al., "Proceedings of a Board of Officers Convened by the Secretary of War to Examine Conditions Existing in the Administration of the Aviation Section of the Signal Corps," Scriven's testimony and Reber's testimony, Records of the War Department General and Special Staffs, 1860–1952, RG165, National Archives at College Park, Maryland (hereafter cited as Garlington Board).

3. General Court-Martial, no. 95565, Lt. Col. Lewis E. Goodier, Kirtland's testimony, 47; and HR 5304 Hearings, Reber's testimony, 28 and 38.

4. General Court-Martial, no. 95565, Lt. Col. Lewis E. Goodier, Kirtland's testimony, 47.

5. Garlington Board, Reber's testimony, 4.

6. Garlington Board, Reber's testimony, 4.

7. Garlington Board, Scriven's testimony, 10.

8. General Court-Martial, no. 95565, Lt. Col. Lewis E. Goodier, Kirtland's testimony, 48.

9. General Court-Martial, no. 95565, Lt. Col. Lewis E. Goodier, Kirtland's testimony, 48.

10. General Court-Martial, no. 95565, Lt. Col. Lewis E. Goodier, Kirtland's testimony, 48.

11. "Round Table Discussion," 80.

12. Chandler and Lahm, *How Our Army Grew Wings*, 256–58.

13. Arnold, *Global Mission*, 42.

14. General Court-Martial, no. 95565, Lt. Col. Lewis E. Goodier, Kirtland's testimony, 49.

15. General Court-Martial, no. 95565, Lt. Col. Lewis E. Goodier, exhibit U.

16. Chief Signal Officer, "Accident No. 2," 111; "Death of Lieutenant Call," *Aeronautics*, July 1913, 32; Chandler and Lahm, *How Our Army Grew Wings*, 257–57; and Hennessy, *United States Army Air Arm*, 79.

9. Beck Makes His Move

1. HR 5304 Hearings, 3. Unless otherwise noted, the citations that follow are from this source and will consist of only the speaker or speakers and page number or numbers.

2. Scriven, 29.

3. Scriven, 29.

4. Reber, 28–29.

5. Foulois, 59 and 61.

6. Scriven, 48

7. Scriven (reading), 11.

8. Scriven, 12.

9. Russel, 24.

10. Nalty, *Winged Shield, Winged Sword*, 10.

11. Scriven, 19.

12. Reber, 28.

13. Garrett-Foulois exchange, 73.

14. Gard-Mitchell exchange, 83.

15. Beck's statement that follows is found on pages 38–45.

10. Cowan's Flight Pay

1. Crowder, "Conditions at Aviation School, San Diego, California, and in the Aviation Section of the Signal Corps," PT14, General Court-Martial, no. 95565, Lt. Col. Lewis E. Goodier.

2. General Court-Martial, no. 95565, Lt. Col. Lewis E. Goodier, exhibits J and U.

3. General Court-Martial, no. 95565, Lt. Col. Lewis E. Goodier, exhibits 62 and 71.

4. General Court-Martial, no. 95565, Lt. Col. Lewis E. Goodier, exhibits 34–54.

5. U.S. War Department, *Regulations for the Army of the United States, 1910, corrected to 20 June 1913*, article 76, paragraph 12921/2, C.A.R. 26, 19 April 1913.

6. General Court-Martial, no. 95565, Lt. Col. Lewis E. Goodier, exhibit B.

7. General Court-Martial, no. 95565, Lt. Col. Lewis E. Goodier, exhibits 62 and 71.

8. HR 5304 Hearings, Scriven's testimony, 34, 85.

9. HR 5304 Hearings, Scriven's testimony, 34, 85.

10. Chief Signal Officer, "Accident No. 2," 112.

11. General Court-Martial, no. 95565, Lt. Col. Lewis E. Goodier, Cowan's testimony, 174–75.

12. General Court-Martial, no. 95565, Lt. Col. Lewis E. Goodier, Cowan's testimony 174–75.

13. General Court-Martial, no. 95565, Lt. Col. Lewis E. Goodier, Cowan's testimony, 177.

14. General Court-Martial, no. 95565, Lt. Col. Lewis E. Goodier, Cowan's testimony, exhibit 15.

15. General Court-Martial, no. 95565, Lt. Col. Lewis E. Goodier, Ned Goodier's testimony, 347–49; Hennessy, *United States Army Air*, 86; and Ed Leiser, typewritten notes on the history of North Island, 72 pages (not numbered, several missing, and several partially damaged by fire), San Diego Aerospace Museum Library, San Diego, California.

16. Loening, *Monoplanes and Biplanes*, 49.

17. General Court-Martial, no. 95565, Lt. Col. Lewis E. Goodier, Dodd's testimony, 143.

18. General Court-Martial, no. 95565, Lt. Col. Lewis E. Goodier, exhibit K.

19. General Court-Martial, no. 95565, Lt. Col. Lewis E. Goodier, exhibit 18.

20. General Court-Martial, no. 95565, Lt. Col. Lewis E. Goodier, Colonel Goodier's testimony, 362.

21. Chandler and Lahm, *How Our Army Grew Wings*, 248.

22. General Court-Martial, no. 95565, Lt. Col. Lewis E. Goodier, exhibits 47–54 and 62.

11. The Seeds of Rebellion

1. General Court-Martial, no. 95565, Lt. Col. Lewis E. Goodier, Cowan's testimony, 178; Hennessy, *United States Army Air Arm*, 102; Foulois, *From the Wright Brothers to the Astronauts*, 91; and Cameron, *Training to Fly*, 46.

2. Loening, *Monoplanes and Biplanes*, 49.

3. Hennessy, *United States Army Air Arm*, 102.

4. Berriman, *Aviation*, 32–33.

5. Berriman, *Aviation*, 31–32.

6. "Round Table Discussion," 46; and Cameron, *Training to Fly*, 45.

7. Foulois, "Early Flying Experiences," Part II, 62; and Hennessy, *United States Army Air Arm*, 50.

8. Hennessy, *United States Army Air Arm*, 50.

9. Loening, *Monoplanes and Biplanes*, 49.

10. General Court-Martial, no. 95565, Lt. Col. Lewis E. Goodier, Dodd's testimony, 123, 152.

11. General Court-Martial, no. 95565, Lt. Col. Lewis E. Goodier, Colonel Goodier's testimony, 367.

12. Chamberlain IG Report, 19 March 1914, 13.

13. Arnold, "The History of Rockwell Field," 29, San Diego Aerospace Museum Library, San Diego, California.

14. Chamberlain IG Report, 19 March 1914, 5–6.

15. The details of the lost tools episode, including the quotes, are found in "Property Submitted for the Action of a Surveying Officer, 24 February 1914 with endorsements," Lewis E. Goodier Jr., private papers; and General Court-Martial, no. 95565, Lt. Col. Lewis E. Goodier, Dodd's testimony, 143.

16. The following exchange between Cowan and Willis is found in General Court-Martial, no. 95565, Lt. Col. Lewis E. Goodier, Cowan's testimony, 175–76.

17. General Court-Martial, no. 95565, Lt. Col. Lewis E. Goodier, 481–82.

18. Loening, *Monoplanes and Biplanes*, 58–59.

19. "Army Aviation," *Army and Navy Register*, 2 March 1912, 2.

20. Arnold, "History of Rockwell Field," 32.

12. William Lay Patterson

1. General Court-Martial, no. 95565, Lt. Col. Lewis E. Goodier, exhibit 33. To save needless repetition, sources from the Goodier court-martial transcript will be identified by only the speaker's name and page number or numbers, or trial exhibit number.

2. Exhibit 33.

3. Colonel Goodier's testimony, 381–82.

4. Kirtland's testimony, 58.

5. Colonel Goodier's testimony, 386.

6. Exhibit 63.

7. Colonel Goodier's testimony, 386, and exhibit 63.

8. There was another Curtiss SC no. 23, which Goodier had built from spare parts, but General Scriven would not allow it to be used. Hennessy, *United States Army Air Arm*, 92.

9. Kirtland's testimony, 50–51.

10. U.S. War Department, *Regulations for the Army of the United States 1913, Corrected to 10 June 1918*, article 87, paragraph 1269.

11. Chandler and Lahm, *How Our Army Grew Wings*, 317.

12. Exhibit V.

13. Exhibit W.

14. Exhibit 63.

15. Exhibits 3 and 4, and Cowan's testimony, 166.

16. Exhibit Y.

17. Exhibit X.

18. Exhibit 55.

19. Exhibit 56.

20. Exhibit 1.

21. Exhibit Z.

22. Reber's testimony and exhibit 2.

23. Exhibit 2.

24. Exhibit 3.

25. Chandler and Lahm, *How Our Army Grew Wings*, 285, and Hennessy, *United States Army Air Arm*, 238.

26. Cowan's testimony, 167.

27. Exhibit 64.

28. Exhibit 4.

29. Exhibits J and S.

30. Kirtland's testimony, 58.

31. Cowan's testimony, 67, and exhibit S.

32. Cowan's testimony, 67; Records of the Office of the Judge Advocate General (Army), RG153, National Archives at College Park, Maryland, 211; Scriven to the Adjutant General, telegram, 15 September 1914, "Amended Memorandum for the Adjutant General, U.S. Army"; and exhibit J.

33. Exhibit 57.

34. Cowan's testimony, 176–77.

13. The Rift

1. General Court-Martial, no. 95565, Lt. Col. Lewis E. Goodier, Cowan's testimony, 227; and Trial PT14. Sources from the Goodier court-martial transcript will be identified by only the speaker's name and page number or numbers, or trial exhibit number.

2. Kirtland's testimony, 227, and Trial PT17.

3. Jones's testimony, 80.

4. Dodd's testimony, 142.

5. Cowan's testimony, 161–62; Dodd's testimony, 139–40; and exhibits 5 and R.

6. Kirtland's testimony, 49–50.

7. Exhibit 17.

8. Dodd's testimony, 146–47.

9. Lieutenant Colonel Goodier's testimony, 435–36.

10. Loening, *Monoplanes and Biplanes*, 58–59.

11. The exchange between Cowan and Kirtland that follows is from Kirtland's testimony, 41–42.

12. Kirtland's testimony, 42–45.

13. Kirtland's testimony, 19.

14. Kirtland's testimony, 20.

15. Exhibits 8, 9, and 10.

16. Exhibit 10.

17. Exhibit 7.

18. Exhibit 8.

19. Kirtland's testimony, 20–21.

20. Kirtland's testimony, 22.

21. Exhibit 16.

22. Kirtland's testimony, 51.

23. Kirtland's testimony, 51.

24. Kirtland's testimony, 51–52.

25. Kirtland's testimony, 22.

26. Kirtland's testimony, 22.

27. Kirtland's testimony, 23.

28. Kirtland's testimony, 23.

29. Kirtland's testimony, 24–26.

30. Kirtland's testimony, 26.

14. Rebellion

1. Fourteen officers, Cowan, Foulois, Patterson, and eight student pilots had not been told about the meeting. One officer, 1st Lt. Virginius Clark, was away at MIT. General Court-Martial, no. 95565, Lt. Col. Lewis E. Goodier, exhibits A, E, 6, 7 (hereafter, sources from the transcript will be identified only by speakers' names and page numbers, or by trial exhibit numbers); Chandler and Lahm, *How Our Army Grew Wings*, 282–85; and Hennessy, *United States Army Air Arm*, 237–39.

2. Bowen, Jones, and Netherwood had been rated junior military aviators on 20 August 1914, well within the sixty-day window. Hennessy, *United States Army Air Arm*, 111.

3. Jones's testimony, 95.

4. Jones's testimony, 73.

5. Jones's testimony, 79.

6. Jones's testimony, 71 and 79.

7. Jones's testimony, 71.

8. Exhibits A and E.

9. Exhibits K and 24.

10. Jones's testimony, 67; Willis's testimony, 357; and Kirtland's testimony, 56.

11. Colonel Goodier's testimony, 370–71.

12. Exhibit B.

13. Exhibit B.

14. Exhibit B.

15. Exhibit B.

16. Exhibit 62.

17. Exhibit C.

18. Exhibit C.

19. Exhibit C.

20. Exhibit C.

21. Exhibit D.

22. Exhibit E.

23. U.S. War Department, *Regulations for the Army of the United States, 1910, Corrected to 20 June 1913*, "Articles of War," article 60.

24. Exhibit D.

25. Exhibit H.

26. U.S. War Department, *Regulations for the Army of the United States, 1910, Corrected to 20 June 1913*, "Articles of War," article 61.

27. Jones's testimony, 78, and exhibit D.

28. Exhibit D.

29. Dodd's testimony, 136.

30. Dodd's testimony, 126–27, and exhibit H.

31. Murry's testimony, 111.

32. Exhibit H.

33. Exhibit I.

34. Exhibit I.

35. Exhibit I.

36. Exhibit I.

37. Colonel Goodier's testimony, 416.

38. Exhibit I.

39. Exhibit K.

40. Exhibit K.

41. Exhibit K.

42. Exhibit K.

43. Exhibit M.

44. The details of what was said and done in Cowan's office are found in exhibit N.

15. The Reaction

1. General Court-Martial, no. 95565, Lt. Col. Lewis E. Goodier, exhibit N; and Colonel Goodier's testimony, 397. Sources from the Goodier court-martial transcript will be identified by only the speaker's name and page number or numbers, or trial exhibit number.

2. Exhibit Ca4.

3. Exhibit 21.

4. Exhibit 21.

5. Exhibit G.

6. Exhibit O.

7. Exhibit 22.

8. Exhibit 23.

9. Exhibit 22.

10. "Army Officer to Answer Charges," *San Francisco Chronicle*, 11 May 1915, 1.

11. Exhibit 24.

12. Exhibit 25.

13. Exhibit J.

14. Exhibit J.

15. Exhibit 25.

16. Exhibit S.

17. Exhibit 25.

18. Exhibit 58.

19. Exhibit 64.

20. Exhibits 23, 26, 29, 32, and Reber's testimony, 303.

21. Exhibit 13.

22. Reber's testimony, 281–82.

23. Exhibit 26.

24. Exhibit 28.

25. Exhibit 28.

26. Exhibit 29.

27. Exhibit 29.

28. Exhibit 63.

29. Exhibit 66.

30. Exhibits 66 and 30.

31. Exhibit 30.

32. Exhibit 31.

16. The Turnaround

1. General Court-Martial, no. 95565, Lt. Col. Lewis E. Goodier, exhibit 25. Sources from the Goodier court-martial transcript will be identified by only the speaker's name and page number or numbers, or trial exhibit number.

2. Exhibit 27.

3. Exhibit 72.

4. Cowan's testimony, 184.

5. Exhibit J.

6. Exhibit 72.

7. Cowan's testimony, 184.

8. Gorrell's testimony, 462.

9. Jones's testimony, 92.

10. Exhibit 72.

11. Exhibits S and 25.

12. Exhibit T.

13. Exhibit J.

14. Reber's testimony, 270, and PT19.

15. Exhibit J.

16. PT18–PT24 and Jones's testimony, 92–94.

17. Exhibit 57 and Gorrell's testimony, 462–63.

18. Exhibit 72.

19. Exhibit 73.

20. Exhibit 74.

21. A law is said to be prospective when it is applicable only to cases that shall arise in the future. Bouvier, *A Law Dictionary*, 389.

22. Exhibit 75.

23. Hennessy, *United States Army Air Arm*, 144.

17. Court-Martial

1. U.S. War Department, *Regulations for the Army of the United States, 1910, corrected to 20 June 1913*, "Articles of War," article 62.

2. General Court-Martial, no. 95565, Lt. Col. Lewis E. Goodier, Kirtland's testimony, 19–28. Sources from the Goodier court-martial transcript will be identified by only the speaker's name and page number or numbers, or trial exhibit number.

3. Kirtland's testimony, 30.

4. Kirtland's testimony, 39.

5. Kirtland's testimony, 39.

6. Kirtland's testimony, 46–48.

7. Jones's testimony, 68.

8. Jones's testimony, 70.

9. Jones's testimony, 79.

10. Jones's testimony, 80–81.

11. Jones's testimony, 87.

12. Jones's testimony, 87.

13. Jones's testimony, 96.

14. Major General Murry's direct testimony and cross-examination, 102–11, and Colonel Erwin's testimony, 112–15.

15. Dodd's testimony, 145–51.

16. Cowan's first time on the stand, 160–241.

17. Geary's introduction of exhibit 72 and arguments, 248–65.

18. Reber's testimony, 279, and exhibit 8.

19. Reber's testimony, 276, and exhibit 2.

20. Reber's testimony, 292, and exhibit 25.

21. Reber's testimony, 292, and exhibit 25.

22. Reber's testimony, 293.

23. Reber's testimony, 293–94.

24. Reber's testimony, 283–85, and exhibit 16.

25. Reber's testimony, 281, and exhibit 15.

26. Reber's testimony, 281, exhibit 15, and Dodd's second time on the stand, 324–29.

27. Colonel Erwin's testimony, 333–35.

28. Colonel Erwin's testimony, Ned Goodier's testimony, 335–51.

29. Ned Goodier's testimony, 335–51, Willis's testimony, 352–59.

30. Willis's testimony, 352–59, Colonel Goodier cross-examination, 433.

31. Colonel Goodier cross-examination, 433, Gorrell's testimony, 462–63.

32. Gorrell's testimony, 462–63, Cowan's second time on the stand, 475–79.

33. Cowan's second time on the stand, 480.

34. Cowan's second time on the stand, 480.

35. "Army Court Verdict Found in 90 Minutes; Sealed Verdict to Be Sent to Secretary of War," *San Francisco Chronicle*, 19 November 1915, section 2, 2.

36. Greer's closing argument, 491–514.

37. Humphreys's closing argument, 515–74.

38. Geary's closing argument, 575–601.

18. The Garlington Board

1. Col. Daniel C. Shanks, "IG Inspection at the Signal Corps Flying School, North Island, San Diego, 2–4 February 1916," 7 February 1916, Records of the Inspector General (Army), RG159, National Archives at College Park, Maryland.

2. Chief Signal Officer to Adjutant General, third endorsement, 9 February 1916, Records of the Office of the Chief Signal Officer, 1860–1982, RG111, National Archives.

3. *Investigation of the Air Service, United States Army*, S. Rep. no. 64-153 at 1–4 (1916).

4. Adjutant General to Brig. Gen. Ernest A. Garlington, 15 February 1916, Records of the Adjutant General, 1783–1928, RG94, National Archives.

5. The proceedings of the board, including the questions and the testimony given before the board, and the conclusions are found in "Committee of Officers Convened to Examine into the Conditions Respecting the Administration of the Aviation Section of the Signal Corps, 17 February–29 March 1916," Records of the Adjutant General, 1783–1928, RG94, National Archives.

6. Hennessy, *United States Army Air Arm*, 154; and "Army Shakeup of Aero Service Started," *New York Times*, 18 April 1916, 3.

7. "Secretary of War to Col. Chase W. Kennedy, 21 April 1916," Records of the War Department, General and Special Staffs, 1860–1952, RG165, National Archives.

8. Exhibit VI, "Letter from Capt. D. B. Foulois, commanding 1st Aero Squadron, 30 April 1916," Report of Committee on Aviation, Records of the War Department, General and Special Staffs, RG165, National Archives.

9. Exhibit VI, exhibit VII, "Committee's letter in reply to VI above, 6 May 1916."

10. Exhibit VII, exhibit XIV, "Proposed Organization of a Flying Corps."

11. Exhibit XIV, exhibit XXIV, "Letter from Capt. Roy C. Kirtland, containing proposed tactical organization and legislation for the Aviation Service."

12. Exhibit XXIV, exhibit XVI, "Notes on proposed flying corps by 1st Lt. H. A. Dargue (from stenographic notes)."

13. Exhibit XVI.

14. Hennessy, *United States Army Air Arm*, 154–55.

19. Separation Achieved

1. Arnold, *Global Mission*, 67–68.

2. Mixter and Emmons, *United States Army Aircraft Production Facts*, 5–7.

3. *Aircraft Production Hearings before the Subcommittee of the Committee on Military Affairs, United States Senate*, 65th Cong., 2nd Sess., 203–18 (1918; hereafter cited as Aircraft Production Hearings).

4. Aircraft Production Hearings, 212.

5. Mixter and Emmons, *United States Army Aircraft Production Facts*, 25–27.

6. Aircraft Production Hearings, 203, 218.

7. Sweetser, *American Air Service*, 46–47; "Plan to Build 3,500 War Airplanes and Train 5,000 Aviators in a Year," *New York Times*, 21 May 1917; and Manufacturers Aircraft Association, *Aircraft Year Book*, 33.

8. "Says with Aircraft We Can Win the War," *New York Times*, 14 June 1917.

9. $640,000,000 Asked for Huge Air Fleet," *New York Times*, 16 June 1917.

10. Taliaferro, *Great White Fathers*, 164; and Howard, *Wilbur and Orville*, 414.

11. Taliaferro, *Great White Fathers*, 164; Borglum to Brig. Gen. George O. Squire, 14 September 1917, as printed in "Borglum Accused of Personal Ends," *New York Times*, 11 May 1918; and Howard, *Wilbur and Orville*, 414.

12. Taliaferro, *Great White Fathers*, 165.

13. Aircraft Production Hearings, 257–70.

14. "Pleads for Haste in Airplane Aid," *New York Times*, 13 December 1917.

15. "Our Army's Work," *New York Times*, 23 December 1917.

16. "Aircraft Program Progressing Well," *New York Times*, 11 January 1918; Sweetser, *American Air Service*, 211; and Aircraft Production Hearings, 211; Mixter and Emmons, *United States Army Aircraft Production Facts*, 9; and Howard, *Wilbur and Orville*, 414. Howard says the change from Deeds to Potter occurred in February.

17. "Overman Bill Expected to Fail," *New York Times*, 8 February 1918; and "Overman Bill Put into Shape for Compromise," *New York Times*, 14 February 1918.

18. "Foe Come and Go at Will," *New York Times*, 21 February 1918.

19. "Seek to Remedy Aircraft Delay," *New York Times*, 18 March 1918.

20. "Enemy Activities in Aircraft Hunted," *New York Times*, 20 March 1918.

21. "Marshall on War Board," *New York Times*, 13 March 1918.

22. Wilson to Borglum, as printed in "Wilson Orders Borglum Charges Sifted," *New York Times*, 7 May 1918.

23. Howard, *Wilbur and Orville*, 414; Sweetser, *American Air Service*, 215; "Board Will Sift Aircraft Charges," *New York Times*, 17 March 1918; and "Aircraft Board Takes up Charges," *New York Times*, 19 March 1918.

24. "Assails Auto Men in Airplane Tangle," *New York Times*, 12 April 1918.

25. Senate Committee on Military Affairs, aircraft report, as printed in "Senators Demand One-Man Control of Aviation," *New York Times*, 11 April 1918.

26. "Shake Up at Hand in Aircraft Work," *New York Times*, 13 April 1918.

27. Wilson to Borglum, 15 April 1918, as printed in "Wilson Orders Borglum Charges Sifted," *New York Times*, 7 May 1918.

28. "J. D. Ryan Chosen to Direct Making of Airplanes," *New York Times*, 25 April 1918.

29. "Borglum Charges Air Profiteering," *New York Times*, 28 April 1918.

30. Editorial, *New York Times*, 25 April 1918.

31. "Borglum Charges Air Profiteering," *New York Times*, 28 April 1918.

32. "Senate Takes Up Borglum Charges," *New York Times*, 30 April 1918.

33. "Baker Is Assailed in Aircraft Report," *New York Times*, 1 May 1918.

34. "Baker Is Assailed in Aircraft Report," *New York Times*, 1 May 1918.

35. Adjutant General to Chief Signal Officer, 29 May 1918, Records of the Adjutant General, 1780–1917, RG94, National Archives at College Park, Maryland.

36. General Orders no. 51, 29 May 1918, Records of the Adjutant General, 1780–1917, RG94, National Archives.

37. John J. Pershing, *My Experiences in World War I*, 1:161.

38. *Aeronautics in the Army: Hearings before the Committee on Military Affairs in Connection with H.R. 5304*, 63rd Cong., 1st Sess., 27 (1913).

Epilogue

1. Foulois, *From the Wright Brothers to the Astronauts*, 69; Hennessy, *United States Army Air Arm*, 39; Chandler and Lahm, *How Our Army Grew Wings*, 262; and Krisman, *Register of Graduates and Former Cadets*, Cullum no. 4460, 297.

2. Paul W. Beck, Military Records, 1896–1922, Records of the Adjutant General, 1783–1928, RG94, National Archives at College Park, Maryland; "Was Beck Shot from Behind?," *Oklahoman*, 7 April 1922; "Lawton Friends Sure Full Story Will Vindicate Beck: Is All Told? Hughes Asks," *Oklahoman*, 7 April 1922; "Beck's Son Coming Today," *Oklahoman*, 8 April 1922; "Coroner's Jury Clears Day," *Oklahoman*, 9 April 1922; "Nephew of Beck Is Not Satisfied with Verdict," *Oklahoman*, 9 April 1922; "Planes Will Say Farewell as Beck Train Heads East," *Oklahoman*, 9 April 1922; "Planes Hum Last Dirge over Beck," *Oklahoman*, 13 April 1922; "Army Board Files Report in Day Case," *Oklahoman*, 29 April 1922; "Weeks Silent in Beck Case," *Oklahoman*, 30 April 1922; "Day's Wife in Divorce Plea," *Oklahoman*, 15 October 1930.

3. Daso, *Hap Arnold and the Evolution of American Airpower*, 85; Krisman, *Register of Graduates*, Cullum no. 3935.

4. Pershing, *My Experiences in the World War*, 1:20, 159, 161, 283; Mauer, *Aviation in the U.S. Army, 1919–1939*, 52 and 107; "Col. Dodd, Our First Commissioned Aviator, Crushed to Death in an Airplane Accident," *New York Times*, 6 October 1918; and Chandler and Lahm, *How Our Army Grew Wings*, 285.

5. Foulois, *From the Wright Brothers to the Astronauts*, 159–83; and "Major General Benjamin Delahauf Foulois," U.S. Air Force, https://www.af.mil/About-Us/Biographies/Display/Article/107091/major-general-benjamin-delahauf-foulois/, accessed April 2019.

6. Interview with Ward Goodier, June 1998; and Lewis E. Goodier Jr., untitled, handwritten, fourteen-page Ned Goodier biography, private papers in the possession of Ward Goodier.

7. Mauer, *Aviation in the U.S. Army, 1919–1939*, 301 and 333; and Krisman, *Register of Graduates and Former Cadets*, Cullum no. 5044.

8. Stephen F. Watson, "From Splendid Aviator to Capable Executive," unpublished thirty-two-page typed manuscript, 22–26.

9. Hennessy, *United States Army Air Arm*, 151–52; and Mauer, *Aviation in the U.S. Army, 1919–1939*, 109.

10. Craig, "Col. Samuel Reber, U.S. Army Signal Corps," 2–5; Hennessy, *United States Army Air Arm*, 154; and Krisman, *Register of Graduates and Former Cadets*, Cullum no. 3113.

11. Krisman, *Register of Graduates and Former Cadets*, Cullum no. 2721.

12. Sloan, *Wings of Honor*, 199 and 365; Wurzburg, *The Battle of Chatillon*, 21–22; and Krisman, *Register of Graduates*, Cullum no. 4833.

13. Hennessy, *United States Army Air Arm*, 80–81, 163–64; and Simpson, *World War I Diary of Col. Frank P. Lahm*, 217.

14. Krisman, *Register of Graduates and Former Cadets*, Cullum no. 4829; and Simpson, *World War I Diary of Col. Frank P. Lahm*, 104.

15. Hennessy, *United States Army Air Arm*, 163; and "Flight Leader Dies in Flaming Crash," *New York Times*, 18 May 1927; Krisman, *Register of Graduates and Former Cadets*, Cullum no. 4664.

16. General Court-Martial, no. 95565, Lt. Col. Lewis E. Goodier, exhibits 8, 9, 20, 26; Brig. Gen. Henry P. McCain to Commanding Officer, Letterman General Hospital, telegram, 29 June 1915; and transcript of partial notes by Bruce Reynolds of taped memoir of Col. L. E. "Ned" Goodier, Goodier papers.

17. "Brigadier General Thomas D. Milling," U.S. Air Force, https://www.af.mil/About-Us/Biographies/Display/Article/106225/brigadier-general-thomas-d-milling/, accessed April 2019; and Krisman, *Register of Graduates and Former Cadets*, Cullum no. 4813.

18. Robert Henry Willis Jr., www.earlyaviators.com, accessed June 2002.

19. "Biographic Memoirs of George Owen Squier," presented to the National Academy of Science General Meeting, transcript in the author's possession; Krisman, *Register of Graduates and Former Cadets*, Cullum no. 3180, 274.

20. Krisman, *Register of Graduates and Former Cadets*, Cullum no. 3184, 274; and Mauer, *U.S. Air Service in World War I*, 2:107.

BIBLIOGRAPHY

Archival and Unpublished Sources

Air Force Historical Foundation, Maxwell Air Force Base, Alabama

Foulois, Benjamin D. Oral history. Typed transcript, 72 pages, K239.0512-766.

"Round Table Discussion with Generals Benjamin Foulois, Frank Lahm, and Thomas Milling." Interview no. 767, 29 June 1954. Typed transcript, 81 pages, K239.0512-767.

Defense Technical Information Center, Washington DC

"The First Army Aircraft Accident Report." ADA382312.

Goodier, Lewis E., Jr. Private papers in the possession of Ward Goodier.

National Air and Space Museum, Washington DC

Thomas DeWitt Milling Collection.

National Archives at College Park, Maryland

Records of Naval Districts and Shore Establishments, RG181.

Records of the Adjutant General, 1783–1928, RG94.

Records of the Army Staff, 1903–1996, RG319.

Records of the Inspector General (Army), RG159.

Records of the Office of the Chief Signal Officer, RG111.

Records of the Office of the Judge Advocate General (Army), RG153.

Records of the War Department General and Special Staffs, RG165.

San Diego Aerospace Museum Library, San Diego, California

Arnold, Henry H. "The History of Rockwell Field." Unpublished, typewritten, 122-page manuscript, 1923.

Leiser, Ed. Typewritten, 72-page notes on the history of North Ireland.

Watson, Stephen F. "From Splendid Aviator to Capable Executive." Unpublished, typewritten, 32-page manuscript in his possession.

Published Sources

Aero Club of America. *Aero Club of America, 1911.* New York: Douglas Taylor and Company, 1911.

——. *Aero Club of America, 1912.* New York: Douglas Taylor and Company, 1912.

——. *Aero Club of America, 1913.* New York: Douglas Taylor and Company, 1913.

——. *Aero Club of America, 1915.* New York: Douglas Taylor and Company, 1915.

———. *Aero Club of America, 1916*. New York: Douglas Taylor and Company, 1916.

Aircraft Manufacturers Association. *Aircraft Yearbook for 1919*. New York: Manufacturers Aircraft Association, 1919.

Air Force Systems Command (AFSC). *Development of Airborne Armament, 1910–1961*. Vol. 1, *Bombing Systems* (paper binding, 66 pages, no page numbers). AFSC Historical Publications Series, 61-52-1.

Allen, Brig. Gen. James. *Report of the Chief Signal Officer, for the Fiscal Year 1906*. *Washington, DC: Government Printing Office, 1906*.

———. *Report of the Chief Signal Officer, for the Fiscal Year 1908*. Washington DC: Government Printing Office, 1908.

———. *Report of the Chief Signal Officer to the Secretary of War, 1909*. Washington DC: Government Printing Office, 1909.

———. *Report of the Chief Signal Officer to the Secretary of War, 1910*. Washington DC: Government Printing Office, 1910.

———. *Report of the Chief Signal Officer to the Secretary of War, 1911*. Washington DC: Government Printing Office, 1911.

Arnold, Henry H. *Global Mission*. New York: Harper and Brothers, 1949.

Beck, Paul W. "Doves of War." *Sunset Magazine*, March 1911, 11–12.

———. "Flying Men-O-War." *Sunset Magazine*, March 1910, 22–24.

———. "Military Aviation in America—Its Needs." *Flying*, October and November 1912, 21–26.

———. "Military Aviation in America—Its Needs." *Infantry Journal* 8, no. 6 (May–June 1912): 798–817.

———. "Military Aviation in America—Its Needs." *Leslie's Weekly*, November 1912.

Berriman, Algernon E. *Aviation: An Introduction to the Elements of Flight*. London: Methuen and Company, 1913; New York: H. Doran Company, 1913.

Bethell, Henry Arthur. *Modern Guns and Gunnery, 1910: A Practical Manual for Officers of the Horse, Field, and Mountain Artillery*. Woolwich, UK: F. J. Cattermole, 1910.

Bouvier, John. *A Law Dictionary Adapted for the United States of America and the Several States of the American Union*. 14th ed., vol. 2. Boston: Little, Brown, and Company, 1880.

Bowers, Peter M. *Curtiss Aircraft, 1907–1947*. Annapolis: Naval Institute Press, 1979.

Brewer, Robert W. A. *The Art of Aviation: A Handbook upon Aeroplanes and Their Engines, with Notes upon Propellers*. New York: McGraw-Hill Book Company, 1910; London: Crosby Lockwood and Son, 1910.

Casey, Louis S. *Curtiss: The Hammondsport Era, 1907–1915*. New York: Crown Publishers, 1981.

Chandler, Capt. Charles DeForest. "Army Aviation: Its Needs." *Aero Club of America Bulletin* 7, no. 1 (January–March 1912): 40–52.

———. "The Lewis Aeroplane Gun." *Journal of the United States Artillery* 38, no. 2 (September–October 1912): 222.

Chandler, Capt. Charles DeForest, and Frank P. Lahm. *How Our Army Grew Wings: Airmen and Aircraft before 1914*. New York: Ronald Press, 1943.

Chief Signal Officer. "Accident No. 2, 2nd Lt. George Kelly: Extract from Proceedings of Board of Officers at San Antonio, Texas, 10 May 1911." Prepared in the Office of the Chief Signal Officer, 28 February 1914. Published as "Mortality in Army Aviation." *American Aviation Historical Society Journal* 9, no. 2 (Summer 1964): 109–14.

Cooper, Edward S. *William Babcock Hazen: The Best Hated Man.* Madison NJ: Fairleigh Dickinson University Press, 2005.

Craig, Howard A. "Col. Charles DeForest Chandler, Air Service, U. S. Army." *American Aviation Historical Society Journal* 18, no. 3 (Fall 1973): 196–99.

———. "Col. Samuel Reber, U. S. Army Signal Corps." *American Aviation Historical Society Journal* 20, no. 2 (Spring 1975): 2–5.

Crouch, Tom D. *Wings: A History of Aviation from Kites to the Space Age.* New York: W. W. Norton Company, 2003.

Crozier, Maj. Gen. William. *Ordnance and the World War.* New York: Charles Scribner's Sons, 1920.

Curtiss, Glenn, and Augustus Post. *The Curtiss Aviation Book.* New York: Frederick A. Stokes, Company, 1912.

Daso, Dik Alan. *Hap Arnold and the Evolution of American Airpower.* Washington DC: Smithsonian Institution Press, 2000.

David, Evan John. *Aircraft: Its Development in War and Peace and Its Commercial Future.* New York: Charles Scribner's Sons, 1919.

Ennis, Earl E. "Wireless Telegraphy from an Aeroplane." *Journal of Electricity, Power, and Gas* 20, no. 4 (April 1911): 36–45.

Fahey, James C. *U. S. Army Aircraft, 1908–1946.* Falls Church VA: Ships and Aircraft, 1946.

Fales, E. N. *Learning to Fly in the U. S. Army: A Manual of Aviation Practice.* New York: McGraw-Hill Book Company, 1917.

Foulois, Benjamin D. "Early Flying Experiences: Why Write a Book?" Part I. *The Air Power Historian* 2, no. 2 (April 1955): 17–35.

———. "Early Flying Experiences: Why Write a Book?" Part II. *Air Power Historian* 2, no. 3 (July 1955): 45–65.

———. "Early Flying Experiences: Why Write a Book?" Part III. *Air Power Historian* 3, no. 2 (April 1956): 114–33.

———. *From the Wright Brothers to the Astronauts: The Memoirs of Major General Benjamin D. Foulois.* New York: McGraw Hill, 1968.

Gardner, Lester D. *Who's Who in American Aeronautics.* New York: Overbook Press, 1922.

Gill, Capt. N. J. *The Flyer's Guide: An Elementary Handbook for Aviators.* New York: E. P. Dutton and Company, 1917.

Goldberg, Alfred, ed. *A History of the United States Air Force, 1907–1957.* New York: D. Van Nostrand Company, 1957.

Grice, Gary K., ed. "The Beginning of the National Weather Service: The Signal Corps Years, 1870–1891, as Viewed by Early Weather Pioneers." National Aeronautics and Space Administration. http://www.nws.noaa.gov/pa/history/signal.php. Accessed 9 January 2018.

Hancock, Cameron, Rebecca. *Training to Fly: Military Flight Training, 1907–1945.* Washington DC: Government Printing Office, 1999.

Hearne, R. P. *Aerial Warfare.* London: John Lane Company, 1909.

Hennessy, Juliette A. *The United States Army Air Arm, April 1861 to April 1917.* Washington DC: Government Printing Office, 1986.

Holley, Irving B. *Ideas and Weapons.* Air Force History and Museums Program. Washington DC: Government Printing Office, 1997.

Howard, Fred. *Wilbur and Orville.* Mineola NY: Dover Books, 1998.

"Investigation of the Air Service, United States Army." 64th Cong., 1st Sess. *Senate Reports (Public),* vol. 1. Washington DC: Government Printing Office, 1916.

Ives, Herbert E. *Airplane Photography.* Philadelphia: J. B. Lippincott Company, 1920.

Jackman, William James, Thomas Herbert Russell, and Octave Chanute. *Flying Machines: Construction and Operations.* Chicago: Charles C. Thompson Co., 1912.

Jakab, Peter. "Eugene Ely and the Birth of Naval Aviation—January 18, 1911." Smithsonian Air and Space Museum, 18 January 2011. https://airandspace.si.edu/stories/editorial/eugene-ely-and-birth-naval-aviation%E2%80%94january-18-1911.

Johnson, Herbert A. *Wingless Eagle: U. S. Army Aviation through World War I.* Chapel Hill: University of North Carolina Press, 2001.

Krisman, Michael J., ed. *Register of Graduates and Former Cadets of the United States Military Academy.* U.S. Military Academy, Association of Graduates, 1980.

Lanchester, F. W. *Aircraft in Warfare: Dawn of the Fourth Arm.* London: Constable and Company, 1916.

Layman, Martha E. *Legislation Relating to the Air Corps Personnel and Training Programs, 1907 to 1939.* Army Air Force Historical Studies, no. 39. Assistant Chief of Staff, Intelligence, Historical Division, 1945.

Loening, Grover. *Our Wings Grow Faster.* New York: Doubleday, Doran, and Company, 1935.

Loening, Grover Cleveland. *Monoplanes and Biplanes, Their Design, Construction, and Operation.* New York: Munn and Company, 1911.

Manufacturers Aircraft Association. *Aircraft Year Book.* New York: Manufacturers Aircraft Association, 1919.

Mauer, Mauer, ed. *Aviation in the U.S. Army, 1919–1939.* Washington DC: Government Printing Office, 1986.

———. *The U.S. Air Service in World War I.* 4 vols. Washington DC: Government Printing Office, 1978.

Miller, Roger. "Kept Alive by the Postman: The Wright Brothers and 1st Lt. Benjamin D. Foulois at Fort Sam Houston in 1910." *Air Power History* 49, no. 4 (Winter 2002): 41–44.

Miller, Roger G. *A Preliminary to War: The First Aero Squadron and the Mexican Punitive Expedition of 1916.* Washington DC: Air Force History and Museums Program, 2003.

Milling, Thomas DeWitt. "Early Flying Experiences." *Air Power Historian* 3, no. 1 (January 1956): 92–105.

Millis, Walter. *The Road to War.* Boston: Houghton Mifflin Company, 1935.

Mitchell, Brig. Gen. William. *Memoirs of World War I.* New York: Random House, 1960.

Mixter, G. W., and H. H. Emmons. *United States Army Aircraft Production Facts.* Washington DC: Government Printing Office, 1919.

Moedebeck, Hermann W. *Pocketbook of Aeronautics.* Translated by W. Mansergh Varley. London: Whittaker and Company, 1907.

Mooney, Chase C., and Martha E. Layman. *Organization of Military Aeronautics, 1907–1935 (Congressional and War Department Action).* Army Air Force Historical Studies, no. 25. Assistant Chief of Staff, Intelligence, Historical Division, 1944.

Morgan, Jane. *Electronics in the West: The First Fifty Years.* Palo Alto CA: National Press Books, 1967.

Morrow, John Howard, Jr. *Building German Airpower, 1909–1914.* Knoxville: University of Tennessee Press, 1976.

The Motor Staff. *Aero Manual.* London: Temple Press, 1909.

Müller, Maj. Hollis LeRoy. *Manual of Military Aviation.* Menasha WI: George Banta Publishing Company, 1917.

Nalty, Bernard C., ed. *Winged Shield, Winged Sword.* Washington DC: Government Printing Office, 1997.

National Academy of Sciences. *Biographical Memoirs.* Vol. 20. New York: National Academy of Sciences, 1938.

Neher, Franz Ludwig. *Das Wunder des Fliegens: Ein Bild von Fliegen und Flugzeugen.* Munich: Kurt Pechstein Verlag, 1938.

Neumann, Georg Paul. *Die deutschen Luftstreitkräfte im Weltkrieg.* Berlin: Ernst Siegfried Mittler und Sohn, 1920.

New York World. *The World Almanac and Encyclopedia, 1912.* New York: Press Publishing Company, 1911.

Office of the Chief Signal Officer. Circular no. 1, *Radiotelegraphy.* Revised May 1915. Washington DC: Government Printing Office, 1915.

———. *Principals Underlying Radio Communication.* Radio Pamphlet no. 40, 10 December 1918. Washington DC: Government Printing Office, 1919.

Ordnance Department. *Army Ordnance, 1917–1919: History of Rifles, Revolvers, and Pistols.* Washington DC: Government Printing Office, 1920.

Peck, Wallace R. "Forgotten Air Pioneers: The Army's Rockwell Field at North Island." *Journal of San Diego History* 52, no. 3 (Summer–Fall 2006): 101–30.

Pershing, John J. *My Experiences in the World War.* 2 vols. New York: Frederick A. Stokes Company, 1931.

Raines, Rebecca Robbins. *Getting the Message Through: A Branch of the Unit History of the U.S. Army Signal Corps.* Washington DC: Government Printing Office, 1996.

Russel, Henry, ed. *A Happy Warrior: Letters of William Muir Russel, an American Aviator in the Great War, 1917–1918; A Family Memorial.* Privately published, 1919.

Scriven, Brig. Gen. George P. *Report of the Chief Signal Officer to the Secretary of War, 1913.* Washington DC: Government Printing Office, 1913.

———. *Report of the Chief Signal Officer to the Secretary of War, 1914.* Washington DC: Government Printing Office, 1914.

———. *Report of the Chief Signal Officer to the Secretary of War, 1915.* Washington DC: Government Printing Office, 1915.

———. *The Service of Information, United States Army: A Review of the Nature, Use, Field of Service, and Organization of the Signal Corps of the Army, with Outlines of Its Methods, and Technical Apparatus, and Notes of the Service of Information and the Organization of the Aviation Service of the Leading Foreign Armies.* Washington DC: Government Printing Office, 1915.

Simpson, Albert F., ed. *The World War I Diary of Col. Frank P. Lahm, Air Service, AEF.* U.S. Air Force Historical Studies, no. 141. Maxwell Air Force Base AL: Historical Research Division, Aerospace Studies Institute, 1970.

Sloan, James J. *Wings of Honor: American Airmen in World War I.* Atglen PA: Schiffer, 1994.

Smith, Laurence Yard. *The Romance of Aircraft.* New York: Frederick E Stokes Company, 1919.

Society of Automotive Engineers. *Aeronautics: Recommended Practices, 1918.* New York: Society of Automotive Engineers, 1918.

Swanborough, F. G. *United States Military Aircraft Since 1909.* London: Putnam, 1963.

Sweetser, Arthur. *The American Air Service: A Record of Its Problems, Its Difficulties, Its Failures, and Its Final Achievements.* New York: D. Appleton and Company, 1919.

Taliaferro, John. *Great White Fathers.* New York: Public Affairs, 2002.

Tretler, David Allen. "Opportunity Missed: Congressional Reorganization of the Army Air Service, 1917–1920." Master's thesis, Rice University, 1978.

Turnbull, Archibald D., and Clifford L. Lord. *History of United States Naval Aviation.* New Haven: Yale University Press, 1949.

U.S. Department of Commerce. *Statistical Abstract of the United States, 1918.* Washington DC: Government Printing Office, 1919.

U.S. Naval Academy Alumni Association. *Register of Alumni, 1845–1992.* Annapolis MD, 1991.

U.S. Navy Department. Bureau of Construction and Repair. *Annual Report of the Chief of the Bureau of Construction and Repair to the Secretary of the Navy for the Fiscal Year 1908.* Washington DC: Government Printing Office, 1908.

U.S. Patent Office. *Annual Report of the Commissioner of Patents, 1912.* Washington DC: Government Printing Office, 1912.

U.S. War Department. *Compilation of General Orders, Circulars and Bulletins of the War Department Issued between February 15, 1881, and December 31, 1915.* Washington DC: Government Printing Office, 1918.

———. *Field Service Regulations, United States Army, 1905, Amended 1908.* War Department Document no. 316. Washington DC: Government Printing Office, 1908.

———. *Field Service Regulations, 1913, Corrected to 31 May 1913.* War Department Document no. 363. Washington DC: Government Printing Office, 1913.

———. *Field Service Regulations, 1914, Corrected to 15 April 1917, Changes 1–6.* War Department Document no. 475. Washington DC: Government Printing Office, 1917.

———. *General Orders and Bulletins, 1913.* Washington DC: Government Printing Office, 1914.

———. *A Manual for Courts-Martial, Courts of Inquiry, and Other Procedures under Military Law, 1915 (corrected to 15 April 1917)*. Washington DC: Government Printing Office, 1917.

———. *Regulations for the Army of the United States, 1889*. Washington DC: Government Printing Office, 1889.

———. *Regulations for the Army of the United States, 1901*. Washington DC: Government Printing Office, 1902.

———. *Regulations for the Army of the United States, 1904*. Document no. 320. Washington DC: Government Printing Office, 1904.

———. *Regulations for the Army of the United States, 1908*. Washington DC: Government Printing Office, 1908.

———. *Regulations for the Army of the United States, 1910*. Document no. 384. Washington DC: Government Printing Office, 1911.

———. *Regulations for the Army of the United States, 1910, Corrected to 20 June 1913*. Washington DC: Government Printing Office, 1913.

———. *Regulations for the Army of the United States, 1910, with Corrections to 3 November 1913*. Document no. 384. Washington DC: Government Printing Office, 1914.

———. *Regulations for the Army of the United States, 1913, Corrected to 15 April 1917: Changes 1 to 55*. Document no. 454. Washington DC: Government Printing Office, 1917.

———. *Regulations for the Army of the United States, 1913, Corrected to 10 June 1918: Changes 1 to 73*. Document no. 454. New York: Military Publishing Company, 1918.

Weigley, Russell F. *History of the United States Army*. New York: MacMillan Company, 1967; London: Collier-Macmillan, Ltd., 1967.

The World Almanac and Encyclopedia, 1912. New York: The Press Publishing Company, 1911.

Wurzburg, Donald B. *The Battle of Chatillon: A Graphic History of the 2nd Corps Aeronautical School*. Grand Rapids MI: Dean-Hicks, 1919.

INDEX

1st Aero Squadron: 1st Company of, 117; 2nd Company of, 121; and Arthur Cowan, 169; and Benjamin Foulois, 139, 147; at Brownsville TX, 200; at Columbus NM, 213, 217; dissidents of, 147, 204; at Galveston TX, 117; and Kennedy Committee, 215–18; and legislation establishing separate flying corps, 216; named, 241, 244, 245, 246; and original Curtiss planes, 215; pilots' poor opinions of their leaders, 214; shoddy airplanes of, 214; and Tom Bowen's crash, 131

1st Aero Squadron (Provisional), 80–82, 169

2nd Aero Squadron, 140, 199, 209, 243

5th Infantry, 26–28

7th Infantry, 61, 82, 182

8th Infantry, 32, 35, 38

8th Pursuit Group, 242

9th Cavalry, 23

10th Cavalry, 22

11th Infantry, 39

13th Cavalry, 213

18th Infantry, 35

22nd Infantry, 217

A-4 Aeroplane Wireless Telegraph, 33

Acme Wire Company, 226

Aero Club of America (ACA), 13, 14, 45, 55, 64–71, 207

Aeronautical Division of the Signal Corps, 11, 12, 53, 63–73, 94

Aeronautical Engineers Society, 217

Ainsworth, Fred, 28

aircraft industry: Air Division of, 223; automobile people dominate, 221; and boards, 221; Construction Division of, 223; Curtiss dominates, 224; Equipment Division of, 221–28, 233, 245; inexperience of, in mass production, 222; infant, 220; problems in, 221, 222–25, 230; standardization of, 221; Supply Division of, 223

Aircraft Manufacturers Association, 221, 224

air meets: First International Air Meet in Los Angeles, 31–32, 93; Harvard-Boston Aero Meet, 46; Nassau Boulevard, 47; San Francisco, 32, 33, 48, 93

air races: Gordon Bennett International Balloon Race, 13; Lahm Trophy Race, 13; MacKay Trophy competition, 137; Second Gordon Bennett International Balloon Race, 13–14; Tri-State Race, 47

air tests, 241

Albuquerque Army Air Base, 243

Alger, Russell A., 24, 25

Allen, James: and the ACA, 14; appointed CSO, 11, 12; and Benjamin Foulois, 19; memos of, 3, 12, 17, 91; and military aviation, 1; moral objection of, to bombing, 49; and Paul Beck, 29, 42; poor management of, 18, 45; and reconnaissance, 2, 14, 53

American Expeditionary Forces (AEF), 224, 237, 241

American School of Aviation, 19

appropriations, 2, 14, 42, 54, 58, 61, 78

Army of Cuban Pacification, 16

army regulations, 9, 96, 120, 169, 173, 177, 202

Army War College, 243

Arnold, Harold "Hap": and air mail operations, 242; and Billy Mitchell, 139; flight training of, 43; as movie stand-in, 47–48; personality of, 43–44; and separation, 61, 76, 85; views of, 3, 45, 46, 79, 80, 82, 115, 222

Articles of War, 154, 155, 184, 198

Augusta GA, 63, 68, 71, 79, 80
Automatic Firearms Company, 50
aviation detachment, 67, 169, 177–79

Baker, Newton D., 214, 215, 229–30, 235
Baldwin, Thomas S., 12, 17
balloons, 7–9, 11, 12, 14, 17, 53, 66, 245
Balloon School (Fort Omaha), 245
Barrett, Joseph E., 11
Battalion of Engineers, 7
Beck, Paul: as author, 27–28, 30, 31, 33, 57;
    and Benjamin Foulois, 36–41, 73; and
    bomb dropping, 30–31; and cash prizes,
    46–47; censured, 27; commissioned; 23–
    25; crash of, 38; and Curtiss Flying School,
    34–35; detailed to Signal Corps, 29; embel-
    lishments of, 25, 33; and FAI pilot's cer-
    tificate, 45; health of, 25–26; lobbying of,
    57–59, 72, 74–75, 77; and Los Angeles Air
    Meet, 30–31; and Manchu Law, 55, 58, 59;
    marriage of, 24; murder of, 240; ordered
    to College Park, 41; promotion of; 35; and
    Provisional Aero Company, 36; quoted,
    12; and San Francisco Air Meet, 32–34;
    and separation, 8, 58–61; and Signal Corps
    administration, 57–58, 72, 78, 85, 91–93
Beck, Rachel, 24
Beck, Ruth (nee Everett), 23
Beck, William Henry, 22
Belknap, William W., 8
Benét-Mercié light machine gun (M1909), 52
Bliss, Tasker, 32
boards: accident investigation board, 40;
    Aircraft Board, 221, 226, 228, 234; Aircraft
    Production Board, 221, 225, 226; board of
    officers, 76, 210, 240, 248; Board of Ord-
    nance and Fortification, 12, 51; board of
    pilots, 217; Garlington Board, 210–14;
    Joint Army-Navy Airship Board, 245; pro-
    motions board, 76; Technical Aero Advi-
    sory and Inspection Board, 246, 247
Bolling, Raynold C., 20, 244
bombs, 2, 6, 90; and bombardment, 30, 49,
    88; discussed, 90, 93; experiments with, 30,
    33, 48; lack of, 5, 210; live demonstration
    with, 33; and Michelin International Bomb-
    Dropping Contest, 48; Paul Beck's, 31; and
    Second International Peace Conference, 49;
    tests with, 48, 129; theories about, 87

bombsights, 5, 49, 53
Borden, P. G., 28
Borglum, Gutzon, 217, 226, 227, 231, 234, 239
Bowen, Thomas S., 119, 122–23, 125–26, 130–
    31, 145, 244
Brandegee, Frank B., 234–35
Breckinridge, Henry, 87
Brereton, Lewis H., 64–66, 70–71, 83, 111–12
Brindley, Oscar, 117, 127
Brownsville TX, 156, 200
Burgess flight school (Palm Beach), 72
Burgess-Wright, 5, 44, 47
Burnett, Charles, 22–23
Bustleton Field PA, 241

Call, Loren H., 71, 83
Campbell, Douglas, 47
Camp Furlong NM, 213
Camp San Luis Obispo CA, 247
Carberry, Joseph E., 107, 109, 248
Carlstrom Field, 240
Carranza, Venustiano, 213
Carter, William H., 20, 41, 71, 80, 177
Central Department, 20
Chamberlain, John L., 5, 107–9, 110, 111
Chandler, Charles DeForest: as ACA com-
    mittee member, 14; as Aeronautical Board
    member, 17; as Aeronautical Division
    chief, 11; in Augusta, 68; bias of, against
    Curtiss pilots, 51, 54–56, 80; as College
    Park commander, 43, as editor, 245; and
    FAI pilot's certificate, 45; and FAI tests sta-
    tus, 68–69; and impromptu Lewis gun test,
    51; and Lahm Trophy Race, 13; negative
    comments of, 56, 80–82, 190; relieved, 82,
    176; in Texas City, 74–82; as unpopular, 78
Chandler, Rex, 83
Chandler Field, 247
Chapman, Carlton G., 145, 197, 245
Clark, Virginius E., 216–17, 218, 247
Cleveland, Grover, 9
Coast Artillery Corps, 48, 52, 136, 186
Coffin, Howard: and the Aircraft Board,
    226; and the Aircraft Production Board,
    221; and board of inquiry, 235; and Gut-
    zon Borglum, 227, 234; lobbying campaign
    of, 225; and production expectations, 224;
    quoted, 222, 225, 229; replaced, 233
Coffyn, Frank T., 37

College Park: bomb tests at, 43, 48; discipline at, 81; and first fatal crash of Wright Model C, 57; first students arrive at, 43; five new airplanes at, 44; Lewis gun tests at, 50

Collier Robert F., 21, 36

Collins, William, 138, 140, 142

Colorado Department, 24, 28

Columbus NM, 213, 217

Committee of Expenditures, 235

congressional acts: Flight Pay Act, 124; National Defense Act (1916), 218; Overman Act, 229, 232, 236

Connolly, Maurice, 97–98

Corbin, Henry C., 24, 25

Corps of Engineers, 4, 8, 18, 239

Cowan, Arthur S.: and bombing tests, 48–49; and Byron Jones, 114; character of, 100; charges served against, 161–63; comptroller's opinion of, 124; correspondence of, 172–73, 194, 196, 208; and Curtiss and Wright camps, 109; and flight lessons, 95–97, 123; and flight pay, 94–98, 100, 101, 109–10, 118, 120, 123–24; and flight records, 152, 177; and Harold Geiger, 136–38; and HR 5304, 97, 118; and Ned Goodier, 129–30; and orders, 83, 177; personality of, 100; and Robert Willis Jr., 112–13; and Roy Kirtland, 128–29, 133–39, 141–44; in Texas City, 13, 80–83; and Tom Bowen, 130–31; and trial testimony, 196–97; as unpopular, 79, 189; and USS San Diego, 130, 152, 156

crashes, fatal: of Arthur Welsh and Leighton Hazlehurst, 56–57; of C. Perry Rich, 101; of George E. M. Kelly, 39–40; of Harold Geiger, 246; of Henry Post, 106; of Lewis Rockwell and Frank Scott, 62; of Loren Call, 83; of Moss Love, 97; of Rex Chandler, 83; of Thomas Selfridge, 18; of Townsend Dodd, 241; of Walter Taliaferro, 185

Crissy, Myron, 33, 48, 92

Crowder, Enoch H., 171, 176–83, 184, 214

Crozier, William, 51

Curtiss, Glenn, 106, 121

Curtiss Aeroplane and Motor Corporation, 224

Curtiss airplanes: D-III, 36; D-IV, 35–44, 83, 104; flight training in, 104; flying boat, 82, 130; hydroplane, 94; JN-2, 200, 203, 204

Curtiss Flying School (San Diego), 33, 34, 101

Curtiss plant (Buffalo), 230

Dargue, Herbert Dargue, 217, 218

Daughters of the American Revolution (DAR), 24

Day, Audrey, 240

Day, Jean, 240

Dayton Engineering Laboratories (DELCO), 227

Dayton flood, 227

Dayton OH (Wright factory), 43

Dayton-Wright Airplane Company, 228

Delano, Mortimer, 64–68

Dickinson, Jacob M., 32, 33

dirigible, 12, 14, 16, 17, 245

Dodd, Townsend: and Arthur Cowan, 130, 132, 136, 166; and Arthur Murry, 165; and Benjamin Foulois, 157; and Daniel Shanks, 173; death of, 241–42; and dissident activity, 100, 145, 147–48, 156–60; and Lewis Goodier, 157–60, 187; and Roy Kirtland, 135; and Samuel Reber, 171; served charges, 161–63; trial testimony of, 194, 201; and vouchers, 157; and World War I, 241–42

Domestic Engineering Company, 19

Downing, Finis E., 22

Dupuy, George, 133

Elkins, Stephen B., 10

Ellington, Eric, 71

Ely, Eugene, 33, 35, 36, 41

Emmons, Harold H., 6, 226

engines: Liberty, 222, 226, 228; pusher, 107, 108; tractor, 108, 117, 122

Ennis, Earle, 33

Erwin, James B., 149, 150, 165, 194, 200

Fédération Aéronautiqe International (FAI) pilot's certificate, 13, 39, 63, 64–71

Fickel, Jacob, 47

Field Service Regulations, 9, 10, 53, 89

Fifth Artillery, 32

First Cavalry, 32

Fisher, Benjamin F., 7

Fletcher, Duncan U., 234–35

flight controls: and ailerons, 44, 105; of Curtiss D-IV, 105; different, 32–33, 44, 103; dual, 94, 96, 98, 104, 117; and elevators, 20, 36, 39, 56, 103, 104, 105; Grover Loening on, 44; instinctive, 103, 105; lateral, 44, 103;

flight controls (*continued*)
of Martin T-2, 122, 131; and rudder, 21, 44, 103, 104, 105; semi-dual, 96; and wing-warping, 21, 44, 103, 104; of Wright Model B, 21, 103–4; of Wright Model C, 104

flight pay, 146, 158, 173, 202; 25 percent, 123; 35 percent, 95, 116, 123, 147; 50 percent, 123; abused, 44; authorized, 55, 72, 78; after first lesson, 96; and Military Affairs Committee, 77; recommended, 76; requirement for, 120

Ford, Henry, 222
Fort Crockett, 82
Fort Duchesne, 23
Fort Frankfurt, 11
Fort Kamehameha, 8, 94
Fort Leavenworth, 16, 21, 29, 61
Fort McKavett, 22
Fort McPherson, 23
Fort Monroe, 25
Fort Myer, 11, 17, 18, 32
Fort Omaha, 25
Fort Riley, 61
Fort Rosecrans, 9, 148, 153–58
Fort Sam Houston, 19, 21, 34–35, 37, 52, 102, 142
Fort Sheridan, 26
Fort Sill, 174, 201

Foulois, Benjamin D.: and 1st Aero Squadron, 117, 139, 140, 174, 204, 214; and Aeronautical Board, 17, 18; and Billy Mitchell, 139, 242; and board of pilots, 107; character of, 15, 34, 147, 156, 157, 158, 201; collateral assignment of, 61, 82; crashed in the Rio Grande, 57; and Curtiss JN-2, 200; as dirigible pilot, 17; and flight pay, 148, 165, 212; and flight training, 18–19, 21; and HR 5304; 85–86, 90–91; and HR 28728, 72–75, 76; and Hunsaker report, 203, 204; and Kennedy Committee, 216–17; and Manchu Law, 42; and Militia Bureau, 42; myths about, 19–20; and Paul Beck, 30, 36–39, 40–41, 61; personal politics of, 75–78; and Punitive Expedition, 215; quoted, 39, 41, 73, 75–76, 80, 82, 90, 109, 113, 163; and request for reassignment, 61; and SC-1 modifications, 20; and separation, 215; thesis of, 16

Frierson, William L., 235

Gallinger, Jacob H., 235

Galveston TX, 117
Gard, Warren, 88, 91
Garlington, Ernest A., 210
Garrett, Daniel E., 89–91
Garrison, Lindley M., 28, 89, 176
Geary, John T., 186, 187, 188–93, 194, 195, 196, 197, 201, 204, 205
Geiger, Harold: and the ACA, 63–66; and Arthur Cowan, 98, 106; and Curtiss detachment at San Diego, 64; death of, 245–46; as dissident, 61; and FAI pilot's certificate, 68–69; and George Scriven and Edgar Russel, 69–71; refused to fly, 136–37; relieved, 137–38; returned to aviation, 245; sent to Hawaii, 94; as U.S. air attaché in Berlin, 245; and World War I, 245
General Myer, 10
Gerstner Field LA, 247
Gibbs, George S., 139, 199
Gilmore, J. C., 24
Glassford, William A., 10, 214
Glenn L. Martin Company, 108
Goodier, Lewis E., Sr.: and Arthur Cowan, 130, 132, 150, 153; and Byron Jones, 153–54; charges against, 186–87; court martial of, 184; and dissidents, 149, 150, 153–56, 158; at North Island, 100–101; quoted, 101; reprimand of, 200, 206, 242; and Roy Kirtland, 149, 150–51; and Townsend Dodd, 157–58, 159, 161; trial testimony of, 201–3; verdict on, 206
Goodier, Lewis E. "Ned": and Arthur Cowan, 98, 99, 111, 129–30, 132, 133; bad landing of, 117; and Curtiss School, 99; death of, 247; and Geiger-Delano set-to, 64; and missing tools, 110–11; relieved from aviation, 246; and separation, 112; trial testimony of, 200–201; and World War I, 246–47; and World War II, 247
Gorrell, Edgar E., 181, 203
Graham, Harry, 71, 83
Greely, Adolphus Washington, 9–12
Greer, Allen J., 186, 193, 205
Gregory, Thomas W., 235

Hamilton, Charles K., 30
Harrison, Benjamin, 9
Hartman, Carl F., 139
Hartman, James F., 111

Hay, James, 6, 7, 12
Hazen, William B., 8–9
Hazlehurst, Leighton W., 57
Hennessy, Frederick B., 71, 74, 76, 81, 85
Hennig, James, 39–41
Henry Farman (airplane), 31
Hersey, Henry B., 13–14
Hess, George E., 41–42
Hickam, Horace M., 242
Hitchcock, Frank, 46
Hitchcock, Gilbert H., 234
Horne, William, 23
Horner, Leonard S., 226
House Military Affairs Committee, 58
Howard, William S., 86
Howgate, Henry W., 8
HR 5304, 85–93
HR 28728, 71–78
Hudson Motor Company, 221
Hughes, Charles E., 235–36
Humphreys, Frederick E., 18–19, 20, 34, 239
Humphreys, William P., 187, 188, 190, 196, 197, 200–204, 205
Hunsaker, Jerome, 203–4

Jefferson Barracks, 22
John Deere, 226
Jones, Byron Q.: and Arthur Cowan, 114; and Benjamin Foulois, 157; at dissidents meeting, 145, 156; JMA rating of, 119, 122, 123, 125, 126; and Kennedy Committee, 216, 218; and separation, 150; and sloppy investigating, 157; and Technical Aero Advisory and Inspection Board, 216, 247; trial testimony of, 191–93; and World War I, 244, 247

Kelly, George E. M., 32, 33–34, 39–40
Kelly, John P., 43
Kenly, William L., 233, 236
Kennedy, Chase W., 1, 215
Kennedy, Frank M., 65, 80
Kennedy Committee, 1, 207, 215–19
Kettering, Charles F., 227–28
Kirtland, Roy C.: and Arthur Cowan, 118, 128, 133–36, 138–44, 189; and Charles DeForest Chandler, 80; description of, 43, 128, 134; and dissidents meeting, 145, 156; quoted, 80, 81, 83; relieved from aviation,

143; returns to aviation, 243; as ringleader, 81, 128; role of, in the revolt, 145, 149–51, 161, 163, 217; and Samuel Reber, 82–83, 151; and separation, 61, 81, 217; stopped flying, 83, 84; trial testimony of, 188–91

Lachambre, 10
Ladd, Eugene F., 178
Lahm, Frank, 12–13, 14, 17, 18–19, 94, 245
Langley Field, 241, 243
Letterman Army Hospital, 99, 122, 138
Lewis gun, 50–52
Lochridge, P. D., 215
Loening, Grover, 44, 105, 115, 132–33, 134, 137
Love, Moss L., 97

Macomb, Montgomery M., 210
Manchu Law, 2–3, 16, 29, 34, 42, 59
Maneuver Division, 21, 34–35, 37, 80, 83
maneuvers, 11, 51, 52
Marshall, H. Snowden, 231–33
Marshall Committee, 231, 232–33
Martin, Glenn, 108, 121, 122, 131, 136, 137, 141, 149
Massachusetts Institute of Technology (MIT), 114, 174
McCain, Henry P., 182, 210
McCoy, James C., 14
McEntee, William, 17
McKinley, William, 17, 24, 25
McLeary, Samuel H., 64, 66, 67, 70, 71
Militia Bureau, 42
Miller, B. F. "Butch," 16
Milling, Thomas DeWitt: accident nearly caused by, 129, 192; and Arthur Cowan, 95, 126, 180; and cash prizes, 47; character of, 44; at College Park, 43; at dissidents meeting, 145, 156; and FAI pilot's certificate, 45; and HR 5304, 85; and Kennedy Committee, 215, 216, 218; promotion of, 247; quoted, 3, 81–82; and separation, 61, 216, 218; and Technical Aero Advisory and Inspection Board, 216; and World War I, 247
Mitchel Field, 242
Mitchell, William "Billy," 88, 91, 139, 214, 237, 241, 242
Mixter, George W., 6, 226
Molineau, Henry S., 43

Molkvar, Colonel. *See* Volkmar, William Jefferson

Moore, Dan T., 215, 218

Morris, Raymond V., 121

Murry, Arthur, 149, 193

Murry, Franklin T., 157

Muzac, 248

Myer, Albert J., 7, 8

Myers, Carl Edgar, 11

National Advisory Committee for Aeronautics, 217, 224

National Guard, 46, 55, 76, 207, 239

Netherwood, Douglas B., 119, 122–23, 125–27, 133, 145

Nicholson, William F. C., 107

Olmstead Field, 246, 236

Overman, Lee Slater, 229, 233

Packard Motor Car Company, 226

Paine, Halbert E., 8

Palmer, Paul M., 215–17

Park, Joseph D., 64–65, 70, 71, 83

Parmelee, Phillip O., 21, 57

Patrick, Mason M., 16

Patterson, William Lay: and 1st Company, 2nd Aero Squadron, 199, 243; and 2nd Aero Squadron, 171; and 2nd Company, 1st Aero Squadron, 121; administration duties of, 116, 117; age problem of, 120–21, 125; and Arthur Cowan, 116–17; could not fly, 121, 127, 171, and flight pay, 116, 117, 125, 212; and flight training, 117, 122, 123, 159, 174, 176; on flying, 117, 118, 214; health of, 122, 125, 176; and HR 5304, 118, 119; JMA rating of, 123, 126, 127, 128, 154, 155, 159, 168, 170, 183, 184, 190, 195, 197, 199, 203, 204, 211–12, 214, 243; lack of charges against, 148; lax attitude of, 173, 174; pilots' opinion of, 126, 143, 146, 151, 159, 170; and the press, 204–6

Paulhan, Louis, 30, 31

Pershing, John J., 213, 236, 241

Phillips Field, 245–46

Plattsburg Barracks, 28

Pope, John, 28

Post, Henry B. "Postie," 106–7, 110

Post Field, 230

Potter, William C., 229, 233

Punitive Expedition, 213, 215

Quinlan, Dennis P., 166–67, 171–72

Radio Corporation of America (RCA), 244

Reber, Samuel: and the ACA, 14, 45, 66; and Aeronautical Division, 82, 94, 97; and Arthur Cowan, 97–98, 120–22, 123, 125, 131, 135–36, 137, 138, 139, 141, 163, 164, 166, 167–69, 170, 172, 194, 196; and bad math, 127; and Benjamin Foulois, 62, 82, 165; and Billy Mitchell, 139; censured, 214; and Edgar Russel, 67; endorsement by, 176–77; Garlington Board testimony of, 211; and Grover Loening, 105; and Harold Geiger, 136; and HR 5304, 86, 88, 90; and James Hay, 123–24; management style of, 138, 142, 147–48, 195, 210–11; and Ned Goodier, 111–12, 200; political strings pulled by, 167, 171–72; relieved, 214; and Robert Willis, 113; and Roy Kirtland, 142, 151; at San Diego school, 97, 135; and "taking scalps," 171, 174, 198; at Texas City, 80–82; trial testimony of, 197–200; and William Lay Patterson, 171, 173–74

Regal Motor Company, 226

Ribot, Alexandre, 224

Rich, C. Perry, 101

Robinson, Joseph T., 207, 209, 210

Rockwell, Lewis C., 6

Russel, Edgar: and the ACA, 14; and Aeronautical Board, 17; and Aeronautical Division, 67, 68; and board of officers, 76; and Geiger-Delano set-to, 67–68, 70–71; and HR 5304, 85, 88, 90, 97; quoted, 88; and Samuel Reber, 82–83, 85; and World War I, 248

Ryan, John D., 233

Saltzman, C. McKinley, 17

Saumur (French Cavalry School), 13

SC-1, 1, 18, 19, 20

SC-2, 36, 39–40, 44, 45

SC-3, 37

SC-9, 117

SC-10, 106–7

SC-11, 83

SC-20, 83

SC-22, 117

SC-29, 13

SC-32, 13

Schofield, John M., 10

Schurmeier, Harry L., 132

Scott, Frank S., 62

Scott, Hugh L., 15, 164

Scott, Riley, 85

Scriven, George P.: and Billy Mitchell, 139; censured, 212, 214, 246; and FAI pilot's certificate test, 68–71; Garlington Board testimony of, 210–11; grounding of Wright Model B and C by, 107; and HR 5304, 86–90; and HR 28728, 76–77; and Lewis gun tests, 51; moral objection of, to bombing, 49; and Ned Goodier, 246; and nonflying Signal Corps officers, 145, 199; quoted, 4, 80–81, 109, 209; and reconnaissance, 2, 49; relieved, 244; and round-robin letter, 79–83; and school commandant post, 97; and Western Department, 164

Second Division, 71, 169, 177–78

Selfridge, Thomas E., Jr., 17, 18, 32

Selfridge Field CA. See Tanforan Race Track

Selfridge Field MI, 243

Shanks, Daniel C., 172–73, 208–9

Shepler, Harry L., 226

Sheridan, Philip H., 26–27

Sherman, William C., 71, 76

Sibert, William L., 186, 193, 200–201, 204, 206

Simmons, Oliver, 38

Sopwith, Thomas, 47

Souther, Henry, 246–47

Squier, George O.: and the ACA, 14; and accident investigation board, 40, 41; and Aeronautical Board, 17; and court of inquiry, 235; disassociation of, with aviation, 233; and James Allen, 3; and Maneuver Division, 37; as "official rubber stamp," 224; and Provisional Aero Company, 36; quoted, 225; and reconnaissance, 2; and Samuel Reber, 214

Stimson, Henry L., 21, 50–51

Sumner, Edwin V., 24

Sunset Field (Spokane International Airport), 246

Sweet, George, 17

Swift, Evan, 186

Talbott, Harold E., Jr., 228

Talbott, Harold E., Sr., 228

Taliaferro, Walter R.: and Arthur Cowan, 156–57, 161–63, 166; and Benjamin Foulois, 157; and board of pilots, 107; as critical of army airplanes, 145; and Daniel Shanks, 173; death of, 185; at dissidents meeting, 145; at Fort Rosecrans, 14; and William Lay Patterson, 126, 174

Tanforan Race Track, 32, 33

Thomas, Charles, 236

Thompson, Richard E., 9

Tilson, John, 77

Tumulty, Joseph P., 227

USS California, 130

USS Los Angeles, 245

USS Pennsylvania, 33

USS San Diego, 130, 152, 155–56

Villa, Francisco "Poncho," 213

Vincent, J. G., 226

Volkmar, William Jefferson, 27–28

Volunteer Engineers, 15

Walcott, Charles D., 224

Waldon, Sidney D., 226

Walker, John, 32, 33–34, 36, 37, 38

Wallace, Charles S., 17, 125, 127

Ward, Edward, 11

Warren, Whitney, 228

Weather Service, 8, 9

Welsh, Arthur L., 56–57

Western Department, 157, 161, 164, 165

Western Wireless Equipment Company, 33

Westover, Oscar, 243

Wheeler, Joe, 24

Wildman, Francis, 130

Willard, Charles F., 30

Williams, Earl, 47

Willis, Robert H., Jr., 112–13, 145, 148, 201, 248

Wilson, Woodrow, 229, 231–35, 236

Wood, Leonard, 21, 62

Wright, Orville, 17, 18

Wright, Wilbur, 18, 19, 227

Wright Model A, 18, 21

Wright Model B, 21, 36–37, 39, 44, 96, 104, 107

Wright Model C, 56–57, 83, 97, 106, 211